FOREIGN AND FEMALE

DORIS WEATHERFORD

Foreign and Female

IMMIGRANT WOMEN IN AMERICA, 1840–1930

Foreword by Lillian Schlissel

SCHOCKEN BOOKS • NEW YORK

First published by Schocken Books 1986

10   9   8   7   6   5   4   3   2   87   88   89

Copyright © 1986 by Doris Weatherford

Library of Congress Cataloging-in-Publication Data
Weatherford, Doris.
Foreign and female.
Bibliography: p.
Includes index.
1. Women immigrants—United States—Social conditions.
2. Women immigrants—United States—History—19th
century.   3. Women immigrants—United States—History—
20th century.   I. Title.
HQ1410.W43 1986   305.4/88   86–6733

Design by Lynn Braswell
Manufactured in the United States of America
ISBN 0–8052–4017–9

for Roy
who means everything
to this book and to my life

Contents

LIST OF ILLUSTRATIONS   ix

FOREWORD   xi

PREFACE   xv

PART I.   The Body and the Soul   1

      FATALISTIC CONCEPTIONS   2
      THOSE UNCONTROLLED BIRTHS   7
      IN SICKNESS AND IN HEALTH   15
      THE IMMIGRANT WAY OF DEATH   20
      RELIGION HERE AND HEREAFTER   27

PART II.   Ambivalence in Morality   35

      COURTING CUSTOMS   36
      MARRIAGE, DIVORCE, AND DESERTION   43
      ILLICIT SEX   56

PART III. Domesticity:The Old and the New   67

      THE FRUIT OF THE LAND   68

OF HOVELS, HOMES, AND HOPES 77
HOUSEWORK AND CHILD CARE 87
CUSTOM IN COSTUME 96

PART IV.   The Contributions of These Women 103

SUPPORTING FAMILIES 104
THEIR WORK AND THEIR WAGES 112
THE WAYS OF WORK 127
FOREIGN DOMESTICS 146
HOMES ON THE RANGE 157

PART V.   The Complexities of It All 171

STANDARDS AND DOUBLE STANDARDS 172
TRAVAILS OF TRAVEL 180
AN OCEAN APART: SEPARATION AND ITS
EFFECTS 193

PART VI.   The Ties That Bind 207

FAMILY RELATIONSHIPS 208
WOMEN'S PLACE IN THE NEW WORLD 223

PART VII.   Content and Discontent 233

VIEWS OF THE NEW WORLD 234

NOTES 250

SELECTED BIBLIOGRAPHY 276

INDEX 283

Illustrations

Following Page 32

Immigrant children received health and hygiene education

Children receiving gifts for their first Christmas in America, Ellis Island, 1918

Norwegian widow Kari Froslan with her teenage children and the casket of her husband, 1897

Jews praying on the Brooklyn Bridge, Rosh Hashanah, in 1909

Following Page 98

The clean, prosperous kitchen of a family influenced by settlement house workers

An early twentieth-century family at supper

A room in a tenement flat, 1910

Laundry hanging between tenements

Milbank Memorial Public Baths provided facilities to those without bathrooms at home

A dugout on the South Loop River, Custer County, Nebraska, 1892

Making a home in the West Coast wilderness

Following Page 166

An old-time sweatshop in New York, 1910 or 1912

A box factory, a poorly paid industry employing many newcomers

Immigrants sometimes found work through employment agencies for servants

A family making artificial flower wreaths in their tenement house

A woman and her children shelling pecans, probably for a candy factory

A woman vendor hawking stale bread

Women parading for improved working conditions, circa 1912

Following Page 204

Immigrants on a ship deck

A vessel packed with newcomers

A woman undergoing an eye examination at Ellis Island

An Italian woman and her children arriving in America

A family on its way to the farms of the Great Plains. Note destination tag on men.

Immigrants in "pens" at Ellis Island; Christmas season, 1906

An aerial view of Ellis Island, 1921

FOREWORD

WIDE-EYED immigrant women beside husbands and fathers at Ellis Island; what did they dream of life in America? Single girls from Italy and Poland who crossed the Atlantic when they would not go unchaperoned to the next village in their own country; what promises had the New World made to draw them so far? Some women came to these shores because there was no alternative, some came "hoping for high adventure and thinking anything in America was better than their present lot." Doris Weatherford's book lays before us the stories of immigrant women who struggled to come to terms with life in this country after centuries of religious taboos, marital subjection, sexual ignorance, and economic dependency. These women held precious few resources for living in this teeming nation. At every turn they found this a society in upheaval. The centrifugal forces of Civil War, of westward migration, of industrialization, of labor strikes and labor violence, of world war—all of these were changing the lives of the entire population. Immigrants were tossed into the streets to fend for themselves. While America has been a generous nation, it has also been unforgiving to those who were vulnerable, and immigrant women were among its most vulnerable new arrivals.

In trying to understand the new world, these women held fast to what they knew from the old. Family was the fixed center of a woman's life. Belief in the family cut across national differences and bound women together even when their languages kept them apart. Like religious belief, the family demanded self-sacrifice. It meant successive pregnancies that killed women before they were forty, the deaths of infants born prematurely or poorly nourished, abandonment by their men, and work that could kill a horse. None of this, however, quenched their passionate determination to keep the family together. One might say an immigrant woman set herself against the grain of American life where the individual, not the family, assumed primacy. She fed her children, prayed for delivery from the next pregnancy, and nourished life with canny wisdom and a morass of superstition.

Weatherford's book recreates some of these themes and new aspects of the lives of these women, particularly in the accounts of those who remained in Europe while their husbands went on ahead. Historians have often marked the nineteenth century as one in which immigration and emigration set populations in motion in western Europe and in America. Here we begin to learn what happened to the women left in "the old country" while husbands, brothers, and fathers went on to make a place for themselves in America. Weatherford shows how they managed to survive in Europe, how they negotiated the obstacles of the immigration system, and how they traveled with hungry children a thousand miles into the heartland of America—a new population of women and children on the move, alone.

Most of the time immigrant women avoided the social institutions—the hospitals and welfare agencies—set up to help them. They mistrusted American institutions and with good reason. Social workers who turned women back at Ellis Island because the relative who sponsored them was an uncle or a male cousin did not act out of concern for an unmarried girl, but rather in fear of foreign women who might fall prey to prostitution. The Vice Commission of Chicago issued a report in 1911 on "The Social Evil" and the U.S. Senate followed suit with a document on "The Importation and Harboring of Women for Immoral Purposes." Immigrant families came under the purview of welfare agencies that saw immigrants depleting the resources of such cities as New York and Chicago. American efforts to help, even when prompted by sympathy, were often hampered by fear and parochial self-interest. Immigrant women were at almost as great a risk from those who would help them as from those who would exploit them.

Yet, in the course of time, these women came to terms with America even as they shrank the marketplace into the circle of a kitchen table where they trained three- and four-year-olds to make flowers. In a harsh world, one learned marketable skills at an early age. These same women learned to limit the size of their families. Slowly, through the prisms of superstition and taboos, immigrant women fought to free themselves from prearranged marriages, rigid parental control, ignorance of their own bodies, subservience to men, and lives of self-abnegation and unrewarded work. For immigrant women, the promise of American life was an idea that very slowly unfolded.

If their superstitions ring strange in our ears, if their vulnerability seems pathetic, Weatherford's work shows us their enormous resiliency, their dogged determination to find a better life. America has never been "a woman's world," and it certainly was not an immigrant woman's world. But their legacy was the determination to meet the new world on its own terms and to give tomorrow to their children.

LILLIAN SCHLISSEL

PREFACE

ON the shelves of almost any library are several volumes each on the Italians in America, the Germans in America, and so on. One can read hundreds of pages in these books to glean a handful of references to women; if one did not know that it was biologically impossible, one could be led to believe that men populated this country by themselves. Similarly, standard works on the history of American women make only slight reference to immigrants. This book attempts to partially fill that lack.

The study covers the era from 1840 to 1930. The beginning date marks the massive influx of starved Irish who were driven from their land by famine in the 1840s, and the ending date was chosen because of the close of free immigration after the enactment of the 1924 Immigration Quota Law. During this era, some thirty-five million Europeans made their way to America. More than one in every three were women. This book is, however, in no way chronological; the arrangement of the material is topical, and these dates indicate only the time period covered.

This study excludes the early colonial women and immigration since 1930, which has been largely made up of political refugees and Latin Americans. Only European women are covered, since immigrants from Asia, Africa, and Latin America have backgrounds and problems that are vastly different. Lastly, the study is of ordinary women, and therefore the famous and those who are too far out of the mainstream (radicals such as Emma Goldman, for instance) are excluded.

Finding appropriate sources was a genuine problem both because the area has been neglected and because the kind of woman the book concerns generally did not feel sufficiently self-important to leave a written record of herself. Most of these women were uneducated, often illiterate and unfamiliar with English, and so primary source material is somewhat scarce.

I began my research by reading dozens of books on the general subjects of immigration and women that are not included in the bibliographical list. The final selected bibliography includes works which fall primarily into two categories: (1) social workers' records of their work with immigrants and/or women and sociological studies of the same; (2) autobiographies, letters, journals, etc., of immigrant women themselves.

Social workers' material must be used cautiously because their contact was often with those immigrants who were most deprived. Nevertheless the studies cited in the book were generally done with statistical care and a sympathetic attitude, and I believe that they give a valid picture of many female immigrants' problems and life-styles. Finally, it will be noticed that I have used quotations freely. I believe that where it is possible to allow the past to speak for itself, that should be done.

Not surprisingly, those who left the best records on immigrant women were often other women. Since much of this book depends on the studies of female sociologists, it seems important to point out that these women were primarily concerned with making a contribution to the budding field of sociology rather than with arguing feminist causes. They used the proper methodology and generally did not set out with their summaries already written. Elizabeth Butler, for example, in writing *Women and the Trades*, surveyed over twenty-two thousand women—a much larger sample than those relied on in modern polls.

Further, these female writers did not always identify with their subjects. Butler, for example, often tells us that women's wages are low because they are unambitious, they do not want promotion, and the like. In all of the progressive admonitions on the status of women in that era, "protection" is the key word, not "equality"; while these privileged women studied the poor and foreign with sympathy, they did not feel sisterhood. Instead of creating a brief for feminism, their overriding concern was to provide information that was as factual as possible.

My aim in writing this book was to reach a wide audience with a survey of an area that has been largely ignored. I am aware that any chapter could be expanded into a volume. There are also chapters on other topics that have not been included for lack of space. I trust that this overview will provide a beginning for further study.

What I hope to have done is to ask some new questions, to raise interest in some new areas of research. These women were courageous people who made an important contribution to America, and while they have been praised in flowery generalities, the honest details of their hard lots have been neglected. They deserve to be remembered.

The Body and the Soul

FATALISTIC CONCEPTIONS

AN annual pregnancy was a fact of life for a great many immigrant women. More than any other factor, this situation determined her life, defined its value, and prescribed its horizons. The word that most fittingly describes the immigrant woman's attitude toward her body, her life, and her world was fatalism. It was a European attitude, developed from long centuries of a class structure that wiped out the peasant who showed any signs of assertion. It was a woman's attitude, formed by aeons of submission to the men who controlled her life—and her body.

The direct result was a fecundity far greater than that of the average American woman. Census figures in 1920 showed that the child of a German immigrant was three times as likely to be the tenth child in its family as the American baby, and other foreigners were comparably more fertile.[1]

The feelings of women on the subject of children form a pattern of ambivalence, but many of these pregnancies were far from wanted. Newspapers in Lawrence, Massachusetts—a city of immigrants—at mid-century had repeated reports of infanticide and abortion. Babies were found thrown in the river; a case in 1866 of the discovery of one such child's maggot-covered body was termed "not unusual."[2]

Most women, of course, did not kill or neglect their children but nevertheless the annual additions were less than welcome. One social worker in 1905 stated succinctly: "All the mothers complain that they have to bear too many children."[3] Yet they were often contemptuous of American women who bore only a few babies. In spite of the physical strain of frequent childbirth, children were seen as an economic asset. Some poor children were put to work at an unconscionably early age. An Italian mother with four preschoolers harshly summarized their plight: "We must all work if we want to earn anything."[4]

In an era when commerce was simple and agriculture predominant, the labor of children was essential, especially on farms. Gro Svendsen, an educated Norwegian on the Iowa frontier at mid-century, had no complaints in her lengthy, intimate letters about bearing five sons in seven years. However, on the sixth pregnancy she wrote, "It took quite a while to get my strength back." The seventh child proved to be the long-awaited girl, but "she is still very small, because she has frequently been ill." More pregnancies brought more sickness and by the ninth one, Gro was fearful enough to need the comfort of sharing her dread: "Next month, if God wills it, I shall have another child. . . . It is difficult these last days because I am always quite weak, but God, who has always been my help and comforter during my confinements, will surely help me this time, too. . . . If I live and recover, I shall indeed write."[5] She lived, but she never really recovered.

The tenth pregnancy was the last, taking the life of this exceptional woman. Gro's first child was born in 1864, and she died in 1878 at age thirty-seven. She had borne ten children in fourteen years. Her husband mourned her sincerely—he was well aware of what a fine woman she was and they had loved each other deeply—and his grief must have been increased by the knowledge that his loving her had, in a sense, killed her.

It is revealing to see that a half century later and in a considerably more urbane setting there was no greater knowledge of birth control. Elizabeth Stern was a Jewish college graduate who grew up in America, yet she seemed to think that all that was necessary to prevent pregnancy was to wish it so. Later, as an older and wiser woman, she wrote:

At that time birth control was a word not spoken. There was a sin called preventing the conception of children, but Margaret Sanger had not yet appeared. Girls became pregnant and had abortions. But married women had as many children as fate chose. If they were much advanced they might live only at certain times with their husbands, and have protection against pregnancy so. That was mentioned, in an awed whisper, by prurient minded, but kindly, married women to young brides. One spoke of it to me, and made me feel as if she had torn the door open on our love by even mentioning my husband and me in this way.[6]

A woman of German origin who also grew up in America had at least a suspicion of the possibility of preventing pregnancy, for she told a social worker that she thought it strange that "rich folks has so few and us poor ones so many." Like other women, the only solution that she could see was celibacy and she decided "it is much better not to marry and to have so many children."[7] Like her, the Italian Lola Anguini believed family limitation ought to be possible, but searched in vain for an answer to the mystery.

> There was always the fear of pregnancy that I had to live with. . . . If you asked a priest for advice, he told you any contraception was a sin, babies were a gift of God. If you could summon the courage to ask a doctor, he would either avoid the question or tell you there was nothing to do but avoid intercourse. Trying to avoid relations with flimsy excuses would create arguments. . . . But there again, all of the women had this problem, and no one would ever talk about it.[8]

There were important variations between ethnic groups on sexual mores, but information on the scientific area of birth control was generally lacking. Although newspaper ads offering relief for "female complaints" were common in the nineteenth century, as the medical profession became better organized and more influential with legislatures, such information (always of questionable value) became even more unavailable. When a newspaper of the more sexually liberated Poles ran an ad in 1911 for a book on what "girls and married women should know," the Vice Commission of Chicago declared the book was written in "indecent and vulgar language. Among other things the advertiser describes a rubber instrument which is to be used to prevent conception. The translation . . . is full of vile and abhorrent information."[9]

But it was not just lack of information that contributed to the size of large foreign families (most Americans lacked information, too); it was a matter of values. It had more to do with the lower status of foreign women and the dominance of the men, with their belief that children were proof of virility as well as potential earners. As length of residence in the United States increased and those values changed, family size decreased. Social workers noted the phenomenon census figures showed: the daughters of immigrants had fewer children than their mothers. One who was familiar with Italian families in New York wrote:

> Children do not appear so frequently in Italian families as they did abroad or among first generation immigrants. The number of offspring now varies from 1 to 4 or 6. . . . Women of the first generation, however, become pregnant every year or so. They are frequently able to limit their brood to 11 or 12 only through abortions. . . . Many young couples make a real effort

to restrict the size of their families. They ordinarily use the simplest and cheapest method known, called "sleeping the American way." This always means separate beds, or more often separate rooms, for the father and mother, with the additional safeguard of having the girls in the mother's bed and the boys in the father's.[10]

But first-generation men were apt to have strong feelings on this subject. An Italian fisherman, speaking of a couple that had been married ten years and had two children, commented tersely, "That man should feel shame to himself." A common view was stated by a mother of twelve children when she said, "If you do anything to stop it, the man he get ill. He get the bad blood. God, he means it to be this way. The woman must do it to keep the peace."[11]

Continence was considered bad for women as well. The belief was common that if a woman of child-bearing age did not regularly become pregnant, she would develop tumors. Continence was also believed to cause illness of the mind. Nervousness in adolescent girls was seen to be the result of chastity, and prompt marriage was the prescription.

If celibacy was too dangerous or made the marital situation intolerable, another method of birth control was a lengthy lactating period. Though undoubtedly they nursed their children for other good reasons, many immigrant women apparently understood that nursing afforded at least some protection against pregnancy: one woman of German background gave as her reason for nursing a long time "so as to keep them from coming so fast."[12]

A third method of birth control was abortion. A writer in 1914 said of the working mothers she studied, "Abortions are common, and unsuccessful attempts are even commoner.... A practice which the women know to be so common they can scarcely regard as immoral, and in any case, they feel it is justified by their necessities."[13] Whether or not they suffered any moral pangs, they almost certainly suffered physical pain and risked death. The blundering way they attempted to end their pregnancies is illustrated by a Syrian woman who said: "I was not happy about my last baby. My youngest daughter was 12 ... and I did not want to start raising children all over again. I did not have an abortion, but I took pills hoping they would help me to lose my baby. Nothing happened and my last child was born when I was about 35."[14]

For many women, abortion may have been part of a commonly accepted, though undiscussed, European background. A rare survey on the subject, conducted around 1910 by a Berlin doctor, "illustrates the extent of abortion. Among one hundred women interviewed, twenty-four had aborted themselves at least once."[15] Midwives also practiced as abortionists. A German midwife uncovered by the Vice Commission of Chicago is perhaps typical; her rooms were dirty, but she showed at least some concern for her patients in that she required a return visit and her fee was a moderate $10, unlike American abortionists whose fees were up to five times higher.[16]

But though there were many women who practiced abortion and what they knew of birth control, most women apparently did not. Many probably wished to but lacked the knowledge, while others had the traditional fatalism of peasant people and agreed with the mother who stated simply, "It is God's will and not man's that the child comes to us."[17]

For educated people also fatalism was dictated by religion. Linka Preus, the Norwegian wife of a Lutheran minister on the Wisconsin frontier in the 1850s, mused in her diary, "In a couple of months, I shall again become a mother. It is indeed, painful and hard, but God's will be done! Hexa [her sister], thy death was the result of bearing a child; Mother's death also; I cannot know what God may have ordained for me; but His will be done; may we all, as Death calls, be prepared."[18]

Plainly Linka's moral convictions did not allow her to avoid pregnancy, and she became pregnant again and again with increasingly deleterious effects to her health. Her diary shows a sad metamorphosis as a gay, bright young woman turned into a sick and fearful creature, her life shortened and pained by unwanted pregnancies.

Though women may have wished to control the situation, the only proven method of birth control—celibacy—was likely to lead to an undesired result. Studies of desertion noted that a husband was most apt to leave when his wife was pregnant. The way to keep your husband, then, was to avoid pregnancy, and the way to avoid pregnancy was to avoid your husband—which was also likely to drive him out.

Social workers whose ostensible aim was to build happy families sometimes had the knowledge that could have given those couples a satisfactory sex life without impairing their health and financial resources, but the moral code of that time would not allow them to give the family the one tool most important for saving it.

Colonial New England families were often so large that several mothers were sent to an early grave in the production and care of a single family. But the real American natives of that time, the Indians, apparently did not indulge in excessively large families. As the Anglo-Saxons became "natives" in the New World, their family size decreased also; they then wrote books and mounted platforms to warn against the growing numbers of "inferior" foreigners. Children are a source of security to people who are trying to make a home of a strange land, and the immigrants of the nineteenth and twentieth centuries were following the pattern laid down by the colonists of the seventeenth and eighteenth.

Security for the group, though, is not necessarily security for the individual. For individual unhappy women the perennial pregnancy was but a step in a swift and tiring march to an early grave.

THOSE UNCONTROLLED BIRTHS

IF birth control was taboo, pregnancy itself was hedged about with superstitions. To avoid the Evil Eye, for example, a prospective Sicilian mother had to hide her condition as long as possible and stay indoors, exercising only in the dark. She had to be careful not to let her eyes glance upon any ugliness, lest her child resemble such. A mother was not told the sex of her baby until the placenta had been delivered; her disappointment at having a girl might delay this process. And to some Sicilians belongs the most bizarre custom of all: intercourse at the onset of labor! Doubtless this practice, which apparently re-affirmed fatherhood, was responsible for a great deal of infection and at least in part may explain the higher death rate of that group.[1]

But Italians were not the only immigrants with peculiar ideas on childbirth; a study of the "older" immigrants—English, Irish, and German—found plenty. Among the more unfounded ideas were the notions that an infant born with teeth would become a murderer and that rubbing a baby's gums when teething would cause him to have a sharp temper.[2]

Unlike Americans who proudly proclaimed their little ones' progress, these Europeans were afraid that any acknowledgment of good aroused the jealousy of the Evil Eye. Even young Italian women adopted these beliefs so strongly that fear could grip their lives:

> A group of women meeting at a friend's house to pass the afternoon noticed with misgivings that a childless woman, said to have the Evil Eye, was present. . . . It is considered dangerous to antagonize such a person. . . . A young mother who had brought her 6 month old baby was especially uneasy and planned to leave as soon as she could without attracting attention. Everyone said something complimentary about the child, carefully adding, "God bless it" afterwards. The childless woman did not say this. . . . A few weeks later the baby died, and its death was attributed to the woman with the Evil Eye. . . . When the baby first began to ail, a doctor had been called in and had said that its diet needed changing, but the mother and her friends knew better. After what had happened, no diet would help. She followed the physician's advice only halfheartedly and depended more on the counsels and practices of every maga she could find. Lemons were stuck full of pins, and the heads cut off; strings were knotted; sacred cakes were baked and placed at the feet of the patron saint. All to no end. It was too late.[3]

The mother, trying to steel herself against the anticipated death, became apathetic and convinced herself that it was impossible to save the child. It seems likely that a major psychological purpose of these taboos was that they would serve as insurance in case the worst happened. Sickness, death, and ill fortune of all sorts plagued immigrants, but if their lives were insulated with manifold taboos, they could be sure of always having some kind of "explanation" for every evil.

Immigrant women could generally expect to have a considerably greater chance of dying in childbirth than their American counterparts, as is shown by the following table.

DEATH RATES RELATED TO PREGNANCY, 1900[4]			
(Deaths Among Women 15 to 45, per 100,000 Female Population)			
MOTHERS BORN IN:			
Italy	121.7	Canada	45.6
Russia	66.2	Ireland	45.1
Poland	54.7	United States	34.7
Germany	52.7	Scotland	33.7
Hungary	52.6	Bohemia	30.6
England	50.7	France	22.5*
Scandinavia	45.7		

* Note that though three nationalities have a better rate than natives, this did not represent many actual women. Immigration from all of these countries was very small compared with other groups.

Many factors contributed to these higher rates of immigrant maternal death: frequent pregnancies; inadequate prenatal care, and dirty surroundings during childbirth. Considering all of this, it is a wonder that so many women did survive and continue to work hard and bear more children.

"The peasant women of the first generation," wrote one expert, "amaze our women by their endurance. One of their own midwives told me that they have as hard confinements as Americans, but that they recover more quickly. In Allegheny [Pennsylvania] a settlement friend went to see a neighbor and found her at nine o'clock barefoot in the yard hanging out clothes. She had borne a child at midnight, after which she had arisen and got breakfast for the men of her family and then done the washing."[5]

But these women aged sooner, their children were more sickly and more of them died, and the mothers themselves rolled up appalling death statistics. They did not return to work because they felt healthy enough to do so, but because they had no choice.

Psychological problems could add to the physical ones. Some husbands, for example, took it upon themselves to criticize if the baby was born sick or dead, and of course there was the predilection for male offspring. Yet, sometimes the psychological problem could be largely of one's own making. Rebecca Butterworth was an Englishwoman living in a very primitive frontier situation, but her negative attitude probably complicated her pregnancy. Part of her letter reads:

> Backwoods of America
> Outland Grove, Arkansas
> 5 July 1846

My Very Dear and Tender Father,

> ... I was taken sick a month since today. Thomas [a friend, who apparently claimed to have studied some medicine] was with me nearly all the time. He did not expect me getting over it. I was almost covered with mustard plasters, had a large blister on my back and I cannot tell you what kind of medicine. ... I had nearly 60 grains of calomel [mercury] steamed bricks put to me . . . On Sunday the 14th of June labour came on. I had a many come to see me expecting it almost the last time. . . . About 3 o'clock Monday morning my dear baby was born . . . crying like a child at full term. Thos. did not like to help me as he had not studied midwifery much. I had to remain in that situation for two hours before the doctor could be got, the dear boy calling all the time . . . Doctor Howard come when he took the little darling [sic] and gave it to sister. In about ten minutes after he took his flight to heaven.[6]

Rebecca Butterworth obviously suffered from anxiety compounded by homesickness. In another case, one Mrs. Pagano,* an Italian who lived in Colorado and Utah at the turn of the century, apparently developed a fairly serious neurosis after several childbirths. Her first baby was born when she was only sixteen and she casually delivered it herself. The following four pregnancies were similarly easy. But by the time the sixth child was on its way, she had developed symptoms of mental illness.

> She had nightmare after nightmare in which she dreamed that the child would be born dead or deformed. If she had been able, by sheer force of desire, to counteract the fact of her pregnancy, she would have done so. . . . After a prolonged and difficult confinement, my brother Carl was born. When they brought him to my mother (he was the only one of the children for whom she had to have a doctor), she burst into tears.

*The real name of this woman is not certain, for although the author's name is Pagano, he uses another name for his family in his book.

Tiny and shrunken . . . he could not have weighed more than five pounds.[7]

Mrs. Pagano had not had such problems as a young immigrant girl, but as she became more Americanized and affluent, they increased. Whereas Mrs. Pagano had her first baby entirely alone in a Colorado coal camp, it was now a catastrophe that her pregnant daughter was in California and she in Utah.

Nearly every day a letter . . . arrived, and my mother lost no time answering. "Now be sure you get plenty to eat," she would say. "There's two of you to feed now!" Or: "be careful not to get frightened of anything. Remember Annie Masto I told you about in Denver? She was frightened by a cat while she was carrying her first baby, and when he was born he had a red mark just like a cat on his forehead." And in return Rose wrote such things as "I can't hold anything on my stomach but peanuts and apples. What should I do?" . . . "Povero me!" my father signed on more than one occasion.[8]

The daughter seemed to feel that as an American woman she had a right to insist on attentions and subservience from her husband that no Italian woman would have dreamed of. By the time the baby was due, she had brought herself to such a state of hysteria that the birth was predictably difficult.

Rosa Cavalleri seemed to go to the other extreme and gave her pregnancy too little attention. She was, like most peasant immigrants, fatalistic about things, neglecting to plan and trusting that the Madonna would "make a miracle" when she got into trouble. Rosa's first child was born in Italy and she experienced such a traumatic delivery that even though she had two doctors, she almost died. When in America her second was due she was seriously frightened. In the lonely mining camp where she lived, there was not even a midwife and her drunken husband could not be depended upon. But Rosa made no plans for delivery. Amazingly, even though this was her second child, she still did not know where children came from! "Domiana said that the husband planted a seed in his wife and it was from that seed that babies grew. I never knew before where babies come from, but it sounded probably true. But even a seed couldn't grow into something alive unless God and the Madonna made it."[9]

When as a young married woman she was pregnant for the first time, her adoptive mother told her much less:

I kept getting bigger and bigger. And then one day I felt
kicking inside of me and I knew it was a baby. How that baby
got in there I couldn't understand. But the thing that worried
me most was how it was going to get out! . . . I didn't want to
ask Mamma Lena, but what was I going to do? That baby was
kicking to get out. . . .

"Well," said Mamma Lena, "You'll have to pray the Madonna . . . Maybe the Madonna will make a miracle for you
and let the baby come out without the doctor cutting.[10]*

Perhaps because Rosa was older, the second child was born nor-
mally. All alone, she cut and tied the cord herself. She had learned
this shortly before when she had to help a friend who was having
a baby, and the patient had given the "midwife" instructions. Having successfully cut the cord, Rosa passed out, and a German
neighbor lady found her and the baby on the floor. She put Rosa
to bed and returned home. Rosa related:

I knew the men would be coming to eat and there was nothing
prepared. . . . I tried, but I couldn't get up. Santino [her hus-
band] came in first. . . . I knew he was angry because there
was nothing prepared. . . . I was hungry and so thirsty. Maybe
if I had something to eat I could get up . . . so I asked Santino
if he will bring me a bowl of warm water from the reservoir
with bread and butter in it. He didn't answer me at first. Then
he started swearing and told me if I wanted something to eat
to get up and get it myself.[11]

It is a measure of Rosa's strength and faith that she didn't allow
these cruel experiences to poison her mind against sex and childbirth. After she left Santino and remarried, she went on to have
several more children without problems or fear. When her last was
born, Rosa's husband was away. The baby was overdue and when
labor at last started, she sent the children to a neighbor's:

I was on my bed all alone by myself. . . . Just when the baby
was born, I saw Sant' Antoni right there! . . . Then the door
opened and the midwife came in to take care of the baby!

*Incredible though it is, the thought occurs that perhaps Mamma Lena didn't
tell Rosa more than she did because she didn't know herself. She had never borne
children—Rosa was adopted—and it could be that she never learned how childbirth
worked. On the other hand, she was married and presumably had sex, but did not
tell Rosa what to expect of marriage, either.

... She washed the baby and put him by me, but then she ran away. She didn't light the fire or nothing.

Oh, that night it was so cold! And me in my little wooden house in the alley with the walls all frosting—thick, white frosting. I was crying and praying, "How am I going to live?"

... My Visella was bringing up the wood and the coal and trying to make that room warm. But she was only a little girl, she didn't know, and ... the ceiling caught fire. I had to jump up from the bed and throw pails of water.... Then God sent me help again. He sent that Miss Mildred from the settlement house. She didn't know about me and my Leo born; she was looking for some other lady and she came to my door.... Then she ran away and brought back all those little things the babies in America have.... Oh, that Miss Mildred and Miss May, they were angels to come and help me like that! Four nights Miss May stayed there and kept the fire going. They were high-up educated girls—they were used to sleeping in the warm house with the plumbing—and there they came and slept in my wooden house in the alley and for a toilet they had to go down to that shed under the sidewalk. They were really, really friends![12]

Most women were better prepared, and put their faith not in the appearance of angels but in midwives. Some immigrants hired a midwife only because she charged less and moved up to a doctor when they could afford to, but others gave sound reasons for preferring midwives. A midwife was more likely to speak the native language; she not only charged less but also accepted installment payments; and she performed other household services, cooking, cleaning, and looking after older children. In 1917 in Detroit, for example, the standard midwife fee was seven to ten dollars and she visited daily for five days or more. Doctors came only once and charged ten to thirty dollars.[13]

The doctors argued that their services were sufficiently superior to justify the higher fee. Upton Sinclair wrote that a Polish doctor in the Chicago stockyards area told him, "I have been practicing for thirteen years in this district, and during that time never a week has passed that I have not been called in to two or three cases of women who have been mangled and mutilated by midwives."[14]

The vivid picture of The Jungle's murderous midwife has taken hold and charges against them have been repeated with more frequency than truth. Immigrants, however, did not have this sinister image. Americans who could overcome their prejudice and look objectively saw, as did this supervisory nurse, that "many of them are well-educated, thoroughly trained women. . . . In Italy none but a well-educated woman can qualify for the training, which covers from two to four years. . . . They are well-trained, scientific women."[15]

A study of the subject much more diligent than Upton Sinclair's "realism" found that public health departments and doctors who were honest about the facts agreed the prejudice against foreign midwives was unjustified: "If the midwife is the cause of much infant mortality we should have a high infant mortality rate, for . . . 88% of all foreign-born mothers are attended by midwives. The maternal mortality in our city among midwife cases is no higher than in the city as a whole."[16]

The death rate in Newark in 1915–17 again shows just the reverse of what most would expect. For every seventy-one women who died with a midwife in attendance, there were eighty who died at home with a doctor and ninety-one dying in the hospital.[17] Of course it is true that complicated cases would be referred to doctors and hospitals, but nevertheless it appears that midwives were not the negligent incompetents they have been reputed to be. Finally, no less a personage than the president of the American Medical Association spoke critically, not of midwives as would be expected, but of doctors:

> Of 116 cases of ophthalmia neonatorum which were treated in the Massachusetts Eye & Ear Infirmary in one winter 22 occurred in the practice of physicians and 11 in that of midwives. Of the 11 midwives, 3 had used nitrate of silver; of the 22 doctors, only 1. According to these reports . . . the doctors should be replaced by midwives.[18]

All of this is especially appalling in view of the fact that doctors charged so much more and gave so much less in terms of time and service. One Jewish mother recognized and preferred the unhurried midwife who encouraged a natural delivery to doctors who hastened births for their own convenience by use of forceps. "The doctor, even the professor doctor," she said, "he comes to your house to get your baby. He hurries you up; he hurries you up, and that is not so good."[19]

IN SICKNESS AND
IN HEALTH

I F women were reluctant to have a doctor around the home interfering with traditional childbirth, one can imagine their abhorrence of hospitals. There, visitors were restricted and no drinks or festive foods could be served. The baby was isolated in a nursery; how then, could Italian babies have pinned on them the charms that friends gave in the wish for a good life? And what of the mother? "Italian women . . . approach their confinement, particularly their first, with wonderful hand-woven sheets, embroidered pillowcases, and beautiful satin coverlets, often made by the mother herself during girlhood."[1]

Women in labor were certainly not the only ones suspicious of hospitals. "It was not an easy thing for my people to send me to the hospital," Rose Cohen wrote of her teenage experience with chronic anemia:

> The very word filled us with fear. . . . It was quite understood that in the hospital patients were practiced upon by hardened medical students and then neglected. Whenever we saw anyone miserable, dirty, neglected, we would say, "He looks like a 'hegdish' " (hospital). And so we saw our neighbors all about us borrow and pawn but keep their sick at home. And when once in a while we saw a person taken to the hospital we looked after him mournfully as if he were already carried to the burial grounds. It was also an open acknowledgement of the direst poverty.[2]

She was Jewish, but these views were shared by uneducated immigrants of all ethnic groups. Social workers, recognizing the immigrants' fear of hospitals, saw outpatient clinics as an alternative and urged their clients to use them, but this wasn't easily done. Some pregnant women avoided prenatal clinics lest the Evil Eye discover their condition.[3] There were other problems as well. Unable to read signs and ask directions, how was she to find her way to the clinic and back in the big city? How could she leave her children, take off from work and lose wages, and spend carfare on the chance that this clinic would prevent some vague problem she couldn't even define? It was better to just get along as she had been.

Doctors not only hospitalized you, they did such terrible things as quarantine you. One family, suspecting their child had small-pox, refused to call a doctor because they had heard of the American system of quarantine. They continued to operate the clothing sweat shop in their home and called a doctor only when it was too late. The child died and perhaps hundreds of people were exposed to smallpox through the clothes from their shop.[4]

Surgery was another frightening thing. Rosa Cavalleri, never re-luctant to express her views, raged on about American doctors and surgery:

> The American doctors they ruin the people. I say, "People don't go to the doctors!" You get a pain in your stomach, and they say, "Take off the tonsils." They tell you to take off those things and they won't cure you till you do. In Italia we don't take off nothing—we keep everything and we are not sick. God gives us all those little things; what for the doctors take them off? The American people ruin themselves by running all the time to those crazy doctors.[5]

A Slavic woman wrote that among her people a witching woman was called first when there was illness, and if she could not produce a cure, the druggist was a second choice consultant. Doc-tors were called only as a last resort.[6]

In Europe it was common for reputable doctors to advertise, and many American quacks took advantage of this. They placed large, eye-catching ads, complete with false testimonials and dire warn-ings. Not only were advertising doctors in Europe respectable, but the newspapers in many countries were so strictly regulated and censored by the government, that anything advertised was taken to have official approval. Here immigrants innocently assumed that the doctors who *did not* advertise were the quacks, for it seemed obvious that these non-advertisers probably could not get permission.

Another factor in choosing a doctor was his fee—and not, as one might expect, necessarily the lowest. Most immigrants apparently believed that one does not get something for nothing and were suspicious of charity doctors. They tended to think that a doctor who charged more was better.

Uneducated immigrants also were apt to call in additional doc-tors if the first one did not bring a quick cure. They sometimes waited only a few hours and if there wasn't noticeable improvement, brought in another. Three or four doctors might be consulted and all of their prescriptions taken—plus, of course, the nostrums of the Old World medicine woman and the local pharmacist. Even among healthy, young working women studied, their medical expenditures for the year was approximately equal to two weeks wages.[7]

This willingness to spend precious money on "better" doctors when free ones were available is illustrative of the devotion of most immigrants to the family. Nevertheless, endless worry over the cost of sickness, especially of a lengthy illness, inevitably made matters worse. One writer observed, "The period of illness is described as such and such number of weeks since he brought anything in. A visit to a doctor who didn't help matters any is reported as a money loss. . . . This constant, open anxiety about the cost is bound to be observed by the sick person.[8]

These ambivalent attitudes produced internal conflict. A woman couldn't let her family's health—and pride—suffer by using charitable services, yet she could not afford to spend the meager income. It was a dilemma often "solved" by indecision and acceptance of the result.

Suspicion of modern medicine extended from hospital to home and preventative health care. Bathing was one such bone of contention: "A young Pole was induced to go into the swimming pool in a Young Men's Christian Association; after that he kept away from the building, and the secretary went to find out why he stayed away. The mother of the lad met him, and gave him a piece of her mind, that he dared to make her boy take a bath in winter time. 'Did you want to kill him?' "[9]

Italian mothers instructed their children similarly. One man, who washed in the river in summer acknowledged that his family never bathed in winter. "My father, who is 80 years old, I have never known to take a bath."[10]

Ventilation was another problem. Many immigrants believed that "even in the hottest weather you must never leave a door or window open at night. The night air will make you sick if you let it get in."[11] Since pulmonary diseases, especially tuberculosis, abounded in immigrant homes, this was a problem that health educators tried to solve over and over again with results coming slowly:

When, on the advice of her doctor, I once attempted to send
an overworked young Italian girl threatened with tuberculosis
to the country, I found myself facing such violent opposition
from her parents that I seemed lost between . . . either tearing
the girl from her family in order to save her life or leaving her
there to die. By slow degrees, and through patient effort, however, the parents were made to realize the seriousness of their
daughter's condition, to provide her with milk and eggs, to
allow her to sleep alone with windows open, to lessen her
heavy household tasks, and to take her regularly for reex-
amination to her doctor.[12]

The home remedies used by women on their families were sometimes useless, sometimes harmful. Elizabeth Stern, writing of her
adolescent years at the turn of the century says that her aunt, a
kindly Lithuanian Jew, "used to fret over me. She fed me goose
fat on bread, made me eat warm dough, and one day put glass
cups on my skinny young arms to bleed me, to 'get the thinness
out' of me."[13] Norwegians in the Midwest thought sheep dung was
effective against tuberculosis when worn as a poultice. Bits of brass
were given to patients with broken bones on the theory that this
would serve as solder to hold the bones together.[14] One of the most
dangerously erroneous ideas of Italians was that "contact with a
virgin was . . . an unfailing cure for gonorrhea."[15]

Many immigrants seemed to feel it was wrong to interfere too
much with the natural course of disease. Americans interested in
public health had to battle with immigrants of almost every nationality over vaccination. Holyoke, Massachusetts, a city filled
with Irish and French-Canadian immigrants, was typical. When
smallpox broke out, public health officials were frustrated at every
turn in their efforts to stem the epidemic. Quarantine signs were
torn down, free vaccinations were refused, and the sick were hidden from officers who would have placed them in isolation.[16] Many
women believed certain diseases were inevitable and that, since
prevention was impossible, the sooner a child got it, the better.

———

Studies of working women often included Americans as well as
foreigners, and there are abundant examples of native women every bit as ignorant as the immigrants they often scorned. Poor
health practices seem to be much more a matter of class than of
nationality. Educated Europeans in America carried out good med-

ical procedures, and uneducated persons who grew up in this country often refused to follow them. It is certainly far from true that American health was clearly superior, for in almost every index of health, some other group outranked natives. For example, although the Irish-born had a scandalously high tuberculosis death rate in 1900—340 per hundred thousand compared with 113 for natives—the Jewish foreign-born had only 72.[17]

In many health indices, Americans are outranked by Scandinavians. As early as 1864, Gro Svendsen wrote home for smallpox vaccine that was unobtainable here. Norwegians also protested the lack of stringent licensing requirements for doctors and missed their own government regulated system, appalled by the fact that "doctors are not appointed to any one district but settle where they see the best chances."[18]

Finally, it is striking that immigrant men and women alike were willing to look to women with only a modicum of training as medical experts. Not only did immigrants respect midwives and nurses, but many placed their first faith in the witching woman—in great contrast to Americans who refused to accept women in medicine even when they had outstanding training.

One study of widows explored the causes of their husbands' deaths, finding that half of them were due to diseases that largely should have been preventable.[19] Respiratory ills were by far the biggest killer—life and breath could have been given merely by opening windows. The frequency of death from tuberculosis is particularly sad, not only because it might have been arrested with rest and fresh air, but also because of its lingering and contagious nature.

Fresh air and rest might have been advisable, but even if a woman accepted that, how could it be done? How could her husband assume the role of a gentleman and give up working when there were mouths to feed and rent to pay? And so a woman would watch the man she loved slowly inch toward death, and with him would go their years of carefully accumulated savings. Working through the day, kept awake by his hacking cough at night, the woman would weep helpless tears. Sickness was sad, but it was also inevitable.

THE IMMIGRANT WAY OF DEATH

L AWRENCE, Massachusetts was a cotton mill town whose looms demanded a constantly fresh supply of labor. At the time of the Irish influx in 1850, life expectancy in Lawrence was a mere fifteen years. By 1880 it had climbed to twenty-five, but epidemics swept through the crowded foreign sections, and in the next decades, life expectancy dropped to twenty and then again to fifteen. After fifty years of "progress," as the twentieth century began, this important vital statistic was at the same level it had been before the Civil War.[1]

A life expectancy of fifteen years seems absurd on the face of it. Obviously the figure is misleading when applied to adults and just as obviously it reflects a huge rate of infant mortality.

Lawrence, with infants accounting for 44 percent of all deaths in 1900,[2] was not alone. In a New York City tenement, of 138 children born in a three-year period, sixty-one had died.[3] Another study of 370 working mothers showed that they had borne 1,758 children of whom 437 had died.[4] Nor were cities the only places where such shocking numbers of infant deaths occurred. The church records of a Wisconsin settlement of Norwegians at midcentury showed that of 194 deaths, 94 had been of children under age five.[5]

Health at birth was only one factor in infant mortality. Women could give birth to well babies, but if they could not care for them adequately, the babies would sicken. The single most important factor in whether a baby grows well is the food it receives, but there seems to have been considerable variation among ethnic groups on the proper nutrition.

A detailed investigation of the subject showed that Italian, Polish, and French-Canadian mothers were especially likely to breast-feed their babies, some of them not beginning solids until the child was a year old. Jewish and Irish mothers were less likely to breast-feed exclusively. Portuguese women in this study exhibited particularly exotic ideas on infant nutrition; many fed their babies solids in the first week.[6]

Even if one had an understanding of what comprised an adequate infant diet, it was a herculean task to provide it. Foods sold before the Pure Food and Drug Act often were adulterated; push-cart merchandise was exposed to flies; refrigeration was unavailable; there were no blenders to puree meat or vegetables. The result was that children existed on crackers, cookies, and pudding—or the milk of a malnourished mother. In more than half of the cases where breastfeeding ceased, it was because the woman no longer could produce milk.[7] The baby would ail and the mother would mourn and no one would ask why except to say it was God's will.

———————

Their acceptance of death is a constant theme. One social worker reported that women started this mental self-protection from the very beginning of motherhood, believing that "the first one has to go."[8] Another confirmed this, saying of the mothers she studied, "They are strangely apathetic toward the loss of their children by death. Almost as soon as the first pang of sorrow is past, the bereaved mother is ready to say that the little one is 'better off' and to speak of death as a merciful release from a life of hardship." Nevertheless she adds, "The same mother who resents the coming of children and resigns them so apathetically to death, will toil fourteen hours a day and seven days a week to keep up a house for the young lives in her charge."[9]

Such toil was a way of life for a Bohemian woman who worked as a maid while her mother cared for her children. Elizabeth Stern, just beginning social work around 1900, wrote that in a dilapidated tenement:

> was an old woman . . . with a baby in her arms, a little child at her knee . . . and a little body of a boy twenty hours dead . . . on the table. Her daughter was working in a flat in the Bronx and would not be home until the following day. . . . I lifted the old woman to the bed, put the dead little boy on two chairs and covered the tiny face, so still and frozen and thin, wrapped the two other children and then ran out to buy milk and crackers and meat at the corner delicatessen. I cleaned up the house, washed the boy and girl and then sat and waited for the mother. . . . [she] came into the room [and] saw me. Her parcels dropped. She came over and pulled back the cover. . . . I helped place the little figure in the coffin. I watched the mother bid it good-by. In those days servants were not ladies of importance; a good job was precious. She could not even

go to see her child buried. . . . I went with the old grandmother
and heard her anguished cry.[10]

The mother's grief took second place to the needs of the present.
Elisabeth Koren, writing in Iowa in the 1850s, was shocked by the
seemingly easy way her Norwegian neighbors accepted the death
of their young son; to her there was an excess of stoicism. "They
must feel or bear their sorrows in a different way from what I could.
As I listened to their way of talking of it, I was not able to say a
word. . . . It seemed as if the main thing they were thinking of was
that the father would not now have his son to help with the
work."[11]

Linka Preus, like Mrs. Koren a Lutheran minister's wife, tried
to be stoic, but compounded sorrow with guilt. When her four-
year-old boy became seriously ill she wrote:

> Some eight to fourteen days ago, I thought Thou wouldst take
> my little Christian Keyser unto Thyself. Never did I believe
> that taking leave of such a little one would be so grievous. We
> all said good-bye to him; then God let him fall into a deep
> sleep; for a day and a half he lay in a death-like coma, breath-
> ing heavily. Finally came a change and to our great joy he
> improved steadily. . . . For Jesus sake Thou wilt forgive me;
> but it seems, now that Thou hast permitted me to keep Chris-
> tian, that my love for Thee is greater than it was before. Alas,
> my Father, forgive me; a very great sinner am I.[12]

Elise Waerenskjold, a Norwegian in post–Civil War Texas, had
no explanation for the sudden death of her son except as an example of God's enigmatic will. She wrote of the Sunday afternoon
Death's Angel called, while her family was out visiting:

> I wanted to go home to bring in the sheep . . . Thorvald wanted
> to go with Mama and on the way chatted quite cheerfully with
> me. We had gone just about 10 steps after he last spoke when,
> without complaint, without a sound, he sank down at my side;
> he spoke no more until Wednesday morning when he regained
> consciousness and could speak a few words and gave Mama
> the last kiss. I was so happy then, for I believed he would
> recover, but that was not to be. At 4:00 he died.[13]

Elise found comfort in the fact that the day before Thorvald had
asked several questions about death and resurrection. Even though
she was an educated and independent woman, she never sought
a medical explanation.

A study of English, Irish, and German women in New York indicated a similar lack of scientific curiosity into the causes of their babies' deaths. A report on a German mother whose four-year-old child died in 1894 stated: "Mother does not know cause of death; died in hospital; mother never thought of asking nurse."[14]

In some cases this fatalistic acceptance of death was the cause of more death. There was, for example, the Irish woman who had borne eight children; four infants died in four years, one lived to be fifteen before pneumonia took him and another died at fourteen in an accident. Of her eight children, only two were alive, but she may have counted herself lucky, for her sister-in-law in Ireland had borne twenty children with only four reaching adulthood.[15]

Their lives were such that they had to believe children were better off dying young. "One son," reminisced an old Irish mother, "would be fifty-two if he had lived through his first year. Another son was born in 1853. In 1855 Katie was born. She died in 1868. Then there was Mike and Stephen and Pat, God knows I don't remember them all, but they is blessed for they died young."[16]

In fact the death of little babies perhaps was sometimes a secret relief to overwrought mothers. Kate Bond, an Englishwoman in Kansas, typifies this; incredible as it may be, her letter seems to say that she will mourn her baby later when she has more time. "We had a little boy born the 23 of December," she wrote. "He lived to be eight weeks old. As soon as harvest is over and things straight I will not forget him."[17]

But when a grown daughter died, she was distraught. This daughter, unlike the baby, was a personality and provided companionship for her mother on the isolated frontier. Her letter read, "I suppose you have heard of Maggie's death. I miss her so much. . . . It is so lonely without her. But I suppose we should have parted if she had lived and perhaps it is better as it is, for I know where she is now and wants for nothing. . . . She was ready and willing to go and missed a troublesome world."[18]

It was as if such women were afraid to be resentful of death, afraid to express a justifiable complaint of their hard lot, lest worse befall. Always there is the rationalization that the child probably would have had an unhappy life. Mrs. Bond and other women like her must have found solace in this reasoning, for they never failed to offer it. When a friend back in England was bereaved, Mrs. Bond comforted her with written beauty seldom seen among Kansas farmwives, an articulateness motivated by strong feeling:

We was sorry to hear of your loss. For I know it is a loss that none but a mother can feel. But, Ellen, when the first pain is over you will thanck God in your heart that it has pleased Him to take him out of this world of sin and sorrow. . . . It seems as though there is extray strength given us for our trials. The other children will miss him, I know, but you must try not to fret too much for their sakes. Peter is in Heaven and at rest and it is those that are here that need our care now. If it had not been for my younger ones I thinck they would have laid me beside her [Maggie] before now. So thinck of yours now and it will help you in your trouble.[19]

Mothers weren't the only ones to mourn, nor infants the only ones to die. When Gro Svendsen died in the delivery of her tenth baby, her husband's grief was deep, as his love had been. He found it very hard to inform her parents. "I must arouse myself and try to write you. . . . It is not so easy to write." Though his letters try to be manly, his unhappiness cannot be hidden:

I also want to send you a lock of my dear Gro's hair. . . . How much I miss her cannot be told. . . . You, too, will feel the loneliness for her who is gone. . . . I want to tell you about Gro's grave. It has a white marble stone, on which are engraved the date and place of her birth, the date and place of her death, and the names of those she left behind. Last of all, a verse from David's Psalms: "In Thee, O Lord, do I put my trust; let me never be put to confusion." . . . I myself planted a tree on her grave to keep the weeds away. Her friends planted flowers. The grave is enclosed by a pretty (white) picket fence.[20]

Gro's husband must have found the reminders of her around the Iowa farm where they had lived too sorrowful to bear, for soon this widower with nine small children packed up and moved to a Dakota homestead. He cared for them alone, not remarrying as was the custom of the day, and his life was hard with frequent visits from death. Only four of the ten children would live to adulthood.

Some women seemed to grow so tired, so achingly weary of their frustrated lives that they only wanted to lay their burdens down. Such was the case with this Englishwoman, whose father writes of her, "Isabella never was well after her baby was born. She knew she was dieing and made all her arrangements, talked about it as calmly as if she were going on a journey. . . . I had all the advise

I could get for her but it was no use. Death was there and we could do her no good."[21]

Likewise, Elise Waerenskjold talked abstractly of her possible death. "The baby arrived well and happy," she wrote at age forty-four:

> I cannot express to you how glad I was that everything went
> well because, after all, I am no longer young, and therefore,
> I was worried for fear I might have to leave my beloved chil-
> dren. Neither Wilhelm nor I have a single relative in this
> country, so it isn't easy to say what Wilhelm would have done
> with the children if I had died, because it is absolutely against
> the custom in this country for a white girl to keep house for
> a widower—and as to a stepmother, well, they are seldom
> good.[22]

Like other women, Elise's concern was first of all for her family. It is as though she is embarrassed to mention any thought—much less fear—for herself.

———

Resignation about death was the usual case because there was no place for any other emotion in lives that were so overwhelmed by the practical. Mourning for a loved one was often cut short by an immediate pressure; where was the money for the burial? "Many a mother," said one charity doctor, "has told me at her child's death bed, 'I cannot afford to lose it. It costs too much to bury it.' "[23]

The bereaved family was under a strong social obligation to provide an elaborate funeral, no matter how poor they were. Funerals among almost every Christian immigrant group, especially the Italian and the Irish, were an occasion. Wakes lasted for days, with food and drink provided; the bereaved was expected to provide an ornate hearse, flowers, expenses for a priest and mortician, burial plot, new clothes, and countless other items. Tradition—and the fear of the neighbor's gossip—prevailed against the practical admonitions of the social workers, and the debts were made. "Funerals of children," reported a case worker in 1907,

> cost from $10 to $90, and for adults $100 to $200. . . . The
> ostentatious display in flowers and number of carriages is
> much to be regretted. One family, which was dependent most
> of the time, insisted on having two carriages for the funeral

of their son, with no one to ride in the second one, but, as the mother said, "Sure, it's all I can do for him." They were burdening themselves with a debt which it would take years to pay. In one case the funeral of a child four years old cost $84, and there was no insurance. The mother has been years trying to pay for it. . . .[24]

A 1913 study of widows showed that approximately two-thirds of the resources available to most widows—insurance, savings, etc.—were used immediately for the husband's funeral. Of the 237 widows who gave information on the cost of their husbands' funerals, all but 86 had spent over $100 to have their mate laid to rest in style.[25] At the average wage most widows could expect to earn, a $100 funeral could be the equivalent of a third of her annual income.

The city, with its established businesses interested in promoting funerals, encouraged this excess, but on the frontier there was little opportunity—or pressure—to bankrupt oneself on behalf of the dead. Among Scandinavians and Germans who largely settled the Midwest, long wakes with heavy drinking at a time of sorrow were scandalous. While they spared widows the expense and worry that complicated grief, perhaps frontier funerals were too bleak for comfort. "Aaste Wilson pictures the frontier immigrant burial custom in stark detail. For funerals, she writes, 'people always had to be invited.' "

There were always two meals, "one before they went to the graveyard and the other after they came back." Simple black homemade coffins were used, with nails driven halfway into the covers. The service opened with a hymn: "Who Knows How Near Me is My Death." Aaste's father, a layman, usually had charge of the services in the Wisconsin settlement where he lived: "He would give a talk in remembrance of the departed one and give thanks for him." Thereupon the people walked past the coffin for a last look, "and immediately afterward we heard the sad sound of the hammering of the nails on the coffin lid". . . . The coffin was put in a wagon, driven to the graveyard, and the mourners walked behind it. Men took turns in digging the grave. When it was ready they placed their spades crosswise on it and sang, "Now the Grave is a Comfort to Me, for Thy Hand Shall Cover Me." Then all said the Lord's Prayer, and that was the end. "It was simple but dignified and there was a Christian spirit and a deep sincerity in it all. . . . They did it as well as they could."[26]

RELIGION HERE
AND
HEREAFTER

ON Rose Cohen's first Saturday in America, her father took her for a walk. He had preceded her here, and no doubt was proudly anticipating the little treat he had in store for her—Rose's first taste of watermelon.

I felt proud of him that he had credit at so beautiful a fruit-stand. As I received the melon in my fingers I saw father take his hand out of his pocket and hold out a coin. I stood staring at him for a moment. Then I dropped the melon on the pave-ment and ran. . . . My father had touched coin on the Sabbath! Oh, the sin!. . . . Then I remembered Yanna, who, on hearing that father was in America, and feeling that perhaps we were too happy over it, came one day to torment grandmother. "The first thing men do in America," she said, "is to cut their beards and the first thing women do is to leave off their wigs. And you . . . you who will not break a thread on the Sabbath now, will eat swine in America.[1]

Her father had indeed cut his beard and now she saw that he violated the Sabbath, too. The poor girl felt that his soul, and prob-ably hers, were doomed. Yet in a few years Rose's father would be admonishing her to remember the old ways as she edged danger-ously away from Judaism.

For some immigrants, the strangeness of America made even more necessary the security to be found in clinging to the old faith. For others, part of the freedom of the New World was the liberty to break away from the religion into which they had been born. For most, of course, the process was an evolutionary one, and the immigrant herself was generally not aware that she was changing her religious views.

To midwestern Scandinavians, the Lutheran church brought the serene remembrance of home. They turned out in great numbers for church services, and even the largest available home empty of furniture could not hold the crowds. Elisabeth Koren describes such a service, "I did not have such a bad seat. . . . until the com-municants had to come forward. But then, with many others, I had to give up my place and go outside. It was out of the question to think of getting in again. . . . There were many more outside than in; they crowded about the windows and doors in order to hear. . . ."[2]

Though apparently devoted to their faith, these people were not quite pious enough to make the financial sacrifice required to build a proper church building, preferring instead to crowd into a home, and naturally the burden fell on the faithful women of the congregation. Gro Svendsen complained that though funds had been collected, "a great deal more is needed in order to build. In America money was said to be so plentiful, and it may be. But it's hard to get any of it when it's to be used for the common good, for such as teachers' salaries, ministers' salaries, and other expenses connected with the church."[3]

Undoubtedly, many people came to church largely for the social purpose it served. Elise Isely, a Swiss-born woman in frontier Kansas, candidly admitted that the social functions of the church were as important as the spiritual:

> City people surfeited with close daily contact with others . . . can hardly understand the hunger for church that pioneer families had. . . . Out of our desire for company as well as out of our need for spiritual development, we dressed our children in their best clothing and journeyed to Fairview. . . . If we could avoid it, none of our family ever missed attendance; if it rained we put up an umbrella; if it snowed we wrapped up in blankets. . . . We were happy in being there. We no more thought of missing church than of missing our meals.[4]

It is understandable why the camp meetings of some of the revivalist American churches held appeal for immigrants. They were not only a glorious social event to isolated frontierswomen, but they were also an interesting change from the stolid state churches of Europe. Ann Whittaker, an Englishwoman living in Illinois during 1840–50, was smitten by the Baptist religion, and its blessings became the lengthy theme of her letters. She said:

> . . . We have had a great revival of religion in our neighborhood. . . . There has been a great many of the wickest characters brought to a knowledge of the truth. . . . I can truly say I feel more satisfied the [sic] I ever did since we came into the country. . . . I find for my own part that there is nothing like living to God for then we have the promise of this life and also of that which is to come. Godliness with contentment his great gain. My dear Brother, if you have not begun to serve

the Lord it is high time to be up and doing. The judgment of his God are abroad in the land.[5]

Elise Waerenskjold was contemptuous of her Norwegian neighbors who deviated from the traditional ways and attended these obstreperous American camp meetings. She had investigated a revival firsthand and was shocked by what she saw. "One after another they begin to sing and clap their hands, crying out Glory! Glory! as loudly as they can. They begin pounding on the ones nearest to them, throwing themselves on their knees or on their backs, laughing and crying—in short, conducting themselves like perfectly insane people."[6]

She was saddened to report that what to her was so repulsive was attractive to others of her nationality. "Several of the Norwegians have abandoned their Lutheran faith. . . . I wish very much," she lamented, "we could get a good Lutheran minister."[7]

But in Elise's Texas, Lutheranism was an oddity and more quickly abandoned. Where one settled had a great deal to do with one's religious development. Those Lutherans who wanted their traditional faith remained amid their neighbors in the Upper Midwest, where both Scandinavian and German Lutheranism grew more conservative than they had been in Europe. (The largest German synod, for example, did not allow its women to form an organization by and for themselves until 1942.)[8] Those who wanted more freedom moved on to the Far West. In the 1860s when the secular Scandinavian Society in San Francisco was large enough to expend over $27,000 on concerts, lectures, and parties, the church membership never exceeded thirty.[9] A pastor commenting on this situation acknowledged that many of the Scandinavians who should have been in his flock had "fallen into free thought and led a gay life." The greatest cause, to his mind, was that "many seem to be ashamed of their homeland and prefer to be— Yankees."[10]

But it was not only the distractions of San Francisco that caused people to abandon their faith; it was a deliberate rejection of something that to them symbolized the Old World. The Reverend Mr. Hvistendahl had to admit that "parents cannot feel strongly drawn to a church to which they cannot take their children." Their English-speaking offspring felt "more at home among Americans, to whose Sunday schools they go. Many are even ashamed of their nationality and regard a Scandinavian church as an absurdity."[11]

These mothers were not neglecting their children's religious education; they were rejecting the old church and the old language. They saw the English language and English church as part of upward mobility. The conservative clergy could not accept the solution of services in English and insisted that religion be tied to nationalism; consequently these women sent their children away from the faith of their fathers.

———

The majority of settlers came for economic reasons, but there is one significant group in the period from 1840–1930 who came because of their religion: the Jews. Millions of Jews escaped the pogroms of Russia and Eastern Europe for the freedom of the New World. It was a great irony for them to discover that even in America they were not entirely free.

Disturbed that her father cut off his beard, Rose Cohen finally spoke to him about it. His explanation was grimly realistic: "They do not like Jews on Cherry Street. And one with a long beard has to take his life into his own hands." Rose asked why they had to live on that street, and again his answer was fiercely practical. "I save here at least two dollars a month. . . . This is not like home. There the house was our own. There, too, we were among friends and relatives. While here, if we haven't rent for one month we are thrown out on the street."[12]

Indeed it was not like home economically, but it was entirely too much like home religiously. Once again they had to choose between their conscience and their physical safety. Rose's eyes were opened to the reality instead of the hope, and she wrote:

> I had seen from the first that Jews were treated roughly. . . .
> I had often seen . . . them attack a Jewish peddlar, dump his
> push cart of apples into the gutter, fill their pockets and walk
> away laughing. . . . And yet as soon as I was safe in the house
> I scarcely gave the matter a second thought. Perhaps it was
> because to see a Jew maltreated was nothing new for me. Here
> where there were so many new and strange things for me to
> see and understand this was the one familiar thing.[13]

It bothered her more as time went on. The violence grew worse, and the girl had visions of her father murdered and herself left alone. Her fear was for her father, for women were immune from the effects of this particular prejudice. That could be a godsend for the men, as she reveals in this memorable story:

I was returning about five o'clock through Clinton Street when
I saw him watching me as I came up. When I was near he
asked, "Are you Jewish?" I nodded my head and stopped. . . .
"You can do me a favour," he said in a pleading tone. "You see
this handful of fish? This is all my profit. If I could get over
to that group of Jewish houses on Cherry Street," he pointed
to our tenements, "I could sell it though it is late. But I dare
not pass those loafers hanging around the saloons. . . . They
have great respect for a lady in America. . . . If you will just
walk beside me while I am passing the loafers, they won't
touch me." I remember now often having seen Jewish men
escorted past dangerous places. And the women would as often be Irish.[14]

While Irish men played at this criminal kind of prejudice, Irish
women, though probably more fervent Catholics, saw the injustice
of religious persecution and humanely registered a quiet protest.

While many hung on to the faith in which they had been born,
others took the first opportunity to abandon it. A German-American
woman left the Lutheran church for a nondenominational one because she thought it "is foolish to have German services, and you
get more Christmas presents there besides."[15] According to a student of the Irish, German, and English families of New York's West
Side, it was not uncommon for women to attend a particular
church for this baldly materialistic reason. A Catholic woman
whose husband did not attend church stated plainly that she went
occasionally because "the Sisters are good to us then at
Christmastime."[16]

Though these immigrants gave the same excuses as Americans
for not attending—that they were too busy or too tired or perhaps
did not have suitable clothes—some gave an interesting reason
unique to the immigrant experience: "nobody cares now if we go
or not."[17] In Old World villages there was pressure to attend
church, but in cities immigrant women were free of this obligation,
and having no innate desire to attend, stayed away. Their husbands
were even more likely to ignore the church, and "husband and
wife rarely attend church together."[18]

A social worker among New York Italians reported a similiar lack
of faithfulness. "Church contributions did not play a large part in
the family expenditures. Though all were Roman Catholic, the

church was not an important factor in their lives. The older generation seldom went to services. The attendance of the girls seemed to compensate for the shortcomings in this direction of the remainder of the family."[19]

As the Italian girls took care of the religious obligations of their families, so Jewish men sometimes relieved their wives in this area. One Jewish girl stated:

> In Poland I and my father and mother used to go to the synagogue on the Sabbath, but here the women don't go to the synagogue much, though the men do. They are shut up working hard all week long and when the Sabbath comes they like to sleep long in bed and afterwards they must go out where they can breathe the air. The rabbis are not so strict as in the old country.[20]

Economic reality took its toll on religious observance. An Italian woman, suffering during an economic depression, expressed her views succinctly: "Bread is bread, and candles are candles. When you have eaten, your stomach is full; when the candle is burned, you are still empty."[21] When a missionary visited a poor Scottish home, the woman responded, "God keep them that's starving us all by bits, if there is a God, but I'm doubting it, else why don't things get better, an' not always worse and worse?"[22]

Bohemians deserted their official faith en masse. Subjected to governmental suppression of religious freedom in their homeland, here they dropped the facade of faith that had been forced on them. According to government figures back home, fewer than 1 percent of Bohemians (Czechs) were "without confession;" here, Thomas Capek, an apologist who was anxious to impress Americans with his people, acknowledged that, "It is within the truth to say that 50 percent of the Čechs in America have seceded from their old country faith."[23] Others put the figure even higher.

Not only did the church become less important, in some instances the importance that remained had a negative effect. During the Great Depression, for example, some Italian couples felt they could not afford a church wedding and were married in civil ceremonies. Problems resulted when the bride became pregnant. Then they had to go to a priest and confess their sin of omission and be married by him—otherwise their baby could not be baptized. Sometimes young wives, desperate to save money, went from priest to priest to see who would marry them most cheaply.[24] Re-

*Immigrant children received health and hygiene education from
the Department of Health prior to World War I. The advantage of
teaching the schoolgirl how to bathe a baby was twofold: her
mother probably spoke no English, and she herself was a future
mother. (Courtesy of the New York Public Library, The Immigrant
Life Collection.)*

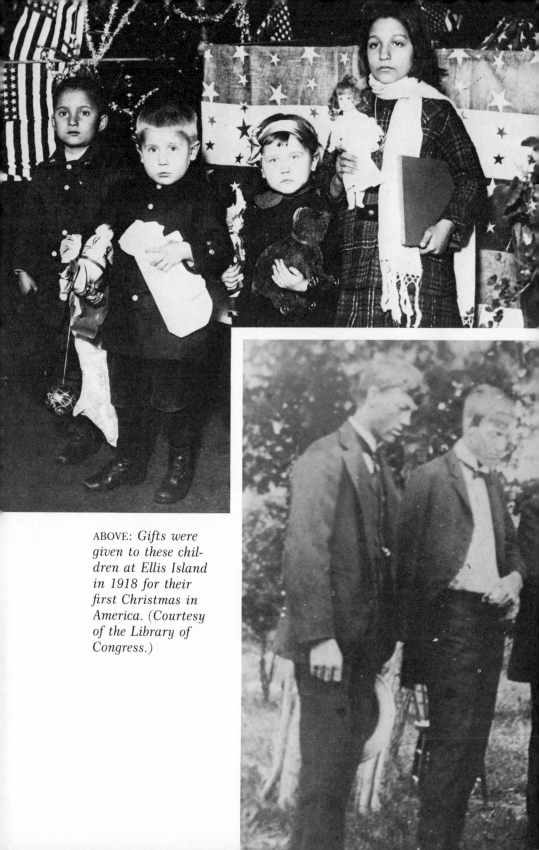

Widow Kari Froslan—who emigrated from Norway in 1871—with her teenage children and the casket of her husband Hans who was killed by a runaway horse in 1897. (Photograph by J. T. Richardson, St. James, Minnesota; courtesy of Elsie Schultz.)

Jews praying on the Brooklyn Bridge in 1909 as part of the commemoration of Rosh Hashanah. Bread was cast into the water as a symbol of shedding one's sins. (Photograph by Bain News Service; courtesy of the Library of Congress.)

ligion became an empty shell where the forms remained, but the substance was gone.

———————

For many Yankees the hordes of immigrants were anathema; and not least among their faults was that they insisted on keeping un-American religions. It was the goal of a good many natives to convert the Jews to Christianity and the Catholics to Protestantism. Their methods were at best insensitive and sometimes cruel.

The Depression of 1893 brought destitution to Rose Cohen's newly arrived family, and they lived on the edge of starvation. Christians controlled the city's public schools, and they provided bread and honey for the hungry pupils—but only for those who would bow their heads and repeat a Christian prayer. Famished Jewish children had to watch others eat. In the Cohen family, finally one day, "As the children were leaving for school Mother asked them without looking at them whether bread and honey was still given to the children at school. 'Yes,' sister said, 'to those who bow their heads and pray.' The boy was already out of the room when mother called after them. 'You can bow your heads and pray.' Then she went into her dark bedroom."[25]

Bessie Pehotsky was a Slavic woman who saw conversion to Protestantism as an essential part of the change from the Old World to the New. She was untiring in her efforts to bring similar enlightenment to her countrywomen. She and her American friends were absolutely undaunted, though she admitted that many times they visited foreign women on a monthly basis for years before they could persuade them to come to one of their meetings. Judging by the slow success of Mrs. Pehotsky's long efforts, these women preferred either to remain faithful to the Catholic church or attend none at all, and had little interest in American Protestant organizations.

While some became lax in the expression of their faith and some even abandoned their native denomination, immigrant women still generally held to traditional views and were careful to use the church in time of need—for baptisms, weddings, funerals, and even confirmation. As shown over and over again, they held strong ideas about "God's will;" they fatalistically accepted whatever happened in this life, considered it at least somewhat sinful to try to change the status quo that God had decreed, and hoped for a better life beyond.

Faith was an individual thing; religion was a group thing. Religion was often determined through what group one had been born into or where one settled. There are striking differences between various ethnic groups and between urban and rural immigrants in the importance attached to the church. For Scandinavians and Germans in the rural Midwest, it was an extremely vital part of their social life. To not belong to the church was unthinkable. In the city it was different. One might or might not attend. There was far less pressure to do so, and there were many other sources of companionship and diversion.

The urban–rural distinction in church attendance was true for natives as well, but an additional factor for the immigrant woman was her remembrance of the church back home. Where the church had been an arm of an oppressive government—as for the Bohemians—they were quick to abandon it. Where the church had been the people's ally against the government—as for the Irish— they held to it with fierce loyalty. And for those whose religion had been a source of deep personal comfort at home—as for the Scandinavian and Italian women—the remembrance of that religion was more necessary than ever, a source of security in a strange new world.

PART II

Ambivalence in Morality

COURTING
CUSTOMS

WHETHER considering courting customs or any other aspect of morality, a woman's official religion did not seem to mean as much as her national mores. The Italians, for instance, were extremely conservative in sexual matters; the Irish were more liberal but still very far from liberated; the Poles generally were willing to tolerate deviation from the accepted moral code; and the French established a notorious reputation for illicit sex as a national pastime—yet all of these groups officially believed in the same Roman Catholic Church.

Ideas that Old World people held about courting customs were of primary importance because a woman's whole life revolved around the courtship period. No decision a woman made in her lifetime would be so vital as whether to accept a proposal—it might well be the only significant decision she ever would be allowed to make, a transfer of subordination from father to husband. The worth of that potential husband was then of the utmost seriousness. For her family, the decision was a momentous one because marriage was not merely a joining of bodies and lives, but a property exchange involving dowries, land, and inheritance.

Therefore courtship was closely supervised. "My parents belonged to the Tuscon Club in Providence," said an Italian woman recalling courtship in the 1920s, "and every other month they would have a social."

> Families took their teenage children. . . . This particular night a stranger came in with a group of gentlemen. He stood out because he was blond and blue-eyed and everyone else in this group was dark with olive skin. . . . I was relieved to hear an Italian accent, though, because I knew that if he were not of our race I couldn't be friends with him. . . . We danced and between dances sat with the family. He bought refreshments for my brothers and sisters.[1]

Having thus paid homage to the family, the young man wrote a note asking to be allowed to call the next Sunday. "This started a ruckus at home. My father wanted to know who was this stranger? Where did he come from? Who were his people? Where did he work? What did he make? And I didn't even know." He called, was thoroughly interrogated and found suitable: "We got permission to go to an afternoon movie in his car but I had to take my sixteen-year-old sister along, and be home before dark. This was the pattern for all of our dates."[2]

Though life in America slowly changed these customs—especially for women whose families were sufficiently poor that they had to allow their daughters to work—parental control remained powerful far into the twentieth century. Guided by the sole object of keeping daughters pure, some parents viewed their every action with suspicion.

One girl told me that her mother made a note of the exact time at which she returned every day from work, and that she had to account for every minute of deviation. . . . Seldom are Italian girls permitted to join clubs or evening classes. . . . When they are allowed this privilege, they are invariably escorted to and from the gathering by a parent or older brother, who must be assured that no mingling of the sexes has been allowed.[3]

Parents intended to keep daughters wholly innocent in knowledge as well as experience. According to one Italian woman who grew up during America's flapper age:

I found out about menstruation when it happened. . . . What little we knew was put together from girlfriends, most of it on the scary side. . . . I never talked about sex with Frank even when we planned our marriage. For him that would be insulting a girl. A girl you married you didn't touch or kiss, you must respect her like a queen. During the ten months we dated we were never left alone except in the parlor when I played the piano.[4]

Though young Jewish women had much more freedom of movement, they shared with Italians the custom of parentally-arranged marriages. Rose Cohen's first date was managed by her mother and a neighbor. She was sent to buy sugar at an unfamiliar store and said a few words to the clerk there. Two days later her mother said, "Well, what do you think of that young man?" A confused Rose asked, "What young man?" "The young man from the grocery store," her mother replied, explaining that he was a potential suitor and that a date had been arranged for them next Saturday. "I was bewildered by what had been happening," Rose wrote. "I was grown up, a young man was coming to see me! I would be married perhaps!... It seemed incredible."[5]

At the "date," her father, mother, a cousin, younger siblings and the suitor's uncle were all present and quickly began to bargain about marriage. When Rose and the young man went for a walk, his conversation was almost entirely devoted to showing that he could support her, and after this one short meeting his family proposed an "alliance." Rose's father was delighted, for she had no dowry and was sickly, so he thought it incredibly lucky that anyone should want her. As for Rose, "I could not understand why father was so happy.... Somehow I had never quite realized that this question would really be put to me and that I should have to answer it." Nor did they give her long to decide: " 'Well,' father said in an easy tone... 'there is plenty of time. Think it over. Take until tomorrow night to decide.' "[6]

Rose bowed to family pressure and said yes. On their second date, Rose and "the young man"—for that is how she thought of him—went to a jeweler to buy a ring. The third weekend, their families held an engagement party. Rose was so little concerned with her bridegroom's feelings, let alone in love with him, that she danced with everyone else and left him sitting alone and neglected. The next time they were together was in his store and he asked her to add some figures. Since Rose had never gone to school, the experience was close to traumatic for her. In a freer form of courtship this grocer might have determined what sort of education a woman had before asking her to be his lifetime business partner. After their fifth date, during which they had absolutely nothing to say to each other, he asked for a kiss and Rose then realized that she could never marry him. Though disappointed, her parents did not try to force her and the engagement was broken.

Despite their added years of experience, there was no assurance at all that marriages arranged by parents would be satisfactory. Rosa Cavalleri's foster mother could not have done a worse job of choosing Rosa's mate, for example. She had always maintained that Rosa needed a lot of discipline and she refused proposals for Rosa from a number of young men, saying that they would let Rosa "have her own way." Rosa then fell in love with a nice young man named Remo, and Mamma Lena gave a reluctant promise to consider marriage for them. After some time she announced that she had discovered Rosa and Remo once went to a dance without her permission, and that Rosa was going to be married to Santino, an older man whom Rosa always hated. She objected, but Mamma Lena refused to listen and that night Rosa ran away to Remo's family. Her mother dragged her back and starved and beat her into submission. Rosa remained true to herself by not saying her vows at the wedding, but the priest was deaf and didn't notice.

The marriage was a tragic mistake, and even Mamma Lena was forced to admit after only a few months that her judgment was wrong:

> The other nights when Santino was drunk and beating me Mamma Lena had sat up in bed and watched, but she had said nothing. This night—I guess she could see it that he wanted to kill me for sure—she jumped up and came over and stopped him. She pulled him away so he couldn't reach to kick me. . . . In the end she put him out the door and he went rolling down the steps. "And don't ever come back to this house!" she yelled after him.[7]

Santino then headed for America, and the two women hoped to be rid of him. Eventually, however, Santino sent for Rosa: "Those men in the iron mines . . . need women to do the cooking and washing."[8] Mamma Lena decided that despite Rosa's fears, she must go; he was her husband and it was her duty. Once again, Rosa had no voice in the decision; her life had been arranged for her.

Some arranged marriages were created by the couples themselves when strangers agreed by letter to marry. In 1907 a Swedish man in America sent a letter via the pastor of the parish where he had lived almost a quarter of a century earlier. Enclosed was a dollar to pay for the trouble of locating his intended, to whom he addressed this note:

Dear Anna,

> I wonder how you have it and if you are living. I have it very good here. It is a long time since we saw each other. Are you married or unmarried? If you are unmarried, you can have a good home with me. I have my own house and I make over ten *kronor* a day. My wife died last year . . . and I want another wife. I only have one girl, eleven years old. If you can come to me I will send you a ticket and travel money. . . . It is around twenty-four years since we saw each other. You must wonder

who I am. My name is Einar, who worked over at Vensta for
Adolf Johanson when you were at Anderson's, and you were
my first girlfriend.[9]

Swiss Jules Sandoz imported three women from Europe to frontier Nebraska to marry him; the first went mad living with this
violent man who refused to work; the second soon left him; the
third stayed to live an unhappy life. The courtships of these women
were marked by fear and irresolution on their part and by an un-
accustomed decency on the part of Jules, which dissipated with
the wedding vows:

> Once more Jules, hunched down on the wagon seat,
> brought home a bride. He had tried to keep Emelia's coming
> a secret—with a fresh shave, a moustache trim, a haircut, and
> a new suit. Every loafer in town followed him to the depot to
> see what got off.
> A pale, slender, rather pretty girl in a well-tailored blue suit
> with fashionably large sleeves hesitated on the car-step. . . .
> "Mlle. Parcel?" a hopeful voice asked at her elbow.
> "Oui—but who are you?" the girl asked in French, drawing
> her arm away.
> "I am Jules," he said proudly, glad to have them all see this
> fine young lady.
> At first the girl could only drop her veil over her confusion.
> Then at last she whispered, "No, no—you are not the
> Jules—"
> But it was he. . . . An old man. Gray under the greasy cap,
> limping despite all he could do. . . . Then she noticed the
> hands: long, fine fingers, smooth almost white. . . . Perhaps it
> was with him as he said.
> Besides, what could she do?[10]

Occasionally one made a more thorough investigation of her intended, as did the German girl who had been living in the United
States without relatives for five years. Since she had substantial
savings, she did not want to risk marrying a wastrel, and she went
to the Immigrants' Protective League in Chicago "to ask advice
regarding a man she wanted to marry. The man lives in West Virginia. She would like the League to find out if he is a good man."[11]
But few women had the inclination or the means to conduct such
investigations; more commonly they took the lover's letters at face
value.

Experts in Polish immigration stated that women from that

country viewed Americanized husbands as so much more desirable that they were more than willing to take the chance of emigrating to marry a stranger: "They risk going alone to America while they are often afraid to go alone to the nearest town in their own country."[12] A Croatian writer agreed that the practice of going to wed strangers was common: "When she comes to America—generally she does not know her suitor—she married. If she is unwilling, not finding him to her liking, she must pay back the money, but it very often happens that another lad pays it for her and takes her for his wife instead."[13] As foreign women preferred to marry Americanized men, so immigrant men often sent back to Europe for an "unspoiled" girl, for as America made men more considerate, it made women more assertive.

Despite indecision and even dread, few women thought there was any alternative to the assumption that young women should be courted and courtship should end in marriage. A German governess who was enjoying her youth saw marriage as an end of freedom, and yet seemed to believe that marriage was nonetheless imperative:

> I don't want to get married yet, because when a girl marries she can't have so much fun. . . . A good-looking girl can have a fine time when she is single, but if she stays single too long she loses her good looks, and then no one will marry her. Of course I am young yet, but still, as my mother used to say, "It's better to be sure than sorry," and I think I won't wait any longer. Some married women enjoy life almost as much as the young girls.[14]

She was not in love and viewed marriage as oppressive, but still assumed one must get married. With the possible exception of the Irish,* this assumption prevailed. Couples entered into the blessed state without the romantic attraction considered important by Americans. Their European heritage taught them that property exchanges and parental approval were the essentials of a marriage contract, not notions of love.

Weddings often were motivated by economic need; a young Chicago immigrant wrote to her social worker in 1913 of her starkly pragmatic marriage:

*see page 221.

Honorable Lady, you are asking me what kind of work I have now. Since I stopped working in that shop, I had no work. . . . I talked to my man about it, and he told me . . . that we rather get married, so I thought it would be better for me to get married. . . . I am only married this week and had many worries over this week. I looked for a rent and it was very hard to find a clean rent. In meantime I live only in a simple rent, pay $6, but the name of the street I do not know. . . . It would give me a great pleasure if you would come to see my household; later I write you a correct address.[15]

She had already begun finishing garments at home, entertaining no illusions that marriage would be an escape from work. But there seem to have been more girls who did view marriage as such an escape—that was the way it was supposed to be according to both the American dream and the heritage of most Europeans. Sometimes the desire to escape from the present through marriage was so strong that women took desperate chances, contracting to marry strangers and dealing with disreputable matchmakers. A Lithuanian girl who came here to marry a dying man turned soon after widowhood to such a matchmaker, who claimed to have "many suitors 'in stock'. I spilled out all my heartaches to her. First she talked me out of marrying a work-worn operator. . . . What I lived through afterward is impossible for me to describe. The woman handed me over to bandits, and when I wanted to run away from them they . . . beat me savagely."[16] Her view of marriage as necessary and her dependency on the matchmaker made her a prime target for sex exploiters.

The need for income that led women to work brought greater freedom from families and matchmakers and helped to make meeting men easier and more pleasant. Courtship changed as American abhorrence of dowries led to their demise, as immigrants saw, from the example of American girls, how demeaning a dowry was to the status of womanhood. Contracted marriages, too, would fade in the freedom of America.

Yet such change takes time and the ambivalence between the old and the new ways continued. The pressure to marry remained long after the fading of arranged marriages. Rose Cohen would pre-date the sighs of many Jewish and non-Jewish girls alike when she complained, "Wherever I went to visit now I was sure to find a young man, and the relative or friend acting as matchmaker . . . What are you waiting for? You are wasting your best years. You are losing your chances."[17] Italians who did not marry were viewed with great prejudice. In one case where a spinster lost her job and was destitute, her brother refused to help even though he could afford to have done so. "She should have got married," he insisted. "She had chances enough."[18] Similarly, a Polish girl found that her aunt back in Europe admired her independence in emigrating and yet could not allow her to remain independent maritally:

It is true that you have been courageous in going so far. . . . I really cannot imagine that you are there at the other end of the world; I should not muster courage enough to do it. . . . I advise you also to marry, not to wait and not to select, for this is the worst. . . . I shall wait soon for news about your marriage. It is to be hoped that such a girl as you are should not waste her time.[19]

To be sure, few parents wanted marriage for their daughters so badly that they would approve courtship with men of another religion or background, but within the group, the pressure to marry remained strong. Courtship then was not like the dating of today; the purpose was not to have fun, but to make a match. Time and money were too precious to be spent simply enjoying a pleasant evening; a man who had no more than that in mind was not to be trusted. The sole purpose of courtship was marriage.

MARRIAGE, DIVORCE, AND DESERTION

MANY factors that did not affect natives compounded marital stress in immigrant families. Since Old World marriages were not for love, but for property, often there was a substantial difference in age. By the time a man had accumulated the property to bid for a wife he had aged, yet was likely to want a young bride. They then had little in common, and husbands tended to be tyrannical, treating their wives like children. A woman might in turn use her only weapon and withhold sex, which to the male European mind was an incumbent "wifely duty" and grounds for withholding household money. According to social workers, some immigrant men were irrationally insistent on "wifely duty," even when a woman was pregnant or sick, and this was a frequent source of violence and family disruption.

The years of separation that many European marriages endured also weakened them. Men frequently came alone to America, leaving their wives in Europe, and couples grew to be strangers. Women realized their independent capabilities and were no longer submissive when they re-united; men often found other women here. The attractiveness of fashionable Americanized women was tempting to a man, who often remembered his wife "as a plain, hard-working, slow-thinking drudge."[1]

Most important was the lack of the restraint that had been provided in Europe by a respected peer group. The families that arranged marriages had an interest in maintaining them, both to protect their social status and their property. A husband who was excessively abusive would find his wife's brothers dealing with him. A woman who neglected her household duties could expect reproof from her own family as well as from her in-laws. Nor did the villages of Poland and Russia provide the opportunities for misbehavior that tempted the Poles in Chicago or the Jews in New York.

Finally, external pressures of life in America had their effect. Financial stress had been more easily borne when one had a garden, a cow, and family to fall back on. The pride of males was assaulted when they could not prevent unemployment and want. When their women could find work, fragile egos sometimes broke. Alcoholism and violence increased, desertion rates soared, divorce became thinkable.

As a result, women who had been reared to unquestionably accept marriage as the great female goal in life began to reject this presumption. Of course, social workers' records tend to emphasize those families whose marital ties were most likely to be eroded, but nonetheless we find endless anti-marriage statements from women of all nationalities. A woman of Irish background stated flatly, "all married women are unhappy. . . . The children keep coming faster than you can get them shoes."[2] A sociologist who interviewed mothers of mainly German and Irish origin reported that, " 'If I had it to do over, I'd never marry,' was the almost universal remark."[3] It was not a whimsical thought, but a deeply held conviction. "More than one woman candidly confessed that her husband's death had been a relief. Mrs. Brunig, a sincerely religious woman, said to me, 'You may think we are having a hard time. But I don't mind it. It's nothing compared to what it was when Brunig was alive. I never had a happy day then.' "[4]

Hattie Reid, an Englishwoman who with her husband ran a grocery store in Brooklyn in the 1880s had borne eight children and wrote, "My life has been one long series of misfortunes ever since I have been a wife." She too advised her daughters not to rush into marriage: "It spoils all their enjoyment and makes old women of them before their time."[5]

Most widows were extremely wary of remarriage. An Irishwoman illustrates the pragmatic approach they took to this question:

> My first husband . . . never drank, but he beat me. Even before I married him . . . I was always dreading it. . . . I would have left him after Henry was born, but he was sickly and I knew he wouldn't live long. I took care of him till he died, but it's God's truth, I was glad when I saw him in his coffin.
> . . . After awhile Samuel Cooley began to come around. . . . But I had had enough of married life. So I left the Greenpoint factory and come back to New York so's to get rid of him. . . . But one day I come home and there was Samuel standing before the door. He told me he was married thirty-two years to his first wife and she never did a day's work outside her house all that time. I left him waiting three months and then I married him in the fall. . . . I didn't mind working in the summer, but when winter came I wished I had a husband so's I wouldn't have to go out.[6]

Blatant financial need seems to be the overwhelming reason for marriage, for most women seemed to expect little out of matrimony except monetary support. Study after study testified that husbands and wives in most immigrant homes did not expect mental companionship or shared experiences.

> After the evening meal the husband frequently goes to . . . the saloon or club. He does not seek the companionship of his wife, even if he stays at home. She keeps house for him and bears his children. He does not ill-treat her, unless he is a brute or habitual drunkard, but there is little spiritual companionship. He does not help his wife in the duty of child

rearing. He does not heed her physical weariness. . . . There is little respect. They refer to each other as "Him" or "Her" or "my man." They do not hide their feelings when speaking of each other, not even before the children. The women speak of marriage as a necessary evil, and yet most of them marry at eighteen.[7]

One can also find these anti-marriage views even in some externally happy marriages. A young Italian woman confided to a sociologist that her husband was so in love with her when they got married that they actually took a honeymoon. She had not loved him when they were wed, but now she did, for he was very good to her. Yet, despite these idyllic circumstances, when she discovered the sociologist's single status, she urged her not to get married. "Wish I wasn't married," she said. "Oh gee! Wish I wasn't married. I'm crazy of my husband, but I wish I wasn't married. See—once you are married—pisht-there you are. . . ."[8]

Women who were more educated and articulate also held reservations about marriage, though again there were no marital problems apparent. Linka Preus's life-style was such that probably none of her contemporaries would have suspected that she had any reservations about her proper wifely role, yet she had considerable misgivings. Linka mused in her diary the night before her wedding:

> There must indeed, be something attractive about being a wife since I have decided to become one; but what is it?
> "Tell me, my cousin Independence, do I enjoy thee more as a wife or as a maiden?"
> "Indeed, as wife you become nothing but a slave."
> "Dear me, then I dare not marry—"
> "Indeed, that is what you ought to do. Very likely you will never feel the slavery of wifehood; rather you will be giving thought to a woman's calling in life."[9]

But Linka, like so many others, expressed her doubts to no one; she did what society expected. Likewise, most of the factory girls who were advised by older women to avoid marriage chose to disregard that advice, and the same women who spoke against marriage as an institution nonetheless usually saw that *their* daughters were properly courted and married. The societal view was as ambivalent as that of an Irishwoman who averred, "Not so many girls would get married if they knew what they were gettin' into," and then went right on to state that the alternative was not acceptable, either: "It is awful to be an old maid or widow. I'd rather take worriment than that." She managed to blend her contradictory views by leaving it all to destiny, as so many fatalistic immigrants were prone to do. "You meet your fate and if you are to be happy, you will be happy."[10] Such fatalism, such ambivalence was the key to their thinking. Marriage was a necessary evil.

Ambivalence and fatalism were part of the intellectual baggage of most immigrants, and more than a few went further to include a strong belief in witchcraft which was often retained for a generation in America. Some couples wore amulets to insure marital harmony, and immigrant newspapers contained advertisements for magical methods of entrapping lovers and potions to improve sex lives.

But in far too many immigrant homes husbands did not use such gentle methods to achieve their aims. The files of social agencies are replete with examples of drunken, violent men who were both rapists of and sadists to their wives, as in this case:

Lena Ziejewski complained . . . that her husband beat her with unusual cruelty, particularly when he was drunk or in the morning when he had not slept well. . . . They . . . had been married only 3 months before their first child was born. He taunts her because she had relations with him before marriage. About 2 weeks after the child was born he tied her hands and feet and bound her mouth. When she was almost suffocated, he released her. His family opposed the marriage and continued to incite him against her. . . . When she put too much salt in his food, he beat her and once because she spilled some lard on the stove he struck her in the face, cutting it, and knocked her down. The neighbors often saw her with dress torn and eyes blackened.[11]

Wife-beating had been sufficiently a part of life in much of continental Europe that neighbors frequently closed their eyes to it, considering it none of their affair. As long as a husband was not too severe, even the victim and her family were willing to consider it unfortunate, but nevertheless a male prerogative.

Sometimes women were driven to violence when their helplessness at last turned to rage. Mrs. Gaszynski was one of many women whose husband interpreted American liberty as license. In Poland he had treated her well, but no longer restrained by family or village reputation, he "began to run around with other women" and finally deserted. Mrs. Gaszynski supported their children alone and heard nothing of him for two years, when she discovered that he was living with another woman. She first attempted reconciliation, but he refused to see her, and finally she went to court for child-support. He did not pay and at last a desperate Mrs. Gaszynski "planned to kill her husband, Mrs. Dujek [the mistress] and herself, but she had only ten cents left. With this she bought some vitriol. She went to the home of the other woman, called her to the door, and threw the vitriol in her face."[12] The woman would lure no more husbands, for she was disfigured for life, but Mrs. Gaszynski and her husband would both go to prison, she for this assault and he for nonsupport.

The obvious end for such broken marriages would seem to be divorce, but most immigrant women were reluctant to take that step because of religious reasons, fear of dealing with American courts, and the expense. Then, too, immigrants were generally more conservative than Americans in all aspects of relations between the sexes, and a lower divorce rate is one aspect of that conservatism.

While divorce through the courts was rare, in practice there were many cases of permanent separation that simply never culminated in divorce. Many people set up a second partnership with another spouse without ever dissolving the first. Social workers bemoaned the foreigners' tendency to ignore these legalities, especially in cases where they had through great effort obtained a divorce for some abused woman who then received her ex-husband back into the house. There were apparently many cases of women who paid no attention to the proceedings of these strange American courts and ended up in legal tangles. Martha Gutowski, for instance, went to a legal aid society and "wished to know whether she was divorced or married."[13] Another woman was shocked to find that she had not been legally married at all; she and her fiance had obtained the marriage license and thought this action alone constituted marriage.[14]

Jewish women were subject to particular problems in the area of divorce. While Jewish law required that the wife consent to the divorce—although the husband was the only partner who could issue it—a wife might fear that rabbi and husband would combine to force her to accept a divorce she did not truly want. The fear that some women had of such arbitrary divorce is shown in this pathetic letter to the *Jewish Daily Forward* in 1912:

> I am a twenty-eight year old woman, married for six years, and my only trouble is that I have no children. . . . My husband eats my heart out with a few words, like rust eats iron. He keeps saying it's "nearer than farther" to the ten-year limit when, according to Jewish law, I will have to give him a divorce if I don't have a baby by that time. . . . A short time ago I was quite sick and he spent a lot of money to cure me. When I got well my husband said to me, "You'll have to earn your own living, so I want you to be healthy."
>
> Dear Editor, I am all alone here, and I ask you to advise me what to do. Can my husband get a divorce after ten years through the court, too? I know he can get it through a rabbi. . . . How shall I act?[15]

(The editor told the distraught woman that United States law did not recognize rabbinical law and that her husband could not get a legal divorce.)

A fairly frequent device of men who wished to end their marriage but had no legal ground was to go to a state where divorce "by publication" was allowed. A notice was listed in local newspapers which the spouse naturally would not see, and one day she would discover herself to be a divorced woman. The Jewish National Desertion Bureau had local representatives throughout the country who took note of such ads involving people with Jewish names. They followed through with legal advice and travel expenses for the wronged woman, enabling her to contest the divorce.[16]

Legal obstacles were not the only problem of women seeking divorce, for certainly religious prohibitions played an important role, too. Rosa Cavalleri, who was married against her will to a man she despised, nevertheless put up with his cruelty. Her fear of physical abuse was so real that she was grateful when her husband Santino began spending most of his time in a brothel. The breaking point of the marriage did not come until Santino spent his savings to buy a bordello and insisted that Rosa manage it since he could not read or do arithmetic. Up until then Rosa believed it was God's will that she obey her husband, but now that there was a clear difference between God's will and Santino's, she refused. Santino threatened her with a razor, and Rosa fled. Taking her children, she went to Chicago to the friend of a friend. Santino followed, trying to get the police to arrest his runaway wife, and she in fact was brought to court:

> There I was, a young Italian girl with a shawl over my head, and I couldn't understand nothing. When we went by the judge, there was Santino from Missouri! He was telling the judge that I was the worst kind of woman—that I ran away and was living with all the men, . . . He wanted the judge to punish me and put me to jail. I can't tell you very much what happened, because the judge was talking English to all those friends of Gionin and Toni [Rosa's protectors]. When he asked me the questions Toni told me what it was and I answered the truth, that's all. In the end the judge told Santino to get out of town. He said if he was not gone by 6:00 the same day he would put *him* to jail instead of me. Then he said, "And don't you ever come back, either."[17]

And so at last Rosa was free of Santino, but she still did not seek the divorce; Santino got it. Rosa's second husband was kind and their marriage was fine—except that the cloud of divorce hung over their innocent hearts. Though Rosa had been forced into the unhappy marriage, though she had not been the seeker of the divorce, still her religion made her suffer for the broken marriage. When she wanted to marry Gionin, "The priest said he couldn't marry us in the church because I had the first husband living— only when he died we could be married in the church. Me, I was crying with tears coming down my eyes and praying to God, 'Oh, God, why do you make it a sin for me to live with this good man Gionin?' "[18]

They were married in a civil ceremony, but the problem continued to plague the marriage:

> After Gionin and me were married together about ten years and have already three children, a missionary from Italy came in our church. He preached so strong against divorce—what a sin it is against God, and the punishment God is going to give those people and all and all—that Gionin he left me alone to take care for all those children . . . [Rosa had two children by Santino as well as the other three]. So then one day he went to confession . . . and Father Alberto told him it's a sin to leave me alone like that with those children. Oh, Gionin was glad to hear that, so he could come back! He said he only left me because he didn't want to go to hell.[19]

Amicable divorce was almost incomprehensible. Much more frequent was divorce after long endurance of abuse and nonsupport. More frequent than that were marriages that did not legally end at all, but simply faded away. Desertion was a far easier way of simply evading a decision; one study of deserters found that most of them did not consider their action to be final; "desertion, instead of being a poor man's divorce, comes nearer to being a poor man's* vacation."[20]

Desertion was harder on a woman than either divorce or widowhood because of the uncertainty it created. Moreover, this generally was a new problem for immigrant women to face, for several commentators noted that desertion was not an Old World phenomenon. A German authority said he was "dumbfounded" by the desertion rate here because at home men just did not abandon their families.[21] Probably this was because European governments, with their passports and workbooks and military service registration, made it much more difficult for men to disappear, whereas lone male adventurers were part of the American tradition. A second factor was that many of these immigrant men had consentually separated from their families earlier when they emigrated. They saw then that their wives managed without them, and having tasted the joys of renewed bachelorhood, perhaps they more strongly regretted having the burden of a family.

The size of the family did not seem to be a factor. Studies showed that fathers of large families were not the most likely candidates for desertion. Seventy percent of the deserted families in one study had fewer than four children. (On the other hand, only 3 percent deserted a wife without children.)[22] Nor did men leave during economic depressions. Apparently instead of leaving because financial pressures were overwhelming, they valued the security of a family in hard times and left when conditions improved.[23]

Male and female sociologists agreed that most desertions were to be blamed largely on the husband. While acknowledging that fault is difficult to assign, one student concluded that in about two-thirds of the cases studied, men were largely responsible for the marital breakdown, with women being at fault in 12 percent of the cases.[24] A common element, said one male sociologist, "is an ex-

---

*We are indeed talking of men here; another study of almost six hundred deserters in twenty-five cities found only seventeen cases where the wife had left. (Lilian Brandt, *Five Hundred and Seventy-Four Deserters* p. 9)

cessive lack of responsibility. A superlative selfishness. . . . He wants to be free to come back when it suits him, and he would be the last to welcome a divorce court."[25]

However, there does seem to be a slight difference in the way male and female sociologists would have solved the problem. Men generally wanted strong laws and jail sentences to discipline the deserters; women, while not disagreeing with the above, put their emphasis on making the family independent.

Indeed, making a woman economically independent often was a more realistic goal than reforming a man's basic character. Of 574 deserting husbands, for instance, 255 were reported as "not working regularly."[26] The desertion brought no economic change and, in fact, might be viewed as a good thing, since the wife would now have control of the income and it would not be spent on the vices that afflicted many of these men. Nonetheless, the financial pressures were great, especially in view of the fact—according to still another study—that more than two-thirds of the husbands who abandoned their families did so before they were thirty-five; "it is obvious that their families must have been composed of young children. They deserted the family when its need was greatest."[27] Because little children prevented her from working, a woman would sometimes have no choice except to search for her man and try to get him back.

She did not receive much societal help with her problems. Social agencies in their early days feared that they would encourage men to desert if they were very solicitous toward the family, so if they aided the family at all, "relief was given . . . in smaller amounts than to a widow or the wife of a man in the hospital."[28] Immigrants were particularly hurt by the residence requirements of some agencies. One Jewish woman poured out her bitterness against these charities in a letter to the editor:

> My husband . . . deserted me and our three small children. . . . The local Jewish Welfare Agencies are allowing me and my children to die of hunger and this is because my "faithful" husband brought me over from Canada just four months ago and therefore I do not yet deserve to eat their bread.
>
> It breaks my heart but I have come to the conclusion that in order to save my innocent children from hunger and cold I have to give them away. . . . I will sell them, not for money, but for bread, for a secure home. . . . Those who are willing and able to give my children a good home can apply to me.[29]

If social agencies were indifferent to the plight of the deserted, the courts were of even less help. Social workers often insisted that women take deserting husbands to court. Their reluctance to do so was to some extent ingrained timidity that made them afraid of both judges and angered husbands, but a large part of it was that these women understood the realities of the law. A man would simply ignore the court order and then the only recourse would be to put him in jail where he could not earn anything. Moreover, immigrants had to be wary of making such complaints; the favorite solution of one Chicago Domestic Relations Court judge for husbands who were cruel or negligent was deportation—a method that could not help but make things worse for the family.[30]

But before a man could be brought to justice, he must be found. If the police did not take this responsibility seriously, some social agencies did. The National Desertion Bureau was a Jewish organization that was superbly efficient at tracking down deserting fathers. Its chief technique was the publication of a "Gallery of Missing Husbands" in the leading Jewish newspapers. Many persons reputedly bought newspapers for the sole purpose of studying these pictures, and the agency received "tips" on their fugitives from all over the country. The deterrent value was doubtless strong, for a Jewish man who left his family knew that he must cut himself off from the life of all Jews in America.

Despite the difficulties of detective work, it was nonetheless easier than social work: the National Desertion Bureau located three-fourths of the men for whom they searched, but of 2,405 deserters they found in their first three years, reconciliations were obtained in only 780 cases.[31] Even when the location of the father was known, he seldom could be relied upon for support. Only 29 percent of the deserters in one study ever contributed anything, whether from conscience or from police force, and those contributions were sparse and irregular.[32]

Women simply had to make their own way, but little in their backgrounds had prepared them for this. A Jewish woman's letter to the editor, intended to reach her husband's eye, shows the fatalism and dependency that made women beg a father for his children's bread:

> Max! The children and I now say farewell to you. You left us in such a terrible state. . . . For six years I loved you faithfully, took care of you like a loyal servant, never had a happy day with you. . . . Max, where is your conscience? . . . You lived with me for six years, during which time I bore you four chil-

dren. And then you left me. Who will bring them up? . . . Have
you no pity for your own flesh and blood? My tears choke me
and I cannot write any more. Be advised that . . . I am leaving
with my two living orphans for Russia. We say farewell to you
and beg you to take pity on us and send us enough to live
on.[33]

In going back to Europe, this woman probably made her separation permanent, but for many women who remained here, desertion was anything but a clearly defined status. Husbands would
return, upset the household, and perhaps take along a child or two
when they disappeared again. The case of Polish Mrs. Kulas,
whose employer sent her to a Chicago legal aid society to get a
divorce, exemplifies the problem. Though her husband earned fair
wages, she always had to pay the household expenses from her
cleaning job. Finally he had deserted, reappeared and deserted
again. "She was afraid he would get drunk, break into her house
and either force her to have sexual relations with him or kill her.
He had often threatened to kill her. . . ."[34]

One must remember that social workers' records are likely to
emphasize the wife's side of the story and that wronged men did
not generally go to a charity agency to complain. Further, there
were cases where the wife was the direct cause of the desertion.
Henry Slokowski had put up with his wife Anna who was a slovenly housekeeper, poor mother, and impossible nag for ten years;
"possibly Henry would have gone on to the end in this humble,
hen-pecked existence had not Martin Pribiloff appeared on the
scene. He had come into the home as a boarder; he remained as
Anna's lover. Obviously Henry was in the way; so as meekly as he
had been a husband, he became a deserter. The charities know
where he is and know that he would go back willingly if she would
give up the lover."[35]

A group of men jailed for nonsupport complained that they too
were wronged, that they had been jailed for "the merest nonsense"
and that "even in the worst times of the Russian reaction people
didn't suffer as the men suffer here in America because of their
wives."[36] Their wives probably were more assertive here than they
had ever been at home, but the evidence does not support their
claim to innocence. Even the male sociologist who told the tale of
hen-pecked Henry Slokowski agreed that Henry was a rare exception and that in most desertion cases husbands were at fault
and were guilty of "a superlative selfishness."[37]

There seems to be one circumstance in which temporary abandonment of a wife was common in parts of Europe. Several researchers reported that some foreigners had a long tradition of pregnancy desertion that continued in America. One study found that almost one-third of deserters had "left a short time before, or just after, the birth of a child."[38] Another sociologist wrote that "some pregnancy deserters take the step in the hope that their wives will bring about an abortion; but this is a modern and sophisticated development and the institution of 'pregnancy desertion' is one of undoubted antiquity. Its prevalence among certain European immigrants would almost point to its being a racial tradition."[39]

In America where there was often no extended family to help, this meant that when a woman most needed support she was most likely to be alone. "Regularly before the birth of each child," one social worker wrote of a client, "Mr. Brady has deserted, and as regularly, when the family crisis was past and Mrs. Brady once more supplied with a paying job, has he returned."[40] A second social worker reported a case where there were seven children in the family and the father "had deserted before the birth of each one, as well as at other times when there was sickness."[41]

Pregnant women became biological wrecks from the strain, as did the Italian woman who worked at three jobs until just a few days before her delivery.[42] The Mrs. Brady mentioned above worked in a laundry from seven o'clock in the morning until six o'clock at night.

> When her baby was born she left off work only a week beforehand and returned when it was two weeks old. She tells the following story of that time to show her employer's good heart:
>
> I went to Mr. Mack in the office . . . on Saturday night. I'd rather died than do it, but I was afraid not to give notice or maybe he wouldn't let me back. "I've got to take a holiday," says I. "Have ye?" says he. Then he says, "Come with me," and he took me downstairs and gave me two sets of clean sheets and pillowcases.[43]

Such charity was exceptional, and of course the idea that she ought to have a right to maternity leave occurred to no woman in this era. But Mrs. Brady would stay at her job, her babies "most grown up in St. Joseph's nursery," and Mr. Brady would eventually show up to impregnate her and leave again.

Obviously many women accepted pregnancy desertion as unfortunate but unexceptional and unavoidable, for some allowed their mates to return and repeat the pattern over and over again. If even disinterested observers noted that "desertion and pregnancy occur together in a great many cases,"[44] the women themselves doubtless were aware of the problem, dreaded pregnancy and wished to prevent it, but such seemed impossible. As the purpose of courtship was marriage in that era, the reason for marriage was procreation. But time and the American example would slowly bring a woman to question the old ways, to make her ambivalent about what her mother had believed, and gradually the institution of marriage would change to accommodate a female partner who had become more free and equal.

ILLICIT SEX

SEVENTEEN year old Anastasia Bazanoff from Russia was not even two months pregnant when she passed through Ellis Island. Morning sickness must have given her secret away to the sharp-eyed arbiters of American morality, for she was detained on suspicion of pregnancy. Her denials were in vain, her condition became obvious and in April of 1915, her baby was born. What she could not achieve by protestations was achieved by war; that circumstance made deportation difficult and Anastasia and her little daughter were allowed to enter.[1]

No questions were asked about the father of Anastasia's child. Even when the officials knew a man was an unwed father, they apparently felt that the moral turpitude clause of immigration law applied only to women. Margaret Heckert found herself detained while the father of her child, Leopold Koenig, was admitted. Leopold had honorable intentions, but the law of his native land insisted he live up to his obligations to the state before he could fulfill his obligations to a woman. Until a young man had served his three years in the military he was not free to marry. With Margaret's pregnancy and the threat of war in the summer of 1914, the young couple decided to flee to America. But America, while unconcerned at that time with male duty to the state, was concerned with female morality, and Margaret and her unborn child were threatened with exile. Leopold appealed to the Immigrants' Protective League, whose agent wrote to immigration authorities: "I cannot protest too strongly against a policy which excludes a helpless and friendless girl and admits a man who is responsible for her condition and for bringing her to this country.[2]

Statistically the officials had little basis for suspicion, for census figures showed that immigrants were considerably less likely than Americans to give birth out of wedlock:

ILLEGITIMATE BIRTHS PER 1,000 BIRTHS, 1920[3]			
U.S. natives	16.7	Germans	6.6
Canadians	15.0	Austrians	5.3
English, Scotch, Welsh	10.6	Hungarians	5.0
Irish	10.1	Poles	4.0
Scandinavians	8.4	Russians	2.5
		Italians	2.5

Domestic workers were the most likely to find themselves pregnant and unmarried. Second to them were young girls who had never worked, while the number of women in factories and commerce who became pregnant illegitimately was very small by comparison. Domestics accounted for well over half the admittances at homes for unwed mothers.[4] The work exposed a woman to a higher risk since the male members of the family would be in a position to take advantage of her and she lacked the safety of numbers that existed in business. Moreover, the loneliness of domestic work made a young girl long for excitement, while work in a group was less boring. Nonetheless, domestic work was constantly recommended to immigrant women. Even more curious is the fact that when managers of homes for unwed mothers were asked what occupations they felt were most dangerous, they invariably replied that those in stores and factories were. On further questioning they admitted that they seldom got girls from those places and had no way to account for the contradiction. Presumably since domestic service was a traditional thing for women to do, they accepted it while questioning the newer occupations.

As might be expected from their life-style and as is borne out by the statistics, unwed Italian mothers were rare. One sociologist reported that in those cases where it did happen, a mother often would conspire with her daughter to keep the girl's father ignorant, both fearing his wrath and the consequences should he seek revenge. The daughter would likely go to visit some distant relative and put the baby up for adoption.[5]

Many unwed mothers did not keep their babies. Jacob Riis, writing in 1890, said the Foundling Asylum of the Sisters of Charity alone had taken in nearly 21,000 infant New Yorkers:

> Years ago the crib that now stands just inside the street door, . . . was placed outside at night; but it filled up too rapidly. The babies took to coming in little squads instead of in single file, and in self-defence the sisters were forced to take the cradle in. Now the mother must bring the child inside and put it in the crib where she is seen by the sister on guard. No effort is made to question her, or discover the baby's antecedents, but she is asked to stay and nurse her own and another baby. If she refuses, she is allowed to depart unhindered.[6]

Cases of premarital pregnancy were tolerated among some European groups—though certainly not all—the assumption being simply that the wedding date would be moved up, since courtship presupposed marriage. Therefore, even though some immigrant groups did not overly frown on premarital sex, their rate of illegitimacy remained low, for families saw that men carried out their obligation to marry.

―――――

While unwed mothers certainly did apply to social agencies for help, there seems to be more emphasis in social records on those illicit sexual relationships that were extramarital. Some cases become so entangled that the truth is hard to discover. Consider, for example:

> Charles Zielinski reported to the Legal Aid Society in December, 1912, that when he went to Canada to find work his wife went to live with another man. . . . Mrs. Zielinski's story was that . . . he often drank and abused her and before going to Canada slipped off to Kenosha and tried to marry another woman, but his previous marriage was discovered. She said he had committed adultery with the wife of the man who was

living with her, and whom she claimed was only a boarder. This wife arrested her husband and Mrs. Zielinski on a charge of adultery.[7]

Social workers might be forgiven if they concluded that some immigrants were amoral. Indeed, they soon learned that the immigrant code did differ from the American—and more importantly, that the moral code of one ethnic group differed from that of another. One sociologist wrote that she was "impressed by instances of the tolerance of the Polish husband and the independence and self-will in establishing sex relations for herself, of the Polish wife."[8] Slavic boarding house mistresses sometimes included sexual relations as part of the board with the full knowledge of husbands. Even such a pious and circumspect woman as Gro Svendsen did not consider it necessary to condemn the moral lapses of her Norwegian community. She wrote noncommittally in 1862 of a friend, "his wife has left him. She is living with another man in a place some 200 miles to the west." Another revealing remark is: "Will you tell Margit Arnegaard that I have made inquiries about her daughter? She is living in comfort. She married the man she left with."[9] Commenting on the English lower classes, one writer noted that prostitutes were not commonly patronized, perhaps because illicit sex was widely available: "Pre-marital relations are very common, perhaps even usual. Amongst the girls themselves nothing is thought of it if no consequences result; and very little even if they do. . . . [Then there is] more pity than reprobation. . . . It is noted by the clergy who marry them, how often both the addresses given are from the same house."[10]

It must be emphasized that not all ethnic groups subscribed to such ideas. An Italian man whose wife or daughter engaged in sex outside marriage would be horrified. Jewish families likewise closely guarded themselves against such shame. Within any ethnic group the closer to middle class Americanization a family was, the more circumspect its sexual behavior. The men might perhaps surreptitiously visit brothels, but the women lost any sexual freedom they might have had.

One reason why illicit arrangements were sometimes preferred was that in Europe—and even in America to a lesser extent—society made marriage a complex and expensive thing. Common-law arrangements were often taken quite seriously, perhaps even more seriously in some cases than marriage. A Lithuanian woman in Chicago was typical; abandoned by her drunkard husband, she moved in with another man because, she frankly said, she had no money and needed support. They felt no need to go through the difficulties of divorce and marriage. Having a marriage license had not made a difference in her first marriage, and the woman saw no point in obtaining one a second time.

Women who "lived in sin" nonetheless could hold firm moral beliefs. An Irishwoman, for example, who lived with a man and had two children by him, did not get married until her brother insisted. Despite her lack of conventionality, she refused to allow her sister-in-law to live with them on the grounds that this woman, who had separated from her husband and placed her children in an orphanage, was immoral.

If their first marriages had been unhappy, some women were especially wary of being legally bound again and preferred a common law arrangement. In the words of one Pole, "That began all the trouble, getting married. A man feels sure of you as soon as you marry him. I'll never marry another man if I get free of this one."[11] Indeed, social workers who nagged unwed couples to marry and took men to court thinking that they were doing the women a great favor, perhaps did as much harm as good. Americans viewed marriage as conferring benefits on a woman, for it was assumed that law and custom then protected her. Immigrant women, however, often seemed to consider marriage as much of a risk as a protection. Realizing American standards, a common-law wife was willing to make a pretense of being married—as in using her mate's name and allowing priests to assume marriage when children were christened—as long as she knew, and more importantly, her mate knew, that she was free.

———

Sometimes illicit sex was engaged in only because a woman felt she had no viable alternative. Women's wages were so inadequate and job security so lacking that sometimes one felt she had no choice except to make "concessions" to her boss. From there she might drift into the sale of the only commodity she had that the world seemed to value. Such cases, according to one sociologist, were "scarcely typical, but far from uncommon."[12] Indeed, sexual crime did pay: in 1906 when the average wage of newly arrived women was $5.58 a week, a "hurdy-gurdy girl" earned $20.00 to $24.00.[13] Full-fledged prostitutes, operating in a house, could earn up to $400.00 a week—though of course they did not keep all of it—while streetwalkers could expect a minimum of $25.00 weekly.[14]

Yet while the wages of sin were attractive, on the whole not as many immigrants as Americans accepted them. The 1911 report of the Vice Commission of Chicago, for instance, shows that immigrants were not sufficiently prevalent in the trade to excite any particular attention. Though the report was done in a time of great immigration and in a great immigrant city, the examples of foreign-born prostitutes among the dozens of case histories can be counted on the fingers of one hand.

The conclusion of another student of immigration was the same: "Nearly all the women in those dens . . . were native Americans, or came from what we call the better immigrant stock. . . . Most of the Slavs who come here do not know anything about the business of prostitution . . . and until a few years ago this was true of among the Jews also."[15] Immigrant women were not represented in prostitution to the same degree that they were represented in the rest of the labor force. Some were willing to ignore the precepts of society when dealing with a man they loved, but fewer were willing to sell their bodies to strangers.

As always, within the immigrant group there are significant variations by nativity. Though the number of immigrants from France was very small throughout the entire era, the French live up to their sexual reputation and come in first in the number of prostitutes they contributed to the United States:

ALIENS DEPORTED AS PROSTITUTES AT TIME OF ENTRY, 1908–09[16]			
French	42	Slavic	3
English	38	Irish	3
German	12	Scandinavian	2
Italian	7	Polish	2
Hebrew	7	Dutch	1
Scotch	5		

A study of New York arrests in the same era confirmed that the influence of the French in prostitution was disproportionate to the numbers: "It seems probable that the percentage of French women who practiced prostitution before arrival is decidedly larger."[17] Most other immigrant women were seduced into the business after their arrival. They agreed with this conclusion:

> The investigation of the United States Immigration Commission into the relation of the immigrant woman to the social evil showed that very few prostitutes are brought into the United States. The great majority of young immigrant women who were found in resorts were virtuous when they came here, and were ruined because there was not adequate protection and assistance given them after they reached the United States.[18]

This "protection" hampered the free movement of many innocent women while doing little to bother the knowledgeable. Women in steerage were carefully checked for any appearance of immorality, while in fact the experienced importers of prostitutes sent them second-class where female passengers were not subject to such insulting inquiry. Unsuccessful suitors sometimes vindicated their hurt pride by maliciously reporting their former girlfriends to the immigration authorities as immoral. Unfortunately, the immigration officials took such reports quite seriously, seemed inclined to believe the worst, and assumed the woman was guilty until she proved herself innocent.

Although foreign women were less likely than natives to enter the trade, evidence indicates that a disproportionately large number of pimps were foreigners and indeed, there did exist a kind of international community of procurers who exchanged letters on likely prospects and warned each other of government crackdowns.[19] The language used in these letters makes the term "white slavery" an apt one indeed, for the writers tell of buying and selling women as chattel, often at high prices:

> . . . statements were made by a certain keeper of a house of prostitution in Chicago that for a certain French girl named Marcelle he had paid the sum of $1,000; that for a certain French girl named Mascotta . . . he had paid $500 . . . that a certain girl named Lillie, also a French girl, was sent from Chicago to Omaha and sold to a keeper of a house of prostitution in that city for the sum of $1,400. . . . that $500 is the ordinary price for a French prostitute when delivered in America.[20]

Indeed, while it was not as common as Americans feared, occasionally naive young women were deceived into becoming friendly with pimps or madams and finally, if they did not join the trade willingly, were brutalized. A common method of madams was to hire European girls as maids, bring them to the United States, and then, when it was difficult for them to escape, break them into prostitution. Consider the case of an innocent German girl:

> On my way to Bremerhoffen in the train Marie G.——happened to be in the same compartment. Marie G.——asked . . . all about myself and my family. . . . She told me that she was a respectable married woman and owned a house in Los Angeles. . . . I thought it quite natural to ask her if she could assist me in obtaining a position. . . . After arrival she told me, "Well, now we go to my house." . . . I saw girls half-dressed, and Marie turned on me right away and said I should not bother about what I saw, and look around so much. . . . I did not know where to go; I had no money; . . . She would not allow me to speak to anyone. . . . I asked Marie G.——for some paper. I wanted to write home . . . she . . . never would give it to me. . . . I was crying and she said she had done so much for me already that I was really ungrateful. I told her I was going to get a policeman, and Marie G.——said if I got a policeman I would get arrested, and not her.[21]

A Lithuanian Jew was also betrayed by a woman who posed as a matchmaker and obtained her trust. When she realized what was about to happen to her, she tried to escape, but was imprisoned and beaten.

> Time passed and I got used to the horrible life. Later I even had an opportunity to escape, because they used to send me out on the streets, but life had become meaningless for me anyway, and nothing mattered anymore. I lived this way for six months, degraded and dejected, until I got sick and they drove me out of that house.
>
> I appealed for admission into several hospitals, but they didn't want to take me in. . . . I had decided to throw myself into the river, but wandering around on the streets, I met a richly dressed man who was quite drunk. I took over six hundred dollars from him and spent the money on doctors, who cured me.[22]

She then got a job as a domestic and the family liked her. Later the mistress of the house died and the man wanted to marry her, but she was unsure because of her past. She wrote to a Jewish newspaper for advice and the editor advised her to tell the truth, and if the man loved her sufficiently, he would understand. The paper, however, showed little sympathy for these unfortunate women, adding, "Such letters from victims of 'white slavery' come to our attention quite often, but we do not publish them. We are disgusted by this plague on society, and dislike bringing it to the attention of our readers."[23]

Not only did the community generally refuse to aid fallen women, but the women themselves felt so degraded that they did not consider their lives redeemable. A rare effort in rehabilitation was made by Sister Blandina Segale, an Italian-born nun. Over a five year period at the end of the nineteenth century she "had restored 157 women [in Cincinnati] to normal living."[24] Almost always, however, the efforts of government and social agencies were aimed at prevention, with little hope of cure for those who were already fallen.

It was unusual for society to forgive and for women to think themselves worthy of forgiveness. Their self-abasement, their fatalism, kept them in the life. "In one of the recent raids," read a 1911 report, "a big Irish girl was taken and held as a witness. She was old enough, strong enough, and wise enough . . . to have overcome almost any kind of opposition." Asked why she did not leave, her reply was:

> Get out! I can't. They make us buy the cheapest rags, and they are charged against us at fabulous prices; they make us change outfits at intervals of two or three weeks, until we are so deeply in debt that there is no hope of ever getting out from under. Then, to make matters worse, we seldom get an accounting . . . and when we do . . . it is always to find ourselves deeper in debt than before. We've simply got to stick, and that's all there is to it.[25]

It was a strange system of morality that convinced a woman that the property rights of her exploiter were more to be reckoned with as a moral obligation than her own human rights. This emphasis on property values as opposed to human values seemed to be one of the strongest of American characteristics. It seemed to be the basic premise of the industrial system immigrants knew so well, and therefore, it is not surprising that daughters of immigrants were statistically more likely to enter into lives of prostitution than their foreign-born mothers had been.

Perhaps the language barrier and lack of knowledge of American techniques of prostitution had some small inhibiting effect on the foreign-born, but more important was a well-defined moral code that enabled resistance. Children of immigrants were more ambivalent in their beliefs, for the conflict between the values of their parents and those of the surrounding American society often left them with no strong standards. Caught up in the syndrome of rising expectations, to many of the second generation the best thing they could do was to make the most money in the easiest way. A government study had to acknowledge that "the foreign born are not so likely to become prostitution offenders as their children are."[26] America had taken away the validity of their mothers' mores and left these girls with none of their own.

PART III

Domesticity: The Old and the New

THE FRUIT OF
THE LAND

CHANGE was the only constant in the life of an immigrant woman. The one thing she could feel sure of was that the future would be different from the past. If she had felt sure of her husband's faithfulness in Europe, in America she saw devastating things happen to marriages. If she had been positive that what the priest or rabbi spoke was the truth in Europe, in America she saw that even these sacred areas were open to question. Everywhere there was change, and with it, ambivalence. Whether the subject was as significant as religion and morality or as mundane as the way she dressed and what she ate, always there was ambivalence about the new ways versus the old. Often the changes that mattered most to her were the ones that were not the most important in societal terms. It is of these personal, seemingly trivial, things that her letters are filled.

Food was one of those things. The change in diet was of tremendous importance, and many an immigrant letter reads like a grocery list. They gloated over the abundance of food in America and considered this the best of justifications for emigration. Jannicke Saehle, a young Norwegian who came alone in 1847 to seek her fortune in frontier Wisconsin wrote:

> I have food and drink in abundance. A breakfast here consists of chicken, mutton, beef or pork, warm or cold wheat bread, butter, white cheese, eggs, or small pancakes, the best coffee, tea, cream and sugar. For dinner the best courses are served. Supper is eaten at six o'clock, with warm biscuits, and several kinds of cold wheat bread, cold meats, bacon, cakes, preserved apples, plums, berries, which are eaten with cream, tea and coffee—and my greatest regret here is to see the superabundance of food, much of which has to be thrown to the chickens and the swine, when I think of my dear ones in Bergen, who like so many others must at this time lack the necessities of life.[1]

Nor did it take a great deal to satisfy them at first. Rosa Cavalleri's first meal in America was unexceptional by our standards, but a banquet by hers. "Bread! white bread! Enough for a whole village! And butter to go on it! I ate until I no longer had any pains in my stomach.!" The next morning she reported, "For breakfast there was white bread again and butter and coffee and sugar and sausages and eggs besides! Mama mia! Did all the poor people in America eat like kings?"[2]

This Norwegian woman, writing from Wisconsin in 1850, plainly thinks that she is inordinately blessed:

> Our daily food consists of rye and wheat bread, bacon, butter, eggs, molasses, sugar, coffee and beer. The corn that grows on large cobs is rarely eaten by people . . . but is used as fodder for the animals. . . . This year we have produced so much foodstuff that we have been able to sell instead of having to buy, and we all have cattle, driving oxen, and wagons. We also have children in abundance.[3]

When they found that they could afford in America foods that had been beyond their reach in Europe, some went wild. Social workers cited examples of children being fed doughnuts, pies, and cookies for all of their meals. When mothers realized that visiting nurses had other nutritional theories, they simply didn't tell them the truth rather than "make that nurse too sad."[4]

Of course they wanted to do what was best for their children, but in this new environment, it was difficult to decide what was best. First it was hard to obtain the accustomed foodstuffs, even if one had sufficient money, which was often not the case. Cooking utensils were unfamiliar, with appliances still stranger. Women were puzzled by the "stoves with no fires in them and no place for the wood, just holes in irons, and if you turn a handle and apply at lighted match, fire comes."[5] Learning the necessary techniques and adjusting the family's preferences to the available foods and doing this in a way that promoted good nutrition was an adjustment that took years.

Peasant women, though untutored in nutritional theory, generally served their families a moderately well-balanced diet. The disruption of life that emigration wrought could seriously disturb these habits. The following anecdote is indicative. A sick baby was brought to a public health clinic and the mother questioned in regard to its diet:

> "What do you give the baby?" asked the nurse through an interpreter.
> "What we have ourselves," was the reply.

"But why should you do that to a little baby?" chided the nurse.

"I always did that in our own country with my other children before we came here."

"But what did you give your children in the old country that you had yourselves?"

"Soup and buttermilk," answered the mother, smiling, apparently at the pleasant recollection of those days.

"What do you give your child now that you have yourselves?"

"Beer and coffee."[6]

Inadequacy of milk was frequent. Milk, often available on European farms, was unreasonably expensive in the big cities of America. As one tubercular woman said when she refused to drink the milk her doctor had prescribed: "The milk comes in a bottle; in my country, I get it from the goat. . . . I do not know what else is in the bottle; there must be something besides milk, to make it cost so much."[7] In one Italian family, the children had so little milk that they were severely bowlegged; their legs had to be broken and straightened to undo the damage caused by rickets.

Milk was a basic element of the Scandinavian diet, where cool weather caused no refrigeration problems. Here, however, women were at a loss in dealing with American summers. Gro Svendsen wrote home:

> I remember I used to wonder when I heard that it would be impossible to keep the milk as we did at home. Now I have learned that it is indeed impossible because of the heat here in the summertime. One can't make cheese out of milk because of flies, bugs and other insects. . . . If one were to make cheese here in the summertime, the cheese itself would be alive with bugs. Toward late autumn it should be possible to keep the milk.[8]

Like cheese-making, bread-baking was part of almost every immigrant woman's domestic knowledge. Of course farm women continued to bake their bread—though they usually changed from rye or oats to wheat for the basic grain—but in the cities, when commercial bakeries were established, this habit soon died, even among nonworking immigrant women. Some Italian women mixed their dough at home and took the loaves to a bakery to be baked, paying ten cents a week for this service,[9] but most budgets of immigrant households were likely to include purchases of bread.

It is seldom that one reads of city immigrants baking anything. They apparently could not cope with American ovens, so different from Old World ones. In addition, women found it difficult to obtain the ingredients for familiar recipes, and in summer, baking made tenement homes impossibly hot. Probably women also were attracted by the novelty of having these foods available in stores.

While they accepted and even praised American food, they also never stopped missing that of the Old World. In 1887, forty years after Elise Waerenskjold had emigrated to Texas, she wrote nostalgically of home-country cooking, wishing she could have "some of the good food you know so well how to prepare. . . . I have not eaten fish cakes since we lay in Drobak, waiting for a favorable wind."[10]

The fear that they would not be able to obtain familiar foods elsewhere was one reason for the existence of immigrant ghettos. European style delicatessens flourished only in cities. Probably many women preferred to stay in their "Little Italy" or "Little Poland" expressly because their shopping needs were met and their language understood. If the importing business was well-established, one could go on cooking and eating much as always.

This was not the case for women who settled outside of cities, especially while the frontier was new. Writing in late winter, Elisabeth Koren complained:

> We cannot say that we live so exceptionally well here. The dishes vary from boiled pork to fried pork, rare to well done, with coffee in addition (milk when we can get it), good bread and butter. To this are added now and then potatoes, which are now all gone; fried onions once in a while, and above all, the glass jar of pickles. That is our meal, morning, noon, and evening.[11]

Because they complained of their tiresome diet and missed their traditional food, it seems very odd to find that Norwegian women apparently prepared little fish. In Mrs. Waerenskjold's Texas it was not easily obtained, but in the upper Midwest it was certainly plentiful. In fact one of Mrs. Koren's friends told her that he lived "next to a river so full of fish, mostly carp and pike, that at times one cannot see the bottom. One evening he himself caught a large mess of fish with his hands."[12] Whether or not this is a "fish story," it is true that fish were abundant in the virgin days of the Midwest. Yet neither Mrs. Koren nor other Norwegian women write of frequently eating fish, even though it was a mainstay of their native diet. Perhaps it was again a simple case of doing what the Americans did.

If their daily diet accommodated itself to American reality, women did try to serve native food for special occasions. Norwegians might not regularly eat much fish, but *lutefisk* was a special treat for weddings and Christmas. Sometimes obtaining the special food presented real problems, not only in locating it but also in paying the greater price that was sure to be charged for what was now an exotic item. Some Italian families ate meager meals for weeks before a *festa* in order to assure having the proper foods then. Even in families that were charity cases, the proper foods often appeared, with the budget carefully reworked to hide this necessary extravagance from the social worker's scrutiny.

Sometimes the problem was not merely adjustment from familiar to new foods, but one of eating to stay alive. Although many immigrants were enthusiastic about plentiful American foods, in other times and places, the situation was the opposite. While Rosa Cavalleri had been exhilarated by the abundance of food when she arrived, when the Depression of 1893 struck, it was a totally different story. They were facing near starvation when one night a kindly neighbor, an organ grinder, shared with Rosa and her children the fifteen cents he had earned. "We ran out and for 3¢ we got the bag of cornmeal; then we got some liver. The liver was cheap in that time—they were throwing it to the cats and dogs. . . . So I cooked the cornmeal with the liver in it and made a nice polenta. My children, when they got that good supper—oh, I wish you had seen it! They thought it was the king's wedding."[13]

Many immigrant families were seriously malnourished during that depression. Rose Cohen's family had arrived only shortly before it struck and had no memories of better days to make it easier to bear. Her mother was anguished at being unable to give her children even the food they had known in Russia.

During economic depressions and even during better times, the diets of many of the underpaid working women were meager. Bread and tea were their mainstays, bread to quiet the stomach and tea to soothe the spirit. In Senate testimony on female factory workers, "Rebecca C., a Russian Jewess, said that during the dull season she had lived many an entire day on a penny's worth of bread, and the landlady added that she had known the girl to go without even that much sustenance for the day."[14]

A clergyman in Lawrence, Massachusetts said that he knew a woman out of work who had subsisted on just two crackers a day.[15] Some women felt that eating decently was a luxury that had to be justified; when questioned about their diet, most of them had only bread and coffee for breakfast, and "if eggs appeared on the menu, the girl usually explained that it was because she was anemic or otherwise run down."[16]

Perhaps it was because they knew that the small meals they could afford would "only whet my appetite for more food"[17] that so many women avoided eating anything except their daily bread and tea. If the stomach could be kept slightly numb and not tempted with food, the mind would fall quiet and the appetite stop its teasing. That would not happen with children. There were sickening pictures of hungry children amid the alleged abundance of America. Holyoke, Massachusetts, at mid-century was a town filled with poor Irish immigrants, and its newspaper editorialized on the degradation some were driven to by their empty stomachs:

> There is one pitiful and miserable sight which we have seen night after night in front of the fruit and vegetable stands. . . . It is a drove of poverty-stricken children, often girls, clad only in one or two ragged garments, down on their hands and knees in the gutters, greedily picking out of the mud and dirt and eating the bits of spoiled and decaying fruit which have been thrown out as worthless.[18]

Yet even though hunger stalked them, most immigrants bore their fate with dignity. Some found that despite a painful stomach, the palate would reject food that was alien. During the Great Depression, many Italians found that they simply could not eat the canned meat and American cereals given them in government relief programs. They traded with Americans if they could, secretly sold them at a reduced price, or guiltily threw them away—but they could not force themselves to eat the unfamiliar food.[19] The prevailing attitude was that women, and especially immigrant women, couldn't be trusted to budget their family food needs wisely.

Despite the suspicions of would-be philanthropists, the evidence is that women generally managed their grocery money quite well. More data is available on this than on most subjects relating to immigrant women; apparently sociologists were concerned that they be able to show the public—legislators and philanthropists in particular—just how efficiently immigrant families budgeted. This quantitative research appealed to the fledgling "science" of sociology. There are reams of data showing grocery lists down to the last ounce of rice—but unfortunately few of the more important questions were asked. Everyone wanted to know how much money a woman earned by the week and by the year and how much was spent on meat and rent and fuel. Few asked her how she felt about America or if she was glad she had emigrated or any questions relating to her personality and opinions.

While it is unfortunate that so few investigators asked these questions, nevertheless we are left with a valuable body of data on the income and outgo of immigrant households. One point that seems to be true is that many immigrant women were delighted at the food available in this country and when their family income was steady, good food was the spending priority.

Analysis of the grocery lists of typical Croatian women in a Michigan mining town around 1910 shows that family food costs for the month were forty-three dollars, of incomes that averaged fifty-eight or sixty dollars[20]—the family spent 75 percent of its income on food! The remaining 25 percent would have to cover the rent, purchases of clothes and any incidentals, and savings. They would live in a hovel where the rent was low and dress in rags, but they would eat well.

Other studies showed similar patterns. Poles and Lithuanians working in the Chicago stockyards spent over 50 percent of their budgets for food, with meat taking the larger portion. For Lithuanians especially, a good steak must have been a glory; they spent nearly one-fifth of their annual income on meat, while spending only 8 percent for clothes. The next largest grocery expense was baked goods, taking 10 percent of the annual income. By comparison, milk and alcohol took about 4 percent each, with slightly more spent on alcohol.[21]

A student of Italians reported, "The general impression gained from a study of the weekly food purchases in these families is that they are more generous in providing food for themselves than for any other need of life."[22] Contrary to the prevailing opinion, Italians ate a good deal of meat and fish in addition to pasta and were wiser than Americans in preferring fresh vegetables. English and Irish accounts, on the other hand, were apt to show much greater expenditures for pastries and sweets, and one detailed study noted that Irishwomen frequently seemed to serve a monotonous diet.[23]

Perhaps the most valid criticism that can be made is an over-emphasis on meat and bread and a shortage of milk and—except for Italians—fruit and vegetables. A Fall River Polish family had a grocery account of forty-five items, twenty-one of which were meat, eggs, or cheese. Despite this abundance of protein, the diet could not be called well-balanced, for cucumbers and cabbage were the only vegetables bought and milk was purchased only once during the nineteen day study period for a family with four young children. Portuguese grocery accounts also showed a complete dearth of green and yellow vegetables, listing only beans, onions, and garlic.[24]*

Immigrants also were plagued by the perennial problem of the poor: having to buy small quantities and paying more per unit. While it could be argued that they were preserving European marketing customs and shopped daily for freshness, the evidence seems to be at least equally strong that this was done because of a lack of money and storage facilities.

———

There were no sociologists studying the dietary habits of farming women, but we have some knowledge from their own pens. Perhaps because of the virgin soil, one could easily raise produce that is a gardener's dream. An Englishwoman wrote that she had raised about 200 bushels of potatoes and was blessed with other bounty, too. "We had a good crop of turnips and an excellent garden. We had beets in our garden that weighed from 8 to 11 pounds. I weighted them through curiosity. . . . Also last year we had a great deal of fruit. It was supposed we had 4 hundred bushels of peaches in our orchard and cherrys and apples. The trees were propped. They could not bear their weight of fruit."[25]

Though they wrote of problems in obtaining familiar seed and young fruit trees, immigrant women were much impressed by the new foods America had to offer. Elise Waerenskjold explained that sweet potatoes "are not boiled in water but are baked in the oven,"

*The study was done in May; too early for garden produce.

and proclaimed them "delicious." Following the habits of Texans, she stopped baking rye and oat bread "because the Americans use these grains only as feed for cattle," and ate instead Southern-style cornbread. She praised the variety of game that could be obtained free. Once, she claimed, her husband had killed thirty quail with one shot: "they come by the millions, they look like a dark cloud."[26] Elisabeth Koren also enthused about the raspberries, strawberries, and asparagus she found growing wild in frontier Iowa.

But the biggest hit was watermelon. Though the varieties must have been much inferior to today's since they were described as being "as big as a child's head," they were dearly loved. Gro Svendsen wrote, "I must tell you something about a fruit called 'watermelon.' We have an enormous quantity of them; I can't compare them to anything I ever saw in Norway."[27]

It was a good thing that much food could be obtained with so little effort, for otherwise the budgets of many frontier settlers would have been stretched to the breaking point with obligatory hospitality to new arrivals. Every spring brought boatloads, and they often were fed and housed by compatriots as they moved toward the interior. A Norwegian Quaker wrote without complaint of this annual influx, "Twelve Norwegians came here today, and are now eating their supper. About two weeks ago there arrived from ninety to one hundred people. They stayed at our house and my brother's house for about a week, and we furnished meals for nearly all of them."[28]

With true hospitality, she makes no mention of the work involved in feeding this horde, nor of the expense. Even if they paid for their meals—and nothing in the letter indicates that they did— there were bound to be costs that would not be repaid. A woman who could feed a hundred people three meals a day out of the tiny ill-equipped kitchens on the frontier had to be a wonder of good management. She would have to have a good heart, too, and an active concern for the welfare of her people.

Immigrant women were, on the whole, good managers and admirably resourceful. Many of them came from a European life-style where the diet had been relatively meager and monotonous. In America, within a generation or two, they adopted each other's cuisine as well as that of the New World, and so developed a country where the diet is more varied and interesting than anywhere else on earth.

Our chief dietary problem today, in fact, has become restraining ourselves from eating all that is available. Mrs. Pagano knew this particular ambivalence before most immigrant women did; Americanized and affluent, she still grew fresh Italian herbs with which to flavor the Old World dishes. But the creator of all this goodness, who had lived on the verge of starvation in Italy, could not enjoy it. The land had blessed her so richly that, as for many modern Americans, a weakened heart demanded that she cease partaking of the bounty. "Eh!" she lamented, "When I was a little girl, back in the old country, I couldn't get enough to eat; and now that I can have all I want, I still can't get enough to eat!"[29]

OF HOVELS, HOMES, AND HOPES

VIRTUALLY every kitchen in an immigrant home served as a bedroom, dining room, and sitting room. Rose Cohen remembered summer nights sleeping in the hellish heat:

There were five of us, the two boys in one cot and we three girls in the other, in the one room filled with the odour of cooking, of kerosene oil, the smell of grimy clothes, of stale perspiration, the heat of the body. . . . As I lay with my two sisters in the sagging cot, with an unconscious limb of one or the other thrown over me, I wept. Then I thought, "Why, need it be so? Why?"[1]

In much of Europe days were spent out-of-doors, with the work being done in the company of other women. But here a woman's place seemed to be literally in the home. Her home, probably more than anything else, caused a woman to wonder if she had made a mistake in emigrating, for usually it left a great deal to be desired.

The kitchen was literally the center of the home; it contained the "central heating system"—the wood cookstove—which was supposed to heat the rooms to the front and rear of it. Consequently, the kitchen was the most inadequately lighted and ventilated room. Only four of eighty immigrant homes in a 1912 study reported any source of heat other than the kitchen stove.[2]

As the house had been impossible to cool in summer, so it was impossible to decently heat. Europeans, accustomed to a more temperate climate, readily succumbed to the malarial fevers of summer and the pneumonia of winter. Many an immigrant woman told her social worker that she went to work even when suffering from colds and fever simply because it was warm at work and freezing at home. Even after wood stoves were replaced by gas, the gas lines sometimes froze in their shabby housing.

The shivering woman could be warmed by huddling close to someone else, for it was virtually certain that her home overflowed with other people. There was a small minority of women who lived alone or with just one roommate, but it was far more likely that one would live in a household as either wife, daughter, or lodger.

To simply say that tenements were overcrowded does not begin to show the situation. For example, one Philadelphia tenement held thirty families in thirty-four rooms[3], an average of four people per room. A Lithuanian woman lived with her husband and five children in a tiny closet of a home that contained only slightly more air space than the law required for one adult.[4] A woman and her child actually suffocated to death sleeping in a miniscule room that contained two other occupants.[5] New York City police, enforcing health department orders, found many rooms similar to one that was less than thirteen feet square and slept twelve men and women, most of them on the floor.[6]

Yet if these cases strain credulity, it is probable that the statistics err in minimizing the overcrowding. Immigrants soon learned that they were in violation of the new housing codes. They certainly understood—if the law did not—that an overcrowded home was preferable to eviction, and they became adept at hiding cots and inventing cover stories to dupe the investigators.

The buildings themselves were jammed together so that the population of many an immigrant city block was equal to that of an entire town. Outside the cities in the small mill towns, immigrant houses also were packed close together. All greenery around the housing was eradicated so the landlord could maximize his investment. While these tenements had windows, they admitted little light or air, since they almost abutted the windows next door. Immigrant women increased their kitchen wall space by reaching out the window and hanging utensils on the outside of the house next door. A woman could even carry on a conversation with her neighbor while both of them were in their own kitchens. But if her neighbor was someone she did not like, the situation could be most unpleasant, for privacy was unobtainable.

Overcrowding did have an adverse effect on mental health, but its physical effects were of more obvious concern. Fire was a constant threat. Most tenements were old, wooden, and had only one exit. The fact that each apartment had its own stove multiplied the danger. Fire escapes were almost nonexistent early in the tenement era—one study found fewer than one in every twenty-five buildings.[7] When fire escapes were required by building codes, the space-starved immigrant family extended itself into this available area. Periodic raids by the fire department could not permanently remove the washtubs, flowerpots, clotheslines, and extra chests packed into their escape way. Once a fire started, the proximity of houses made them a death trap for hundreds of people who were jammed into the same block. Many of the victims of the great Chicago fire were immigrants; their poor wooden shacks made ideal fuel.[8]

A second danger was epidemics, which spread as rapidly as fire. In New York's Gotham Court, a cholera epidemic which barely touched the rest of the city killed at a rate of 195 per 1,000 residents. The health department lamented, "There are numerous examples of tenement houses in which are lodged several hundred people that have a pro rata allotment of ground area scarcely equal to two square yards."[9] Although public attention was drawn to the problem when an epidemic hit, few realized that these tenements were constant disease mills. It was a rare person who was not exposed to tuberculosis. A third of a million rooms in New York City were without windows—"pitch dark and unventilated."[10] One national health authority said of the rooms where women lived day in and day out,"If we had invented machines to create tuberculosis we could not have succeeded better."[11]

But the aspect of overpopulation that worried investigators most was the moral danger of such close proximity between the sexes. There were, for example, the case of a Russian-Polish home in which a thirteen-year-old girl slept in the same bed as her father and brother,[12] and that of a newly arrived young Polish woman who lived with a male relative and a dozen young men who boarded with him.[13] Yet while the upright Americans worried over the orgies that they thought must naturally result from so many bodies so close together, the actual result of overcrowding probably was directly the opposite. Where privacy was so unobtainable, a free and healthy sex life was unlikely.

Rats lived in these overcrowded buildings along with the people. Women hung food from the ceiling in the hope that rats wouldn't be able to reach it and watched their babies carefully. Even the enlightenment of the social workers who made their home in the Chicago Commons settlement house could not keep the rats from their abode in a neighborhood that teemed with them. Rosa Cavalleri, who was a cleaning women there, said it was, "all full of rats—three pounds, five pounds, I don't know how many pounds to make those rats, but they were big! The residents used to wait in line by the bathroom door, and when somebody didn't come out, they'd push the door and there it was the rats playing tag with themselves. And when the residents were all sitting down eating dinner, those rats chased between their legs."[14]

The rats were there because filth was there—or was, at least, nearby. Indoor toilets were rare, and when available, were located in dark halls and shared by many tenants. Since no one was responsible for their cleanliness, their usual state was one of filth. New flush toilets proved to be worse than the old outhouses, for the cold of the halls caused pipes to freeze. With water and sewage lines backed up sometimes for weeks, the stench could be overpowering. Before the twentieth century the usual arrangement was to have privies in the backyard; later flush toilets were often installed there, where they were practically certain to freeze.

If they were in working order, their location was greatly inconvenient, and women suffered most from this. Women had the frequent bladder demands caused by pregnancy. A mother was responsible for nursing the sick and for taking young children to the toilet. It is small wonder that women told social workers they had bladder problems caused by trying to delay nature's call.

These personal hardships for women seldom occurred to investigators. They were concerned with cleanliness. Even when a janitor was in charge, she often gave up the task as an impossibility. One such woman took an inspector out to the yard closet, "confident of our approval because she had scrubbed it an hour before. She was embarrassed to find a thick, filthy pool upon the seat."[15]

City slums were bad enough, but probably worse were the hundreds of company-dominated mill and mining towns. These companies transformed a pleasant meadow by throwing up a three-

or-four story fire trap of a factory; they ravaged the earth with strip
mines; and everywhere they dotted the landscape with bleak, gray
shacks. Nowhere did they take any responsibility for sanitation.
Raw sewage almost always drained directly into rivers, and when
the water was high, sewage backed up into cellars—which were
often immigrant homes. Emma Huhtasaari, a northern Swede
whose native tongue was Finnish, wrote in 1905 from her Han-
cock, Michigan mining town: "There is never a birdsong in America. . . . There is only coal smoke and dusty streets. Coal smoke
from many factories so that the air gets heavy. It feels so bad when
you have grown up in Norrland's fresh air."[16]

The people in these towns were powerless, dependent upon a
governing class that did not care about their needs. Those who
lived alone on the frontier had more control over their lives. Yet
sanitation there too often left a great deal to be desired. People did
not grasp the correlation between sanitation and disease. They
built their outhouses and wells conveniently close to the house,
and dangerously close to each other. In the early days, privies were
often not even constructed: "No one thought of building a log
house for so simple a purpose. The discharges of both the sick and
well were deposited in the open, where they were accessible to
hogs and chickens, as well as to the myriads of flies which always
infested the homes, for no window screens were used."[17]

The result was fevers, which, since they arrived with summer,
the new arrivals blamed on the climate. Mosquitoes abounded and
foreigners quickly developed diseases to which Americans had
built up immunities. Elise Waerenskjold wrote of a group of Norwegians who disregarded advice and settled in bottom lands: "Almost everyone became ill. . . . Consequently many were discon-
tented, and some had died." The group had consisted of "eight
families crowded into two small rooms."[18]

Though surrounded by miles and miles of empty land, the farm-
house itself was often as crowded as its city counterpart. Usually
the motivation of the city housewife who accepted boarders was
extra income, but the country women more likely felt obligated to
take them because they had nowhere else to go.

Elisabeth Koren, as the wife of the only clergyman for a hundred
miles or more, was invited to stay at the best available home. Yet
it was only a one-room cabin, partitioned with curtains for a little

privacy. She stayed with another couple and their two toddlers, and her husband made a sixth person in that one room when he was not circuit riding. Personalities clashed and after several months of forced companionship in the snowbound Iowa house, Mrs. Koren was asked to leave. Spring came and construction began on her own home, while she lived more fretful weeks in another crowded household. When she was able to move into her own home, she was as ecstatic over a rough three-room abode as she would have been over a castle back in Norway. "How pleasant it is to have a bedroom, and in the morning to go into a tidy room to a breakfast table all set, instead of first having to clear away the toilet articles . . . We really learned to prize all such little things, . . . which at home it never occurred to us to think about."[19]

Linka Preus also came from a fairly wealthy family in Norway, but though accustomed to a large house and a staff of servants, she accepted her crowded Wisconsin home cheerfully. It was one twelve-by-twelve-foot room, in which were squeezed one-and-a-half beds; a "sofa" (actually two clothes chests covered with pillows); a chest of drawers "with a cupboard for a hat"; two easy chairs ("my treasures"); another chest of drawers; and a storage chest under the bed. The room, she wrote, was "well-filled, . . . two persons can barely pass."[20] Later a table was added, a truly unique furnishing which filled Linka with marvel:

> My kitchen table consists of a box we brought from Norway. . . . This we inverted and provided with four legs, beautifully trimmed and polished by nature herself, from a poplar tree growing in the woods just outside our door. To be sure they were frozen and raw, but what of it? . . . To my great delight, I discover that the legs have been sprouting lovely green side branches, covered with green leaves. Behold, thus our kind God causes summer to flourish in our home while winter still prevails outside.[21]

Besides being crowded most homes were not well-built. They had been hurriedly constructed by husbands who were not professional carpenters. Floors sagged, doors and windows—the few that they had—hung crazily, and roofs leaked. The home that Elisabeth Koren had been so happy to have soon proved how poorly built it was when she lamented after a thunderstorm, "The floor was a pond, so I had to tiptoe about with great caution, holding up my dress. . . . The rain streamed in through the curtains and across the table, soaking them thoroughly. We had to pull the bookcases and bed away from the walls and cover them with towels, for the rain came through the walls and ceiling . . . and soaked the bed-clothes and other clothing."[22]

Cold, like rain, poured in through the countless cracks. Many women slept in beds that were fully occupied all night and yet awakened to find frost on pillows and sheets frozen stiff. Mrs. Brandt wrote that her North Dakota kitchen was so cold that "I often put on overshoes and tied a scarf over my head before pre-paring breakfast."[23] In the great blizzard of 1880 her neighbors had to bring chickens and pigs into their homes to keep the ani-mals from freezing. Straw and manure were piled around the foun-dation to prevent freezing, with doors and windows covered by black tar paper and sealed tight, making the house dark and gloomy.

Yet to have a log cabin, as these women did, was something of a luxury. Many settlers lived in the dark earth itself. On the tree-less plains west of the Mississippi they had no choice—no other building materials were available. The Norwegian women who commented on these earthen homes nonetheless found them sur-prisingly pleasant. Mrs. Koren wrote that a dugout was "not as bad as one might think."[24] More common than dugouts—which re-quired a hill or cave-like terrain—were the sod houses that sprang up. Homes made of dirt and grass may actually have been more of a shock to Yankees than they were to immigrants, who were usually familiar with thatched roofs made of similar natural ma-terials. The women set out to make the best possible home. Mrs. Brandt wrote of her friends who lived thus, "It was wonderful how neat and cozy sod houses could be made. When floors were scrubbed, walls freshly whitewashed, and the broad window sills filled with blooming geraniums, such homes were by no means unattractive. . . . I must admit, however, that such houses had their drawbacks. They were apt to become damp and in time would settle so that the roof and walls would become lopsided."[25]

Settling and dampness were not the only drawbacks. Snakes and burrowing animals thought this sod no different from any other; overcrowding was apt to be more severe, and livestock in the home more common; windows were scarce and wintertime depression was worst of all here on these unprotected plains where the wind swept down from the polar north. Blizzards howled for days and snow swirled, often burying the little house.

Still they survived. When spring came, they set about their

housecleaning with fervor. Down came the tar paper and the manure insulation and up popped the flowers women forethoughtfully had planted in the fall. Linka Preus and Elisabeth Koren both wrote in their diaries of long searches in the American woods for wildflowers similar to those they had known back home; Elise Waerenskjold, after forty years in Texas, was still writing back to Norway for plants she could not obtain here. Women set up their woman-to-woman networks of exchanges and as the years passed Linka and her friends grew such difficult houseplants as callas, fuchsias, chrysanthemums, and primroses. Indeed, when Linka's diary was printed in 1952, the editor revealed that her descendants grew plants, "which, through a series of transplanting of slips, trace their ancestry back to her bay window."[26]

The sod house was only temporary. Life in it was easier to bear because of the conviction that it would not be permanent. One year would be the bonanza—a good grain crop and high farm prices—and the family's little hoard of savings would go over the top. Then they could place their order for lumber and the railroad would bring their new home. Eventually this did happen for almost everyone on the plains. Likewise, the city immigrant tolerated her tenement because she, too, did not believe she would be there forever. This was not the promise of America.

The reasons for getting out of the ghetto were economic as well as esthetic. It did not make sense to pay the rents that slumlords charged for these wretched hovels. With rent high and maintenance nil, the profits on this human misery averaged 40 percent, and examples of 100 percent and more were cited.[27]

Almost all city immigrants moved often from one tenement to another in the hope that one of these "temporary" homes would offer a little more for a little less. Rose Cohen explained, "We liked moving from one place to another. Everyone . . . moved often. It meant some hard work but we did not mind that because it meant change in scenery and surroundings. None of the places were pretty and most were dingy. But moving even from one dingy place to another is a change."[28]

Immigrant women found themselves criticized for the appearance of their neighborhood by Americans who did not stop to reflect that these buildings were owned by other Americans. The exteriors were very shabby and the interior impossible to restore to decency, yet surprisingly many women did do quite well. Social workers consistently reported that many homes were neat and clean despite obstacles.

Building codes, sewage systems, and control over landlords were needed, yet political consciousness, economic power, and even the vote were lacking. A woman continued to be judged by the home she kept, and too often she was condemned as lazy and slovenly by Americans who had no comprehension of her powerlessness.

The solution that seemed most viable was individual ownership. Peasants who had been the chattels of a propertied aristocracy now had one burning desire—to own for themselves. To own one's house was to be secure, to be at last free.

This explains their resentment of efforts of well-intentioned reformers to ameliorate their lot. The tenement was temporary. They were content to live in a hovel if the rent was low and they could save. They recognized that "improvements" in the tenements would only raise their rent and prolong the time to their ultimate goal.

As soon as they could afford it, they bought that home even though they might carry two or three mortgages for the rest of their lives. While nativists accused them of irresponsibility, they were putting down roots at a fast rate. In Paterson, New Jersey, for example, where silk mills had long attracted female immigrants, these weaving women put their paychecks into housing. Twice as many foreign-born employees owned their own homes compared to their native co-workers.[29] The pattern held in other mill towns. In smaller localities where buying a home was more conceivable than in the great cities, these immigrants quickly made reality of their dreams.

Nevertheless, statistics on home ownership may prove misleading in terms of the comfort they brought. While many did buy and enjoy a single-family home, others bought a home and rented most of it, continuing to live as poorly as before. A Lithuanian family, for example, bought a house containing four apartments and rented them all, while they lived in a tiny attic room, sharing it with chickens.[30] A report concluded, "One schedule after another showed that it was not uncommon to find the owner occupying the least desirable apartment in his tenement."[31]

Women generally did have considerable control over family financial matters and made the arrangements in the frequent moves and new rentals. We can only conclude that this self-privation reflects the woman's idea of the proper way to do things. They were willing to buy security at the cost of comfort and even health.

Those who lived in squalor despite a rising income were common but still a minority. More often the drabness of the usual rented home changed after a woman had her own place, and a bit of discretionary income. Often it was decorated with more zeal than taste, but the overall effect was one of color and cheer. Social workers among Slavic women observed their taste in decor:

> The floors are . . . , especially among the Poles, scrubbed to an amazing whiteness. The walls are hung with gorgeous prints of many-hued saints, their gilt frames often hanging edge to edge so that they form a continuous frieze around the walls. The mantel is covered with lace paper and decorated with bright-colored plates and cups, and gorgeous bouquets of homemade paper flowers are massed wherever bureaux or shelves give space for vases. Gayly colored cotton curtains at the windows . . . and numerous canaries in cages—I have found as many as ten in a single kitchen—lend vivacity to the scene.[32]

Nor was this solely a characteristic of Eastern Europeans; a student of Irish, English, and Germans in New York reported the same pattern, indicating that perhaps this was more a matter of class than of nationality. "Everybody," she wrote,

> had drawings of relatives done by itinerant artists who sold their portraits on the installment plan. Most homes also had copies of sentimental pictures and the Catholic ones inevitably had images and prints of saints. Pictures of Washington, Lincoln, and McKinley were common, many of them obtained with coupons. The most common attempts at original decoration were samplers done by the women and pictures drawn by children, one of which was done in chalk on the kitchen wall and was entitled, "The House My Aunt is Going to Live in When She Gets a Feller."[33]

HOUSEWORK AND
CHILD CARE

A curious language pattern was noted by social workers: while immigrant women "could discuss their factory work in English quite fluently," they "lacked a vocabulary relating to their home life."[1] It is indicative of the extent to which women are isolated in this area.

There was no one to teach women American methods of housework. Gro Svendsen wrote home, "Life here is very different from life in our mountain valley. One must readjust oneself and learn everything all over again, even to the preparation of food. We are told that the women of America have much leisure time, but I haven't yet met any women who thought so!"[2]

Some aspects of this readjustment were pleasing. One Minnesota writer was thrilled by the ingeniousness of Yankee inventions:

> Our milk pails are so made that we can strain the milk as we pour it out of the pail. Churning butter is also very easy and seldom requires more than ten minutes. . . . Our washboards are also covered with zinc and designed to make washing very easy and quick. . . . We heat [irons] by putting them on a stove lid, and they are much better for ironing than those we had in Norway.[3]

Emilie Koenig, who came as a bride from Germany to frontier Indiana in 1853 (and who was to die a few days after childbirth in 1854), was fascinated by American housekeeping and especially her new home. "We will, of course, live according to German custom as much as circumstances will allow," Emilie wrote, and yet she rushed to elaborate on the wonders of the new: "You should see the cooking stove we selected. . . . It is the cutest stove one can think of. . . . A great show is made of the beds here, for they frequently have them in their living rooms. . . . They have a variety of covers, the best-liked being the quilts. But it takes much time to make them!"[4]

The new housekeeping methods were not always easily learned or appreciated. Landlords complained that ignorant peasant women didn't know how to care for their housing and were especially untutored in the functions of plumbing. Bathtubs were put to strange uses and damage was done through ignorance. The method of scrubbing floors by throwing water on the floor and then swabbing it with a broom (which had worked fine in European homes), was "disastrous to the ceiling of the apartment below."⁵

The standards of many immigrant women in housekeeping were alien to those of middle-class America. Samuel Chotzinoff, who went beyond the ghetto to become a concert pianist, wrote in his memoirs of a traumatic visit to his music teacher's home when he inadvertently brought along a bedbug. His hostess screamed at him, "There's never been a bedbug in this house before!" He wrote, "I could not believe she was telling the truth. I had never heard of a house that had no bedbugs." His mother's response to the desperate unhappiness of the boy was to call his hostess an "all-right-nick" who was putting on airs. "Yet," he added, "the incident was not without its effect on her. She engaged more frequently in housecleaning. I would find my underwear and socks removed after a single week's wear. . . . "⁶

The women themselves sometimes complained about the extra work necessitated by these new standards. "We had no blinds and no curtains and the floors were all made of stone," a Sicilian woman fondly recalled. "You have no idea how simple life is over there. Here one must wash two or three times a week; over there once or twice a month."⁷

Occasionally the adjustment to new household ways was dangerous. The Norwegian Mrs. Brandt had her gasoline stove running for several hours heating water for a large wash, while her four children played. "I had never heard of such a thing as carbon monoxide," she wrote. "Suddenly I felt a little faint, and things seemed to grow dark before me. I looked through the open door into the living room, and saw all four of the children lying on the floor motionless!"⁸ She barely managed to get into the fresh air, revived herself, and brought her children to safety, but they very well could have all been dead as a result of the seemingly innocuous American machine to aid housewives.

Even after adjustments were made, housework American-style was still no easy chore, for there were so many jobs that had to be done that are forgotten about today. Water had to be drawn, carried, heated, and emptied again; kindling wood had to be chopped and brought in, fires made, ashes taken out; oil lamps had to be cleaned and trimmed.

Laundry was a job spoken of more frequently than any other aspect of housework. Water had to be pumped, carried to the home, lifted to the stove, a fire built to heat it and then each garment scrubbed on the washboard. These garments had to be rinsed, starched (after the starch was cooked), wrung, and hung to dry. In tenements where pullied lines or porches were not available, women carried the waterlogged clothing to the roof to dry, worrying about it being stolen or covered with city soot. Finally it was taken down, sprinkled, and ironed with a heavy flat iron that had to be heated.

Many women made the observation that it was easier for them to go out and do someone else's housework than to do their own. Women who did "day work" enjoyed the conveniences of modern appliances and running hot water at their employer's house, making their own homes look even bleaker by comparison. "I don't mind the work at Mrs. Van Hoozer's," said one. "Her family is small and things are convenient in the laundry. It's the washing here at home for him and the boys that breaks my back."[9]

Despite their many hardships, women managed to keep good homes. As Edith Abbott, a premier sociologist, said:

> Day by day social workers are going in and out of the dilapidated tenements where they find familes obliged to live under conditions of great privation and discomfort. They report that the tenement mothers not infrequently make efforts that are little short of heroic to keep their homes and their children clean and neat. That these women of the tenements so often succeed in making their miserable flats into real homes is evidence of their courage and their almost inexhaustible patience.[10]

Many writers held a similar brief. A student of Slavs wrote of their homes: "everything is spotless."[11] Another student agreed, until she reevaluated her data and conceded how misleading such generalities can be. "It is with something both of surprise and resentment," she wrote, "that one faces figures (albeit gathered by one's self) which assert that over thirty per cent of Polish homes and over forty per cent of Russian and Ruthenian homes vary from 'dirty' to 'very dirty.' "[12] Despite many dirty homes, the accomplishments of women in creating pleasant ones in the face of seemingly insurmountable barriers were so striking as to elicit admiration and wipe out the negative impressions investigators may have had.

Whether or not a woman got any help with housework seemed to depend on national origin. Bohemian women, for example, had worked outside the home in the Old World and this tradition plus the generally liberated attitudes of Bohemians combined to make sex roles less rigid and the work load more equitable. A study of them noted:

The most noticeable effect of having the mother go to [the] factory is that the ordinary masculine aversion to doing women's work is greatly moderated. The boys run home from their play after school hours to start the kitchen fire, so that the water may be boiling when their mothers come home. They make beds and sweep and clean house. I have known a boy of 11 to acquire sufficient knowledge of housework so that, at his mother's death, he was able to do all the housework for a family of four. Several times I have come into a home and found the strong young husband washing, and not at all embarrassed to be caught at the washtub.[13]

It was not so in other immigrant families.* "Strong, young" or any other type of Italian man seldom stooped to help his wife or mother with housework. One Italian woman recalled bitterly, "Washing was woman's work. Cleaning was woman's work. Cooking was woman's work. Babies were woman's work. Everything was woman's work.... The only thing that my husband did was the shopping and that was because he insisted on handling the money himself. Also, he could meet his cronies and talk and gossip for awhile."[14]

Scientific investigation into the question yielded varying results. A government study of women and girls in New England textile mills showed that 60 percent of them said they did no housework, a remarkably high percentage that is probably questionable because of the inclusion of "girls." This study also "ascertained that often the unemployed husband ... had taken charge of the house," and added that "the standard of housekeeping ... among the foreign operatives, ... is very low."[15] Another study of working mothers (no "girls") showed the opposite. Of seven specific tasks listed, in all but one the mother did over 50 percent of the work alone. (The one exception was lunch preparation.) The mother employed full-time did 77 percent of the mending by herself, 72 percent of breakfast preparation alone, etc. When the column of figures for

*Margaret Byington in *Homestead: The Households of a Mill Town,* (p. 87) mentions that when some of the more affluent immigrants there bought washing machines, which were not yet electric, the men of the household would "turn the machine."

It seems to be true that when machines are introduced—and a job therefore becomes easier—it becomes acceptable for men to do that job. For example, for centuries women have been hired as "cleaning ladies" to scrub the floors of public buildings on hands and knees, but when vacuum cleaners and power scrubbers were introduced, men were hired to run them.

"mother with help" is added to her work alone, the result shows that it was extremely rare for these women not to do, at least partially, all of the tasks of homemaking.[16]

A final study confirmed the differences between ethnic groups in willingness to ease housework burdens. Use of a commercial laundry, for example, was one of the first signs of a rise in standard of living. Yet only 12 percent of Italians used this service, and their numbers did not rise as income increased. On the other hand, 86 percent of the emancipated Bohemian women used laundries. Jewish mothers, who, like Italian women, seldom worked at outside jobs after marriage if it could be avoided, nevertheless were more assertive in freeing themselves of the laundry burden, using commercial laundries as frequently as Bohemians.[17]

It was not only women and female sociologists who noted the inequitable distribution of household tasks in immigrant ghettos. An Americanized male observer wrote of a street scene there:

> Down the street comes a file of women carrying enormous bundles of firewood on their heads, loads of decaying vegetables from the market wagons in their aprons, and each a baby at the breast supported by a sort of sling that prevents it from tumbling down. The women do all the carrying, all the work that one sees going on in "the Bend." The men sit or stand in the streets, on trucks, or in the open doors of the saloons smoking black clay pipes, talking and gesticulating.[18]

Marketing was another aspect of housework, and immigrant homemakers were often valued for their ability to haggle. Their daughters soon learned, however, that it was a skill unappreciated by Americans and that a lady did not bicker over prices. One recalls her Italian grandmother:

> At the pushcarts, she would haggle and bargain with the peddlers and I hated to shop with her. I'd be embarrassed as she'd take a piece of fruit with some spots on it and say, "Look at this, it's gone bad, you don't want to sell this—no one would buy it—give it to this poor little kid here, her father doesn't make much money." And she'd push it to my mouth while the peddler yelled. Or she would complain that the vegetables were 2¢ cheaper on the next street and get her price reduced.[19]

Haggling had been a real necessity in her youth, and though she was now quite wealthy, she still took pride in her skill, which

was totally unappreciated and humiliating to her Americanized offspring. Haggling had become a lost art, exchanged for other, more
valued skills in the new way of housework.

———————

Rearing children in America brought many new problems. In
the Old World children joined their parents in the fields or in the
family occupation. In some urban families here, children did spend
their days helping at contracted home work, but flower-making and
finishing-sewing were not enjoyable or healthful nor even very
profitable, and finally became illegal. This arrangement resembled
European life, but the common adoption of American ways called
for parents to work outside the home. In the Old Country a child
would have been supervised by an extended family and watchful
villagers; here he was often left unsupervised amid strangers.
Crowded city streets offered no swimming holes or fields for ex-
ploring and very few playgrounds. Recreational opportunities for
girls were even more scarce than for boys.

Many of the girls had no chance to think of play, for they were
already busy mothering at a tender age. The situation of Rosa Cavalleri's family is typical. "I was all the time gone to work and my
children were alone on the street. My Visella was 8 or 9 years old
and she had to be the mother to the other children. And I had
more trouble because the landlord was so mean. He was all the
time beating the children. One day he kicked Visella and beat her
terrible because they were playing house in the back alley and
moved some boxes."[20]

Leaving children in charge of children was not unusual. A study
of working mothers found that the second most common "method"
of child care was for the children to be uncared for.

PROVISION FOR CHILD CARE OF WORKING MOTHERS[21]	
Philadelphia, 1918	
Total	1,430
Adult in Household	742
No One	408
Nursery	165
Neighbor Runs In	64
Neighbor in Her Own Home	51

The profit-making day-care center was unknown. Women's wages made it impossible for them to support such centers. Some charity nurseries did charge a nominal fee such as a dime a day,[22] but they remained philanthropies, not businesses. Moreover, most immigrant women were reluctant to use what nurseries did exist, preferring the services of relatives and neighbors. Women viewed these institutions with suspicion, a distrust grounded in the immigrant's experience with almost any sort of institution in Europe.

Their suspicion of the American nurseries also had some basis in fact, for much of this charity came with strings attached. If she once placed her children in a nursery, a mother was made to feel that she had surrendered her control over them and had given social workers the right to interfere with her life. Many cases show appalling pressure by social workers to consign some children to orphanages or to foster homes after they had been taken by a nursery.

The pettiness of nurseries' rules shows the extent to which the institution controlled its clients. In one, mothers were forbidden to bring their babies in carriages because the look-alike baby buggies had caused confusion. After a long day's work, the woman had to carry her children home instead of letting them ride. Nor were the mothers consulted on anything. Some mothers worried about the baths given their children, but nurseries seldom took this opportunity to educate them and calm their fears. One social worker, sympathetic to the mothers in this power struggle, summarized: "It must be said that the attitude of the management too often shows the strain of autocracy with which we are prone to dilute our charity."[23]

Even more than petty rules and annoying attitudes, the women feared the damage nurseries might do to their children's souls. To understand this, one must recall that until the influx of foreigners at the beginning of this era, the United States had been almost wholly Protestant, and to entirely too many natives, Protestantism and Americanism were synonymous. Rabid anti-Catholicism existed and it sank to violence and deception in its efforts to "save souls." Even when Protestant intentions were good, Catholic fears could not be allayed. In Holyoke, Massachusetts, for example, a day nursery was opened in the 1880s but soon had to be abandoned, for the working mothers, most of whom were Catholic, would not leave their children in the care of Protestants. (The Catholic Church, on the other hand, did nothing to meet the needs of these women and it was not until 1916 that a nursery run by nuns was set up.)[24]

One fear that immigrant mothers had was that their children might be shipped off to the West by these agencies. In fact, neglected or orphaned children were sent West to foster homes, where their labor was valued on farms and where, presumably, they received a good (and Protestant) home. Further, the report of one such society in 1875 indicates that immigrants predominated in its interests: they sent off 2,124 foreign-born, compared with only 1,509 American children who were sufficiently neglected to merit this change.[25] While it is true that immigrants were disproportionately represented in the poorer class where children would need charity, these numbers are so disproportionate compared with the numbers of foreign-born children in the population as to indicate a genuine racism.

Catholics objected that so-called nonsectarian agencies involved in this work were in fact fiercely Protestant. They believed that one of their aims was to tear Catholic children from their faith by separating them from their families. The following view of a priest, though it probably exaggerates the facts, exhibits the honest emotions of Catholic immigrants:

> I heard a distinguished philanthropist of Boston, and member of the City Government, say, that the only way to elevate the foreign population was to make Protestants of their children. . . . To aid the work of perversion, societies were formed to receive Catholic children, and provide for them, till a number should be collected sufficient to fill a car; when they were swiftly steamed off to some Western state, and there sold, body and soul, to farmers and squatters. Missionaries, both male and female, were hired to prowl about certain quarters of the city, to talk with children . . . and urge them to leave their friends and homes, picturing to them vistas of food, clothing, and money.[26]

In one case a priest reported that he had accidentally come across Catholic children who were to be shipped West that very day, despite the fact that many of their "poor mothers had paid their board in advance just to avert this catastrophe."[27] Whether or not these reports are valid, it is certainly clear that most immigrant women were extremely wary of placing their children with an agency of any kind.

Many social workers, once they got hold of a client, could be incredibly arrogant about managing her life. The records of social agencies dealing with widows sometimes read more like the agency is fighting against the woman rather than aiding her.[28] Again and again they show that an agency urged the widow to commit her children to an orphanage and she refused. The way the records are written, of course, makes the widow sound obstinate. Undoubtedly the woman felt she was trying to do what was right, not only because she did not want to be separated from her offspring but also because she understood that they would be better off in their own home than in an impersonal institution. The agencies, on the other hand, were quite ready to label the mother "unfit" if she did not cooperate with their ideas. The frequency with which widows and unsupported mothers had to accede to placing their children in orphanages is seen in the assertion that only about one-sixth of the inmates of such asylums were full orphans.[29]

For a woman to preserve her individualism and do what her conscience told her was right for her children took courage, for agencies often refused aid if clients did not submit to their plan— which often included giving up some of her little children. Having lost the argument and with it the charity aid, a woman then had to make heroic efforts to support her family alone.

Rose Schneiderman's mother became a widow at an early age and for a time kept her family together by working and taking in lodgers, but they still "often went hungry to bed." After a year her four-year-old son was committed to an orphanage run by the Hebrew Sheltering Guardian Society. The next summer Rose joined him as an inmate. "When I first saw him I could have wept, for he looked so woebegone wearing a dress." The place was not a happy one. The matrons, she said, "were very strict and even very cruel." Nor was it less cruel for her mother, for visits were not regularly allowed. When Rose was able to return home after a year, she and her mother went surreptitiously to see her brothers who remained. They obtained permission from a farmer whose land bordered on the institution, took a picnic lunch there, and the boys "would steal down the hill to where we would be waiting. We always had sweets and fruit for them, which we handed over the fence."[30]

When she contrasted this to the warmth of a European village where uncles, aunts, cousins, and friends looked after each other's offspring, a woman had to question the American way. Surely this was wrong; surely monetary values were again supplanting important human values. This time she knew she was right. The questions became instead what could be done about it, and was it worth it? Only the future could tell; only the child—too young to know now—could say whether or not the heartaching decisions his mother had made were the right ones.

CUSTOM IN COSTUME

T HE adjustment in dress began before they left Europe. Americans had jeered at the curious clothing of new arrivals in the early days of immigration, and, having felt themselves the objects of scorn, immigrants passed this message back to their sisters in Europe. By the height of the immigrant era one expert reported:

> Few of those who wear a peasant costume at home arrive in it at Ellis Island. They leave their beautiful embroidered garments behind, carefully instructed to do so by their friends in America. They know that such things would excite derision here, and indeed they themselves are prone to despise them in comparison with the cheap, ready-made goods which they buy at the port where they embark.[1]

These elaborately embroidered garments were handcrafted; sometimes the maker had even shorn the wool from the sheep. Doubtless many of them had been part of a bridal trousseau and were associated with happy memories. But they sold them, or if one was too precious to part with, it remained stored in the trunk in America. Shedding her old dress was symbolic of a woman's intention to become a new person.

"Once established here," this writer goes on, "the process of expansion of wants is a rapid one. . . . Nothing is too good for them, especially for their children and their young women."[2] During the first year expenditures for dress were a serious problem for many. They soon learned that Americans required conformity in clothing. An expert on American industry reported that she often saw women turned down for jobs because of their dress, even when a good appearance was not necessary, as in dirty factory work.[3] One candy manufacturer stated that he would not employ a woman who came to apply bareheaded or wearing a shawl, for he felt that if they had not adopted American hats, they were not properly assimilated.[4] Dress became another factor limiting employability; one could not afford to ape American style in order to get a three-dollar-a-week job.

But when they could afford good clothes, they bought them. An Irish shopkeeper in a Pennsylvania mining town said of the new arrivals from Eastern Europe: "They want the best goods and they want them up to date. If they do not know themselves what is the style, or if they do not speak English, they bring a friend with them who does."[5] A student of Italians said that they soon bought silk underwear for their girls and that competition in dressing children reached burdensome heights in some neighborhoods.

Vain ambition it might have been, but it also may have been a realistic acceptance of American values; "Italian girls in particular realize that they are judged largely by appearance."[6] Cornelia Parker, a sociologist who masqueraded as a working-class woman, was shocked to find that no man offered her a subway seat when she was dressed as a worker and not as a lady.

A most important part of a lady's ensemble was the hat. This nonutilitarian, much-decorated item was the symbol of similar characteristics in its owner. A woman who wished to be treated as a lady never appeared in public without one. For immigrant women, there was even more symbolic importance attached to the hat. At home, only women of social status were allowed to wear hats. Wearing a hat, then, meant to them "stepping out of the serving class, and out of the ranks of the peasants."[7] "Tell me," said one Slovak lady of her former servant, now in America, "it can't be true, can it? She writes that she wears a hat. Of course even in America that is impossible."[8]

Now that one was socially free to dress in style, the only remaining problem was economic. There were some girls who preferred to spend their money on education, but most saw stylish dress as the best road to advancement. Sadie Frowne, a sixteen-year-old Jewish orphan in a garment factory, said:

Some of the women blame me very much because I spend so much money on clothes. They say that instead of a dollar a week I ought not to spend more than twenty-five cents a week

on clothes, and that I should save the rest. But a girl must
have clothes if she is to go into society at Ulmer Park or Coney
Island or the theater. Those who blame me are the old country
people who have old-fashioned notions, but the people who
have been here a long time know better. A girl who does not
dress well is stuck in a corner, even if she is pretty, and Aunt
Fanny says that I do just right to put on plenty of style.[9]

It is important to note that Sadie saved the same 25 percent of
her income. Virtually all young immigrant girls put savings for
their family ahead of personal desires. Steamship passage, feeding
the family, education for brothers, all came ahead of their new
dress. But when money for style was available, they saw this as a
practical investment in the future.

———

Clothing, like food, took a relatively larger portion of one's budget
than it does today. A writer on Italian working women reported
that "when earnings were less than $7 a week the women appar-
ently were unable to get more than the barest necessities of the
cheapest grade. Shoes could not cost more than $2 a pair, suits
$8 or $10. . . ."[10] But, if the "cheapest grade" of a suit cost eight
or ten dollars, it was over a week's wages for these women. That
these shoes were cheaply made is evidenced by the fact that budgets of frugal people show expenditures for three or four pairs of
shoes in a year. Women put cardboard over the holes in their soles
and wore them as long as possible, but the shoe life was only a
couple of months.

Women knew that quality clothes would last longer, but then
they had to pay the extra cost of buying on installments or somehow do without while they tried to save. One Italian girl did decide
that a quality suit would be worth the cost and paid twenty-two
dollars for a suit—on an income of six dollars a week.[11] A study
of living costs reported that women spent very little on clothing,
but the few purchases they made proved to be very expensive compared to their income. There were many examples of women buying one suit for the year and that costing twelve or fourteen dollars—two or three times their weekly income.[12] The average
clothing expenditure in another study was nearly as much as the
average expense for rent.[13]

It was no wonder then that wardrobes were limited to a few
garments and that these were laundered nightly. Rose Cohen

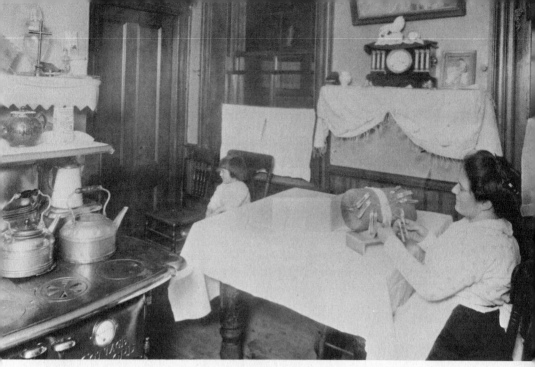

The clean, prosperous kitchen of a family influenced by settlement house workers. (Courtesy of the Schlesinger Library, Radcliffe College.)

An early twentieth-century family at supper. (Photograph by Lewis Hine; courtesy of the George Eastman House Collection.)

A room in a tenement flat, 1910. (Photograph by Jessie Tarbox Beals; courtesy of the Museum of the City of New York, Jacob Riis Collection.)

Laundry hanging in an immigrant courtyard. (Courtesy of the Library of Congress.)

Milbank Memorial Public Baths provided facilities to those without bathrooms at home. Some women took a sandwich along and viewed an evening at the bathhouse as a recreational opportunity. (Courtesy of the Library of Congress, Bain Collection.)

A dugout on the South Loop River, Custer County, Nebraska, 1892. (Courtesy of the Solomon D. Butcher Collection, Nebraska State Historical Society.)

Making a home in the West Coast wilderness. (Photograph by Darius Kinsey; courtesy of Ralph W. Andres.)

wrote, "I used to hang my dress on a string over Mrs. Feleberg's stove to dry over night. In the morning I pulled it straight and put it right on."[14] It is ironic, too, that she, like so many other ill-clad women, was employed in the garment trade.

Once a woman was married, appearance ranked very low in her values. Marriage was for life and the practical investment she had made in fashion had paid off. She no longer had to be concerned with pleasing men by being stylish. Her major concern now was to dress her children, especially the girls, in fashion, and to dress her husband warmly. A study of family budgets in New York showed that expenditure on clothing for the mother was consistently the lowest.[15] This frugality of women was illustrated by one notation of the investigator: "One hat, bought long before she knew him"—and the subject had been married ten years.[16]

An Irish cook stated proudly, "The McNabbs are no wasteful folk. I've worn one dress nine year and it looked decent."[17] Rosa Cavalleri, the Italian cleaning woman, laughingly acknowledged that she was so fat that when the residents of the place where she worked gave her their old skirts, she had to sew two or three of them together to make one big enough for her. "And nearly always she wore a neckerchief pinned with a safety pin, for in her girlhood in Bugiarno to expose a naked neck was a sin."[18] For married women, modesty was the only dress requirement.

Some might find it surprising that many of these women could not sew. Even those millions who worked in the garment industry often knew very little, for they repeated only one small part of the complex task of designing, cutting, and stitching a garment.

A study of working women found very little sewing other than mending; these women said they didn't have time and thought it cheaper to buy clothes from a pushcart. Sometimes a very poor woman would be seen in expensive tailored clothes—a discard from the lady for whom she cleaned. "Mrs. Reilly, walking out in a tailor-made suit which was worn last year by the well-to-do woman for whom she washed, would give no hint of the tea and bread diet on which she and the children might be subsisting—which was exactly what Mrs. Reilly wished."[19]

While they adopted American dress with alacrity, there was nostalgia for the colorful native costumes worn at home. Slovak women remembered with pride their concession to spring mud;

they had worn short skirts and high-heeled boots, fitted to the leg and crafted of soft, patterned leather.[20] Far superior this was, they thought, to the long American dresses whose hems were encased with dirt. Sicilians recalled the daily visits the hairdresser had made to their homes, brushing and arranging the hair of the females while serving as a courier of local news.[21] A pleasant practice among some Slavs that also disappeared here was for a betrothed man to outfit his intended with a new wardrobe. She spent the day shopping, while he stood about waiting to pay the bill.[22]

Unquestioning acceptance of American ways was the usual pattern, but educated immigrants were more likely to be critical. Gro Svendsen wrote frankly:

> Norwegian clothes ... are better and much warmer. We can get nothing but cotton goods. ... One advantage, at least, they do have. They get new clothes more often than we did in Norway, simply because the clothes here don't last. Working people wear out their clothes in just a few weeks. ... Everything Norwegian is of better quality than what can be bought here.[23]

When Americans sneered at the newcomers, little did they suspect that among the more sophisticated Europeans there were women scorning them. Linka Preus, after going to a fair, wrote of "Yankee ladies with fans and parasols, puffing with the heat; at the same time many were made-up, pale as porcelain dolls—Excellent style indeed! You are welcome to it. Yankee fashion remains in poor taste."[24]

These educated people were especially critical when they saw their compatriots adopting this tasteless dress. There also seems to be some resentment and discomfort at seeing servant girls rise above their former state. "I was displeased," said the usually charitable Linka, "with the country girls—some of whom no longer wore their embroidered Norwegian costumes—to see them sitting with their fans."[25]

Others were even less kind. The *Irish-American*, a New York newspaper of the 1850s, devoted editorial space to chide Irish domestics for not staying in their proper place. It asserted that these young women attired themselves "too expensively and showily for their calling," adopting "unbecoming airs."[26] Many men agreed with the one who wrote home for an "unspoiled" woman to marry, saying that he would not have one of his community, who wore new dresses to church the second Sunday after their arrival and hats and parasols the third.[27]

And yet in their quick adoption of American ways, they did lose more than cantankerous prospective husbands. In their rush to become Americans, they threw out the good with the bad, exhibiting only their strong desire to belong to their adopted land. To succeed in America, one simply had to look like an American.

Ultimately that would be the solution to all of the questions, all of the ambivalence. To some extent, the immigrant would shape America to more closely resemble her values and life-style. She would have some influence on American cuisine, for example, and immigrants must have helped change American child-care methods—but largely the ambivalence about America and its ways would simply fade with time. The need of conformity for success would overpower the remembrance of the old ways; sentimentality would step aside to practicality. A mother might question, but a daughter would accept—and a granddaughter would probably never even notice.

PART IV

The Contributions of These Women

SUPPORTING
FAMILIES

PROVIDING food, shelter, and clothing for her family and herself has ever been a woman's life-work. Immigrant women generally controlled the family budget and made the decisions of how to proportion the usually insufficient income. "The men are inclined to trust all financial matters to their wives," was the report from Slavic steel mill families. "It is the custom . . . for the workman to turn over his wages to his wife on pay day and to ask no questions as to what it goes for."[1]

> She pays the rent [the receipt was made in her name]; she buys all his clothes as well as the children's; she decides whether cash is to be paid, and the curses of the small unpaid tradesman falls upon her; no one thinks of holding the man responsible. She gives him each morning his carfare and his lunch-money, if necessary. If he wants ten cents for tobacco or five cents for a beer he gets it out of her if he can; if he can't, he goes without. It isn't a case of hen-pecking. The man thinks it is the only way to hold the home together. Women's economic position in the slums is high.[2]

Nonetheless, it was not really an enviable position, for even if all husbands lived up to this model, the needs usually exceeded the funds. It was particularly a problem when the woman was new in America and unfamiliar with what goods were available and their comparative cost. It took real managerial ability, and these women have not been given sufficient credit for their effectiveness as family financiers. In an era when both food and clothing were far more costly in relative terms than they are today, women managed well.

What also has been ignored is the tremendous contribution that women made in earning. The image of a "typical" family in which the husband worked, the wife stayed home and two or three children went to school was almost never found in an immigrant household. The idyllic picture clashed with reality with a frequency that surprised the statisticians themselves, as one recorded: "A preliminary canvass of six industrial sections of Philadelphia revealed the fact that the majority of 11,073 families were not supported by the husband alone. . . . Only six per cent of this entire group was of the conventional statistical type, husband, wife and three children, supported by the husband alone."[3]

A study of artificial flowermakers, most of whom were immigrants, showed how far these people were from the American notion of fathers supporting a family. In 128 families, there were 807 members and 545 of them contributed to the family income.[4] In another study of 200 Greenwich Village families, "there were only 23 in which the earnings of the father were reported as the only source of income."[5] And if the figures lie in any way, it is probably in overestimating the fathers' contribution, for men sometimes saved their pride by reporting larger earnings than they received. A mason who gave his wages as twenty-four dollars a week, for example, was found to have earned that only four weeks of the previous year, and for forty-four weeks he had not contributed one cent to the family budget.[6]

What is even more startling is the size of women's contributions. Since women were always paid less than men, they could work harder and their monetary contribution would be less. Nevertheless, this study shows that the average Italian family received 48 percent of its income from male wage earners and 44 percent from female wage earners. When the 6 percent of the average income obtained from homework and lodgers is added to the contributions of females— and it ought to be, since they did nearly all of this work—the contribution of women becomes slightly higher.[7] This is especially significant because it is not percent of contributors, but percent of *income*.

The above studies might be accused of bias because the investigators were women, and because the studies were of families in which there were known to be employed women. Yet, male sociologists studying "typical" families agreed that the contributions of women were very necessary. "It is a significant fact that, considering all the families together, the husbands contributed on the average. . . . 54.4 per cent of the average family income. . . . It was very difficult for most of our families to live upon the income which they derived from all sources. It would have been almost impossible for them to live upon the income from the husband alone."[8]

Another male investigator set out to study those families he considered to be "typical," i.e., both parents present and having two to four children under sixteen, passing by the doors of the numerous homes who did not fit into his preconceived mold. These women would be least likely to work because of their young children, yet even he had to admit that the fathers alone did not support the families. The only ethnic group that received substantially more than half of its income from the father was the long-resident Irish.[9] Thus, even with this arbitrary standard of selecting families where the mother and children could *least* be expected to contribute to its support, they still accounted for more than half of its income!

———

It was an exceptional woman who lived outside a family unit; single women almost invariably were attached as daughter, sister or lodger to a home. Those rare ones whose circumstances allowed them to support only themselves could sometimes manage a decent sort of life, low though their wages were. A fifteen-year-old Jewish orphan described the frugal yet pleasant life she and her roommate shared at the turn of the century:

> We had the room all to ourselves, paying $1.50 a week for it . . . We did our cooking on an oil stove, and lived well, as this list of expenses for one week will show:[10]

ELLA AND SADIE FOR FOOD (ONE WEEK)

Tea	.06	Butter	0.15
Cocoa	.10	Meat	0.60
Bread and Rolls	.40	Fish	0.15
Canned Vegetables	.20	Laundry	0.25
Potatoes	.10	Total	2.42
Milk	.21	Add Rent	1.50
Fruit	.20	Grand Total	3.92

Since their combined earnings totaled nine dollars weekly, they had a considerable surplus after food and lodging were paid for, and yet their diet was better than most. Sadie acknowledged, "Of course, we could have lived cheaper, but we are both fond of good things and felt that we could afford them."[11] Examples of this kind of maturity are not uncommon among immigrant girls. At an early age they developed a strong sense of accounting and knew exactly how much it cost to live and how every penny could be spent to the best advantage. Nevertheless they were sometimes accused by sociologists of being ignorant of budgeting, perhaps because they kept their accounts in their heads instead of on paper.

The single woman, then, who had no one but herself to support might live fairly well in good times. However, when industrial depression or sickness befell, her singleness was a great disadvantage. Few women had enough savings to carry them for very long and even fewer had any health insurance. In those times she might starve. Many women apparently were so afraid of such catastrophes that they could not separate themselves from the backing of some sort of family.

Katia Halperin, for example, paid more than Sadie for her board and yet lived much more unsatisfactorily. Like Sadie, she was a fifteen-year-old Jew, six months in America. She paid $3.00 of her $3.50 earnings to her aunt. Not having enough for carfare, she walked forty minutes to work, put in a nine-and-a-half hour day, and made the long walk home. She then had to help her aunt with the housework.[12] Her family thought she was old enough for adult work but not old enough for independence, and many other girls were caught in the same situation. Their families wouldn't think of allowing them to live alone, and one cannot really be sure if this is because they wished to protect them or to exploit them.

During the Wilson era, progressive states undertook to determine just what salary was needed for a decent life-style, in order to agitate for a minimum wage. Exhaustive studies were done. A summary reported that, "In every item the estimates seem to have been pared down to the lowest possible figure." But even then, most women did not earn enough to meet them. A board for Massachusetts industry, for example, estimated the cost of living for female employees at $8.71 a week, yet a shocking 89 percent of their women workers earned less than $8.00.[13]

Further, these minimum standards included no provision for savings. To an immigrant woman that was often the most important reason for a paycheck. Virtually all of them tried to save a large portion of their earnings to support a family overseas or to pay for passage of relatives. The lack of any savings item in these estimates shows the attitude of American industry toward a female worker. She was important as long as she was working—and the devil help her when she became ill or had an accident or grew old or was laid off by that industry she sweated to serve.

———

Young women lived in situations of grave responsibility and little reward. There was, for instance, seventeen-year-old Louise Trentino, whose father was usually idle and whose six dollar weekly income was the mainstay of him, her mother, herself, and a brood of younger children.[14] Louise's number was legion, and social workers' reports are replete with such cases. There was the Bohemian girl who went to work at age eleven in an artificial tooth factory.[15] Her father was a tailor, but the occupation was low-paid and there were eight children, four of whom were sickly. Among the saddest cases was that of an Irish girl who earned a pittance in a department store—another occupation infamous for low wages—and tried to support a family of nine. Her sickly father finally went mad with worry over the family's debts and tried to murder the children.[16]

Other fathers did not worry; the home situation of one such father is far too typical:

> The family had an [annual] income of $907 with which to support a family of twelve. The father, a peddler of cheese, whose earnings were casual and spasmodic, preferred bullying every cent of their wages from his two young daughters, who were the chief support of the family, to going out himself in disagreeable weather to sell his wares. During twenty-eight weeks of the year he had made nothing, and his total earnings were somewhat less than a fifth of the entire income.[17]

This family had the dubious distinction of being chosen as having the lowest living standard of any in this study of Italians. The one chosen as having the highest was headed by a widow. She had regular and well-paid employment and maintained her family of six pleasantly.[18] Why these fathers did not do better at supporting their children is a complex question. In many cases, ill health prevented them; in some the unemployment that plagued women also was a genuine cause; in others, they worked steadily but earned too little because they were unskilled or the skill they knew in Europe was not relevant here; often there were simply too many stomachs to be filled. But there also is evidence that many men did not try to feed the children they brought into the world. A student of the German-Irish West Side wrote:

> In . . . the building trade there is always "slack time" or no work in the winter months. The men know about this beforehand, but they refuse to work at something else for lower wages. In several cases the husband was offered work in the wood yard and at street cleaning. He refused to take the job; it was "beneath him." The men either sit at home and as one German woman said, "refuse to put on their shoes," or they go to the saloon and spend a day in loafing.[19]

Laziness, alcoholism, gambling, all played a part in leaving families destitute, but the particular experience of immigrant men
probably was a strong factor. Many of them had urged their wives
to emigrate with extravagant promises, and when they found that
conditions were not what they had dreamed, the loss of pride was
too much for them. Aagot Raaen's father was one of these. He had
been an aide to the king of Norway and now the abject poverty of
his North Dakota family was too much for him to take. Aagot's
memoirs are one long, sad record of the struggle made by her
mother and the children:

> . . . She thought how hard everyone had worked and how Far
> [Father] had sold the grain as soon as the threshing was done,
> intending to pay the money on the mortgage. Instead he had
> gone away and had not returned until all the money was used
> up. Then he had sold three steers and two cows and used that
> money, too. The worst of all was when he took the cream
> checks. Kjeresti shivered as she remembered how angry Aagot
> had been as she threatened: "After this I'll milk the cows onto
> the ground; I'll not carry those heavy milk pails up and down
> that steep hill for the saloon!" But Aagot had not carried out
> her threat.[20]

Of course it should be emphasized that most men were not of
this sort. Most were hard-working, sober people who wanted the
best for their families. Nevertheless, circumstances were such that
very few could survive without the help of female wage earners,
and occasionally men simply gave up and left the job to women.
The women went to work—no job was "beneath" a woman—yet
they received little recognition for their efforts.

The sons followed in their father's footsteps. The sacrificing attitude was inculcated early in girls, and they soon understood that
less was expected of their brothers than of them. One investigator
wrote, "It was assumed as a matter of course that the girl's pay
envelope should be turned over to her mother intact. 'It wouldn't
look nice to pay board to the mother that raised you,' was the common view of the girls, while the question as to whether the brothers also contributed everything they made to the home received
the answer, 'Oh, no, he's a boy.' "[21]

The result was not only passive girls but spoiled boys. The notation was made in a report on an Italian family that the girl gave

her "pay envelope unopened to the mother," while no one in the family even knew how much her brother made. It was not as though the family didn't need his income; they were so poor that even the three- and four-year-old daughters had to help at flowermaking. Even though the son was on probation from the court, there apparently was no increase in discipline at home. "You know how it is with a boy," was the mother's explanation. "He wants things for himself."[22] More was expected of sons in other nationalities, yet there were still inequities between siblings based on sex. Girls received less money for spending, and one study showed that while the employment rate for working children was higher than that of their fathers, boys still were more likely to be unemployed than girls. In explanation the sociologist talks of boys who "won't work" and adds, "There are also girls on the West Side who 'won't work,' but they are rarer than the boys. . . . The mention of a 'wild son' is not uncommon."[23]

Yet most sisters showed little resentment of the favoritism given their brothers, and many a girl sacrificed that his life could be better. One who had always worked while her brothers studied, said that during the years one of them was in medical school, she had "brought home flowers from the shop at night and had worked sometimes until four or five o'clock in the morning. 'When he graduated,' she said, 'I cried all day and was as happy as though I had graduated myself. I often say to my mother that we treat my brother as if he were a king—but I can't help it.' "[24]

It is particularly sad to think of the constant inequity in wages. Women were inevitably paid about half as much as men; even if a woman worked all of her waking hours, she could not equal the wages her brother got. The hard reality is that a family might be poor only because their firstborn—who became the wage earners—had been daughters instead of sons. For the girl it was a double tragedy to be oldest, for not only did she work hard for little appreciation, she knew if she had been born later, her life would have been much more pleasant.

Perhaps the one good aspect of the situation is that it took off some of the pressure European families had placed on their daughters to marry young. The opposite soon became true; if a daughter married, it would mean a substantial cut in income. Of course for the girl who wanted to marry, this was by no means a happy change in mores. Unless she could convince her prospective husband to take on the burden of supporting her family, she probably would have to give him up. Immigrant girls did in fact marry later than their mothers; in part this probably showed a disillusionment with marriage, but it may also be that their families pressured them to remain single in the same way they had been urged to marry in the Old World. In either case, what a girl wanted was not so important as what her family wanted.

Immigrant women not only supported families here, but also often maintained relatives overseas. Of 894 newly arrived Italian women interviewed by the YWCA during 1912–13, 164 had relatives abroad wholly dependent on these women for support, and 266 others were partially supporting a European family—a total of 430, or almost half of the group. Of course, all of them had to support themselves, too. The median wage of newly arrived women was $5.49, at a time when $9.00 weekly was "generally accepted as the lowest wage on which a girl can live in New York City and maintain a decent standard."[25]

"When Molly Davousta was thirteen, her mother and father, who had five younger children, had sent her abroad out of Russia, with the remarkable intention of having her prepare and provide a home for all of them in some other country." Molly went first to London, "to seek, not only her own fortune, but that of seven other people."[26] She had worked there four years when her father died and the pressure on Molly increased. She came to New York in hope of better wages, and at age seventeen with four years of experience, earned $5 to $9 a week. Nevertheless she managed to send home nearly $100 that year, often going without lunch and breakfast to do so. With this money, her sister Bertha joined her and together they supported the family in Russia until passage could be saved. Finally, Molly Davousta had her family with her, and now she could look forward to supporting them until she was too broken for a life of her own. Suffering from backaches and headaches, Molly was old before she was twenty.

Like Molly, Getta Bursova had been self-supporting since she was twelve. Born in Russia, she had already worked six years in London and two in New York when interviewed at age twenty.[27] Sarah Silberman, an Austrian Jew, had started work at age nine. She had been entirely on her own since age fourteen, having done machine-sewing in Vienna, London, and New York.[28] There had been little reward for her effort, though; she lived with virtual strangers, sleeping in the kitchen, and was quite alone in this world in which she had traveled so far.

Nor were Jewish girls the only ones to begin work so early. A Polish girl had supported herself since her mother died when she was thirteen.[29] A Swedish woman began to earn her living when only ten as a nurse girl in Sweden, then she did domestic work until she emigrated at age twenty. She kept a boarding house for ten years after that, and finally worked in a laundry.[30] It is important here to note that only the last job would show up in occupational statistics—yet she had worked since childhood. It is indicative of the serious underestimate traditional accounting makes of women's work.

Rose Cohen was one of those who made the voyage to America and began work as a child. Still growing, underfed, and working long hours, her strength was sapped before she really began to live. "During those days," she wrote, "I could not seem to get enough sleep."

> Now on coming into the room I would light the lamp and the kerosene oil stove and put on the soup to cook. Then I would sit down with my knees close to the soap box on which the stove stood, to keep myself warm. But before long my body relaxed, my head grew heavy . . . and I longed to lie down. I knew it was bad to go to sleep without supper. . . . But it was no use. I could not eat then. . . . The cot was so near. . . . I would rise a little from the chair and all bent over as I was, I would tumble right in. . . . It was on these nights that I began to forget to pray.[31]

THEIR WORK
AND
THEIR WAGES

LARGE numbers of women of every immigrant group were employed decades before American observers began to take note of the phenomenon of working women. As early as 1855, "two-thirds of the New York dressmakers, seamstresses, milliners, shirt and collar makers, embroiderers, . . . and artificial flower makers were foreign-born."[1] Women of the "new" immigration in later decades also worked; one student of early twentieth-century immigrants asserted: "In my investigation of several thousand unmarried immigrant women and married immigrant women without children . . . fully 90 percent were found at work or looking for work."[2] Some industries were almost entirely composed of these newcomers: garment manufacturing was overwhelmingly Jewish; the textile mills of New England were run by immigrants; they made up over 75 percent of the employees of the silkmill centers;[3] even in Pittsburgh cracker factories, seven of nine female workers were born across the sea.[4]

Yet most women had no consciousness of themselves as workers, no awareness of careers, no initiative to make changes that would improve their situation. Rosa Cavalleri, for example, had been a skilled silkmaker in Italy, but apparently thought so little in terms of careers that she never considered finding that work in America. The immediate was more important; the family needed the five dollars a woman could earn, hence she took the nearest job at hand.

The work that was available varied by locality. Often jobs that were considered too complex or laborious for women in one place would be allotted to them in another. In Paterson, New Jersey, silk mills, for instance, only 18 women were employed as skilled spinners, but in the competing Pennsylvania mills, there were 729 in 1919.[5] The explanation lies in the fact that in Pennsylvania, the men worked in coal mines. Similarly, in New York Jewish male tailors had the best jobs in the garment industry, whereas in Chicago women were discovered to be capable of holding these positions—because men there worked in industries such as meatpacking.

Flowermaking was an industry that employed many foreign women. Artificial flowers not only were used in home decoration, but they also adorned the elaborate hats of the era, and there was consequently a large demand. It was a trade peculiarly suited to women, both because they could do it better than men and because it could be done at home.

It was one of the worst industries in terms of wages. More than half of the women employed in flower shops in 1905 earned less than six dollars weekly in the busy part of the year—and there were months with little or no work.[6] Early in the era, flowermaking was divided among various ethnic groups, but between 1900 and

1910, the Italian population of New York more than doubled, and by the end of that decade Italians made up 72 percent of this trade.[7] Flowermaking appealed to them, for they could do traditionally feminine work in an atmosphere that was almost entirely female.

Ultimately, it was the whim of fashion that ruined the trade. For most of the immigrant era, no respectable woman appeared in public without a hat and thousands were employed in adorning them, but in 1920 the flapper arrived. She flung away her hat, and with it the symbol of forced femininity, the artificial flower.

In the packing room of a candy factory where she worked, Cornelia Parker found "one Hungarian, two Germans, four Italians, two Spaniards, a Swede, an Englishwoman, and numerous colored folk,"[8] as well as two white Americans, both of whom claimed to have seen better days. A Senate study around 1910 indicated that two-thirds of the workers in this industry were foreign.[9]

The specific job a person held in a candy factory made a great deal of difference in status. Most chocolates were hand-dipped, and the "dippers" were recognized as artists. Packing candy also required considerable skill, for each of the dozens of pieces was assigned a specific spot in the box, and the boxes had to be packed with speed. Lowest on the scale were women who bagged children's candies and those who carried the heavy boxes and trays.

Dippers were paid a cent-and-a-half a pound in Pittsburgh in 1909. Experts could do 100 pounds a day, which gave these women, the acknowledged artists of their trade, a total of $9.00 for a six-day week. Girls who packed "prize bags"—little sacks of a few peanuts, candies, and a trinket—were paid four cents a hundred. Fast workers could pack 3,000 a day (300 an hour or one every twelve seconds) to earn $7.20 a week. Those who spent their days putting sticks in suckers were paid the least. Each box contained seventy-two rows with twelve suckers to a row in this factory, and workers were paid three cents a box! That is a total of 864 suckers for just three pennies.[10] Sociologist Cornelia Parker stood packing candy from eight o'clock in the morning till six o'clock at night. At the end of her first day she wrote, "When the bell does ring I am beyond feeling any emotion. . . . During the summer I had played one match in a tennis tournament 7–5, 5–7, 13–11. I had thought I was ready to drop dead after that. It was mere knitting in the parlor compared to how I felt after standing at that table in that candy factory."[11]

Like the candy industry, cigarmaking was stratified into three distinct levels: the skilled "rollers," or "makers;" the "bunchmakers" who arranged the tobacco into roughly the shape desired; and the "strippers" who devined the leaves. Packing was also considered a highly skilled position in this industry.

Cigarmaking was a most unusual immigrant industry—at least for a time—because of the extraordinary position of a particular group of women. "The customary method of Bohemian immigration was for the women to come first, leaving the men to work in the field. Five or six wives would come over together, work at cigarmaking as they did in Bohemia, and send money back for their husbands' passage and the entire family would take up the manufacture of cigars, emulating the industry of the mother."[12]

These women began preceding their husbands and children to America in the late 1860s; by the 1870s more than half of New York's cigarmakers were female. One writer says of the men, "Their wives taught them, after they came over, the relatively unskilled work of bunchmaking, while the women still did the more skilled and better paid rolling. . . . The women were considered by Americans to be more intelligent than the men."[13]

Technology in the form of cigar molds was to blame for displacing the craftsperson, yet many American men were adamant in their belief that it was the entrance of immigrant women into the industry that had ruined it. As cigarmaking became less of a craft, women of other nationalities also found their way into it. A circa 1912 study reported only one out of twenty-seven women in cigarmaking giving America as her birthplace.[14] Most were older women who considered themselves unassimilable, and who, inured to rough field work in Europe, did not object to the smell or the tobacco stains on their hands.

Although the percentage of immigrants who settled in the South was very small throughout the era, Tampa, Florida, became an exception in the 1880s when cigarmakers were recruited to go there. These were primarily Cubans of Spanish descent, with lesser numbers who came directly from Spain as well as a third group of Italians. Women worked alongside men in the dozens of cigar factories that flourished in Tampa. "Prized for their nimble fingers and patience, Latin women earned impressive wages for their labors."[15]

Besides the wages, there were other advantages to this work. In the early days at least, there were no noisy machines and employees could listen to lectors who read to them as they worked. Skilled women were "allowed a good deal of latitude as to their hours."[16] Yet there was the pressure of demanding speed, eyes were subject to strain, and there were illnesses that were "the direct result of nicotine poisoning."[17] A U.S. Labor Department writer noted, "A young woman who had been working in a cigar factory since her arrival . . . pointed to her framed passport picture, which showed her to have been plump at that time. When her father met her three years later, "He not know me, I so thin and skinny. Never sick before I came to America. Cigars not good to work."[18]

———————

Keeping America clothed employed more immigrant women over the decades than any other single industry. When the Irish arrived in the 1840s, they began to replace Yankee farm girls as laborers in the textile mills of New England. Experienced British workers joined them, as did Germans and French-Canadians. By the end of the century, these mills employed Poles, Italians, various Balkan peoples, even Greeks, Syrians and Armenians.

Because textile work required nimble fingers, women were early employed and long made up a majority of the workers. At times European women were recruited for this industry, particularly skilled Englishwomen. Immigrants who came in response to this recruitment, however, were not entirely happy with American mills; they considered them tyrannous in hours and pace of work.

Textile mills also were exploiters of children. Many women began in the mill when still children. Mary, a Fall River weaver, said, "My mother, she was sick all the time. She worked in the mills in England since she was nine years. I had to stay home and tend the children and help round ever since I was little. . . . I got a job [as] 'spooler-tender' when I was twelve—there wasn't the law then."[19]

Though women like Mary were skilled workers and considered themselves careerists, and though the companies preferred to employ women, men still were paid more. Women in the Holyoke mills in 1871 averaged $.75 to $1.60 a day, while men got $1.00 to $2.25.[20] A U.S. Senate study added, "There are no promotions as far as female employees are concerned. Women never become section hands . . . or overseers." They approved of this on the ground that "under such a system an overseer can not offer girls higher pay or more desirable positions" and thus tempt them into immorality.[21]

Mill work was hazardous to health. A study done in Lawrence in 1912 (when that city was 90 percent immigrant) painted an appalling picture: one-third of the spinners in the mills died before they had worked ten years. They died of respiratory diseases— pneumonia and tuberculosis—which were promoted by the lint and dust and machine fumes of the unventilated mills. That the cause was a simple lack of fresh air can be seen from the fact that only 4 percent of the local farmers died from these diseases.[22]

The sound level also had serious effects, as Fall River Mary said, "At first the noise is fierce . . . but you get used to it. Lots of us is deaf. . . . It's bad one way: when the bobbins flies out and a girl gets hurt, you can't hear her shout—not if she just screams, you can't. She's got to wait till you see her."[23]

When the raw cotton had been woven into cloth, it generally headed south out of New England for the immigrants of New York and other cities to sew into garments. Until the Civil-War era ready-made clothing, expecially for women and children, was rare. In many communities in this still largely agricultural era, the only employment a woman could get other than domestic service was dressmaking. New York seamstresses in 1845 worked fourteen to sixteen hours a day to earn a pittance of $1.25 to $1.50 a week.[24] Even when the garment industry began, much of the work was done on home contract. In the 1860s, German, Scandinavian and Irish households began to take in this work. The cut clothes were brought home and all members of the family worked at sewing them together. The "sweatshop" had begun.

In the 1880s "revolutionary changes entered" the garment business. Electrically powered machines, national markets created by railroads, and legal restrictions on sweatshops played their parts, but "the greatest single factor" was immigration. "This is affirmed by manufacturers, who say that without the immigrants the industry could not have assumed its present proportions."[25] Most important among these immigrants were the Jews who brought not only legions of young women into garmentmaking, but also thousands of male tailors. As usual, these men took over the best positions in what had been formerly considered "women's work." A government study concluded, "On the whole the changes of the period reshaped the industry in such a way as to assign a less important place to women."[26]

Women from all countries worked in laundries; half of the women in Chicago laundries around 1910 were foreigners.[27] It was another job easily seen as "women's work," an extension of their work in the home and acceptable even though it was extremely heavy and tiring. The most important product of laundries in that era were men's cuffs and collars that were starched to the point of rigidity. Getting limp cloth to resemble cardboard in stiffness required a strenuous ironing process:

> The cuff is placed over the saddle-shaped padded head; pressure of a treadle raises the head against a stream chest, and pressure of another treadle causes the head to drop back as the cuff is finished. Only by violent exertion can hot metal and padded head be forced together. . . . The whole body of the girl is shaken by the force. . . . In one laundry the manager said, "No American can stand this. We have to use Hungarians or other foreigners. It seems to be unhealthful, but I don't know. The girls don't stay long enough for us to tell.[28]

This was only one of the perils of laundry life. Hands and hair could be caught in mangles. Laundries were terrifically hot and humid before electric fans became available. Windows had to be kept shut in some cities lest the surrounding soot dirty the clothes. In winter the contrast between indoor and outdoor temperatures brought on colds; "most of the girls had colds most of the time."[29]

The conditions in this occupation were so poor that bright young women usually left quickly. The jobs remained for the newly arrived, the older women, the mentally mediocre. These people were aware that laundry was poor work. When asked her earnings one Irishwoman warned, "Now don't faint when I tell ye: I git *seven cents* an hour!"[30] Not only were wages low, but this industry was infamous for taking away from the toiler the mite she earned, as this collar starcher revealed:

> When I go to work . . . I am given a slip of paper marked on one side, "Received" and on the other "Returned." I mark on one side. . . . When the collars are starched I turn them over to . . . boys [who] mark on the other side. . . . If a boy makes a miscount or if for any reason at all the numbers do not tally on both sides of the slip, the starcher is docked. . . . She is charged from fifty cents to a dollar. . . . The great majority of the girls are docked every week. . . . The boys are never docked, it being assumed, apparently, that they never make mistakes.[31]

THEIR WORK AND THEIR WAGES

Worse, starchers were docked *five dozen* collars if they dropped *one* collar, and absurdly, "the starcher is even held responsible after the collars leave her hands. If the bars on which the collars are dried happen to be dirty the starcher is fined, although the bars are supposed to be cleaned by other workers."[32]

There were probably millions of women who worked at money-producing jobs, yet never made the census statistics as wage-earners because the work they did was not in an organized industry. Women not only worked at home industries such as flowermaking, they did other odd jobs for factories at home such as threading wires through tags or crocheting over curtain rings.[33] They cared for the children of factory women. They did "day work" as cleaning women. They took in laundry. They worked as seamstresses. They made items for sale such as fancy cakes. They raised gardens and poultry and sold their produce. They did countless tasks that earned money important to the sustenance of their families. One such job that was common in the immigrant community was that of the boardinghouse mistress.

In the early days of any ethnic group's migration chances were that dozens of men had left their families behind, and they gravitated to the one or two available women of their national group who could cook their food in the familiar way and spoke their language. A sociologist in the western Pennsylvania coal and steel area in 1910 found that, though Slavic homes were still crowded with boarders, conditions were much improved from a decade earlier. "From 50 to 100 of them used to live in one house, not a big one. There were no women among them, and other people would not take them to board. If there was a man who had a wife, all flocked to him. There would be 25 boarders in a family. . . . Ten years ago they used to have plank shelves for bedding round the wall."[34]

A boardinghouse mistress would begin her day before dawn, packing lunch pails and fixing breakfast. The night shift would then arrive to occupy the beds during the day. Another meal would have to be prepared for them, dozens of dishes done, and the laundry begun. Clothes soiled by sweat and ingrained grime had to be rubbed on a scrub board, and the water needed to do this had to be drawn and heated. In the evening there were more meals to fix, more lunches to pack, dishes to be done again. In the midst of this a woman had to care for her children, keeping them quiet in the interest of the day sleepers. Doubtless she fell into bed exhausted, but that was provided she could find a bed, for "the lodgers are given the best sleeping rooms while the rest of the family sleeps on the floor, the mother getting the most undesirable spot."[35]

In some communities, women cooked to individual tastes. Each man would place his personal order and the woman would shop for and prepare a dozen different suppers, tagging each piece of meat with the name of its owner. In other cases, men did their own shopping and women prepared the food, while sometimes the men cooked, paying only for laundry and the use of bed and kitchen. One especially curious method was found among Chicago Poles who paid two dollars a month for lodging and bought their own food. The food, however, was cooked by the landlady, who was not paid for this service but was entitled to the leftovers, "and this is usually all that the family need."[36]

The earnings for this work varied, but it could be quite good. In western mining communities circa 1910, a woman who boarded ten or fifteen men could earn eighty dollars monthly—as much as her husband made.[37] Nevertheless, the woman who did the work often did not get the credit; it was her husband who was known as the "boarding boss."

One priest said that "when the children get to be five or six years old, the parents leave the mining or factory settlement. . . . By the time the eldest is six, there are enough little ones to keep the mother busy."[38] As the immigrants became more aware of American standards, they tried to decrease the number of strangers who lived in their homes. A Protestant minister reported that a man:

> whose wife kept 18 boarders sleeping in two shifts came one day . . . and asked him if he thought it would do to take to fewer boarders; his wife had no time to go to church. The minister naturally encouraged him to do so, and he cut the number down . . . to four men, trying to give his wife more time so that he could teach her to read. Finally he said that he wanted to live like the Americans, with no boarders and a parlor "where no one slept."[39]

A final factor in ending the practice was that, as one Slavic woman reported, "The keeping of boarders has had a great tendency to break up homes and families."[40] The loss of privacy was harmful to a family, as was the close contact of a lone woman with males who lacked any feminine companionship. One survey found that more households without husbands than with accepted lodgers,[41] and while it is plain that the husbandless woman would have greater need of income, one can also see that this could give the appearance of immorality. Another reputable sociologist said that in fact sleeping with the boarding mistress was a sufficiently common practice "to bring into use a special term to describe it—full board."[42]

Occasionally boarding houses began catering to Americans and the Americanized. Elise Isely's Swiss aunt started one in St. Joseph, Missouri, a jumping-off place to the west. Because her cooking was good and the beds clean, men stayed for weeks. Grossinger's, the famous Catskills resort, had similar beginnings. Jennie Grossinger was born in Vienna and her father became one of the myriads of Jewish tailors in New York. When his health collapsed, the family moved to a Catskills farm for fresh air, but neither the soil nor they were suited to farming. Jennie suggested that they take in boarders, Jewish workers like themselves who needed a fresh-air vacation and who would be subject to discrimination in other resorts. The idea worked, but not before Jennie and her family put in a lot of hard labor, as she recalled: "We did all the work ourselves. . . . Mama cooked and so did I. Harry, my husband, recruited guests in New York. Papa took care of the farming, marketing and meeting the guests at the railroad station. I remember we all put in 18-hour days until the midsummer of 1915 when we hired one chambermaid."[43]

For most, however, the boarding business was a temporary stage of life to be abandoned as soon as possible. Those who operated them did not consider themselves businesswomen, but exceptionally overworked housewives. They were anxious to lay this burden down and obtain the American dream of living in a single-family home. "With a house on the outskirts of town, and a garden about it, and a glimpse of the larger out-of-doors, they begin to feel that the dreams of their emigration have come true."[44]

These were the most typical jobs, but unusual ones existed also. The range of jobs which immigrant women found or created for themselves ran the gamut from the uniquely womanly to the heaviest of traditionally masculine labor. One exclusively feminine job was that of wet-nurse; mothers with a sufficient milk supply some-

times took on an additional baby to earn the money paid by orphanages. Nor was this a rare thing; the Foundling Asylum of the
Sisters of Charity in New York alone sent out more than 1,100
such "pay babies" in 1889.[45]

At the other extreme was rough manual labor done by immigrant
women in the metal industries. A 1909 Senate investigation found
4,500 women working at coremaking in foundries. "The work done
by women," they reported, "is distinctly skilled," but it was also
strenuous—some of them lifted over sixty pounds. English speak-
ers accounted for less than one-fifth of this group.[46] A similarly
large number of women operated power-presses and riveters, did
soldering and machine-tool work. Again all but 13 percent were
foreigners.[47] A third group was composed of some 2,600 women—
largely Polish, German, and Hungarian—who worked at nut- and
bolt-making. The report summarized:

> Much of the work is singularly unpleasant in character. . . .
> The action of the machine spatters oil or water over every-
> thing . . . , including the operator and her clothing. . . . A
> woman . . . turning out the maximum number of one-fourth
> inch nuts must press the treadle 50 times a minute—a rate
> which, in view of the fact that it is to be kept up for 60 minutes
> an hour and 10 hours a day, needs no comment.[48]

Since Pittsburgh men gravitated to the steel mills leaving all
other manufacturing jobs to women, it comes as something of a
surprise to find that in fact the metal industry there was the third-
largest employer of females, following only laundries and cigar factories. Two-thirds of these women were Slavic—Hungarian, Polish,
or Croatian.[49]

> Fifty core makers work in the largest . . . room. All are women.
> Through the narrow entrance you can see them moving about
> among wreaths of coal smoke and black dust. . . . They strike
> you as an incarnation of the activities of smoking ovens, boil-
> ing crucibles and iron soft with fierce heat. The dim light
> through windows encrusted with black dust . . . cannot dispel
> the impression of unreality.[50]

Slavic women also worked alongside men in the steel mills as
"openers." Sheets of steel came from the furnace welded together;
their job was to take the sheet and "beat it on the ground to separate the parts; then with the lead piece in the glove, they make
an opening. They forcibly tear apart the plates, holding part of the

sheet down with one knee, while tearing the metal with the other. The violence of this work takes all the strength of even the earth-toughened peasant women . . . from Poland."[51]

"We never use American women on assorting work," a Mid-western manager of metal works averred. "These Hunky women are strong. They come to work with their husbands in the morning. They don't mind working . . . where the men have to work 'stripped.' They can pull sheets of metal apart as well as any man can. No American woman would want this kind of work."[52]

There was other hefty toil outside of metal mills done by women. A study of working mothers in Philadelphia included "7 laborers employed by an oil refinery for heavy work."[53] In Yonkers, women worked at tanning skins, while in Connecticut, they packed fuses in "imminent risk of explosion."[54] Immigrant women did "men's work." Obscurely and without recognition, they quietly toiled at hard labor, while Americans debated whether or not women should work outside the home in any job.

There were other jobs not typically remembered. Some women worked in mining and others washed railroad cars and there were Europeans who worked as crop followers. At the opposite pole, we find a number of fortunate Italian girls who made use of their native background by singing in the choruses of professional operas. There were occasional women editors of immigrant publications and of course there were nurses, midwives, and teachers, especially in parochial schools. The 1915 Chicago directory of Bohemians listed nineteen female and thirty-six male physicians.[55] There were multiples of women fruit- and vegetable-hawkers, pushcart sellers of dozens of products, operators of corner stores. Vestiges of the Old World remained with women who refurbished cornstalk mattresses or grew medicinal herbs. Whether the job was self-created and informal or part of the rigid industrial scene, whether it was as masculine as steel production or as feminine as wet-nursing, immigrant women worked.

The acceptance of vastly lower pay rates for women was un-questioned throughtout the era. The inferior mentality was so deeply ingrained in some that even when they were the victims of blatant inequality, they could not see the wrong. An Italian widow with five children began work in a Providence bakery in the early twentieth century for one dollar a week and finally worked her way up to seven dollars. "Since business was good, he hired another baker, a man. We did the same work, the same hours. He was a widower with three children. His pay was $10.00 a week right from the start, which was just and fair, after all he was a man."[56]

In 1905 when the immigration wave was cresting, the Census of Manufacturers reported that three-fourths of male workers received more than eight dollars weekly, while over three-fourth of female workers received less than that. The disparity varied from industry to industry, but in no case did an average man earn less than an average women. The *highest* average female wage was $7.60 and the *lowest* average male wage was $7.71. The least disparity was in the country's oldest industry—cotton goods—where the weekly gap between the sexes was only $1.68.[57] Women's skills were responsible for this, but never were women skilled enough to overcome the handicap of sex. The International Silver Company replied to a job inquiry from a skilled British woman saying they would be delighted to employ her, and continued unabashedly to tell her that skilled female help was paid twelve-and-a-half to twenty cents an hour, while unskilled male labor received seventeen-and-a-half to twenty-five cents.[58] An industrial expert summarized, "Where skill and occupation are comparable, alike in skilled trades and in unskilled occupations, the man's wage is double the women's."[59]

To some extent, one was paid what one was successful in bargaining for, and women who did not have the courage or ability to demand raises never got them. One who started in a box factory at age eleven had worked there nineteen years and still earned the same $5.50 she made as a beginner.[60] In artificial flower factories women with ten years or more of experience were found to be earning six or seven dollars while workers who had been there just two or three years were getting ten and eleven dollars.[61] Elizabeth Hasanovitz was a courageous woman who successfully insisted upon pay commensurate with her capability. After a trial week in a dressmaking shop,

> I asked the foreman for a price. He nearly fainted when I told him I wanted fourteen dollars a week. It was fortunate for me that two girls had left in the middle of the week, for the foreman, being very busy and having few skilled workers, was afraid to lose me, too. So after two hours' bargaining, I remained there for thirteen dollars a week, but was strongly forbidden to tell anybody in the shop of the "extravagant amount" I was getting. I was the highest paid worker.[62]

Few had the self-confidence to proclaim their worth for two hours as she did. There was in Elizabeth Hasanovitz's shop an interesting contrast to her: Sadie, also from Russia, also a talented and experienced dressmaker. She got only ten dollars a week and was a real sycophant, staying at this nonunion shop because the boss had vaguely promised to reward her some day while she exploited her compatriots to please him. "Almost all the girls," Sadie said, "I brought here, as soon as they come over from Russia." The boss wanted her "to get him green girls for help. You know he does not like Americanized girls—they fuss too much . . . while green girls don't kick about the pay."[63] Sadie went on to say that the first three weeks her green girls worked for nothing and after that they earned three dollars a week.

It was a common practice to take jobs without knowing what one was to be paid. The subservience of many newly arrived Italian women was seen by YWCA workers interviewing them who frequently found that the Italians did not know what their wages were, as the first payday had not come yet.[64] "Many times you don't ask," said a subject in another study, "for you know the bosses sometimes get sore about it." Another responded, "I'm not privileged to ask. . . . It is what they give you."[65] Some workers had their own form of retaliation against this system; if after a week they found they were getting less than they had in their old place, they returned to their former jobs saying they had been sick.

Some employers admitted women could not live on the wages paid. They purposely hired only girls with families "because the trade does not offer a living wage."[66] Other employers deceived the public—and occasionally even themselves—into believing their wages adequate. There was often a disparity between what firms said they paid and what workers said they earned. A study of Italian women circa 1912 found that 54 percent of them made less than eight dollars a week, but only 22 percent of the firms employing them reported their wages to be so low.[67] One enthusiastic young executive, while escorting sociologists through his factory, stated that the hundreds of women working there were paid twenty dollars a week. A visitor doubted this, and he insisted that it was true. Finally he sent for the payroll records and discovered to his surprise that the women earned from five to seven dollars. The forelady earned twenty dollars, and he had fixed that figure in his head for all of them and sincerely believed it to be so.[68]

In contrast to this would-be humanitarian were the many employers who cheated their workers and attempted to prevent the payment of the little they earned. Legal aid societies cited many cases of "ridiculous pretexts to defraud" workers, among them:

> . . . a Lithuanian girl . . . employed as a scrub woman in an office building. During the influenza epidemic the other scrub women employed were unable to work. The janitor offered to pay this girl $16 per week if she would work double time and do their work. She usually received $8. When her week was finished he gave her only $8, although she had worked not only her usual time from 8 to 11 but also from 11 to 3. When she demanded what he had promised he told her that he was only joking with her.[69]

Deliberately making mistakes in writing paychecks was another practice. "Sometimes the employer may have no funds in the bank . . . [and] promises to give another check. . . . When he finally gets the check it may be for the original amount only, payment of the amount earned after that time being postponed."[70] Rose Cohen had the unfortunate experience of working for an employer who allowed wages to accumulate and then skipped town.

Danish Anna Walther had a somewhat similar experience. She decided to do millinery work outside New York for a season and went to Indiana, thinking it was the Far West and she would see Indians. After three weeks she was called to the manager's office and curtly informed that her model hats were not up to their standards. She knew this was not true because the hats were selling well, but since she had only a verbal contract and since the season was too far advanced to return to New York, she had to suffer a reduction in wages.[71]

Anna stoically accepted the situation, for she had no choice. Women would learn from these experiences, though, and in time would be less exploited. Meanwhile she, like millions of other immigrant women, would work.

T H E   W A Y S
O F   W O R K

THE industrial manager of that era believed in exercising harsh discipline. Stiff fines were imposed for minor infractions. Being five minutes late commonly cost an hour's pay, even when a woman may have stayed up until the wee hours with work she had taken home. The garment factory where Natalya Urosova worked was on the twelfth floor of a building with 2,000 employees and two ancient elevators. Sometimes Natalya got to work at 7:30, but it was 8:30 when she reached the twelfth floor; often she lost a dollar of six dollar earnings through late fines.[1] Most outrageous was the practice of fining a pieceworker for being late, even when she had no work to do and would earn nothing—she actually could accumulate a deficit in wages during her first hours at work.

Many companies charged employees for supplies necessary to do their work. In the garment industry workers had to buy thread and needles, and they routinely supplied their own scissors, thimbles, and such. One Italian woman reported that she had thirty-five cents deducted from her paycheck to compensate for the electricity to run her machine.[2] Sometimes women owned their sewing machines. Rose Schneiderman had just begun to pay for hers when the factory burned down. "This was very hard on the girls who had paid for their machines. . . . The bosses got $500,000 insurance, so I heard, but they never gave the girls a cent to help them bear their losses."[3]

A moment of negligence could cost the worker an amount disproportionate to the harm done. One who made kid gloves had to pay for them if the machine stitched incorrectly. Two pairs were damaged one week and she had to pay $2.50 each: "It took nearly the whole week's pay."[4]

One of the few New York stores which complied with the law requiring seats be available for women workers, fined the women if they were caught using them. Department stores were infamous for low wages, long hours, and arbitrary rules. The irrationality of their unbending regulations was illustrated by the case of a girl who had worked at one for several years. When her father died and her consumptive mother was unable to work, they had to move further out of town where the rent was low. But:

I have to be at the store at eight o'clock. The train that leaves
home at seven gets me to the store two minutes after eight,
but though I've explained this to the manager he says I've got
to be at the store at eight, and so, summer and winter, I have
to take the train at half-past six and wait till the doors are
open. It's the same way at night. . . . The rules are that I must
stop five minutes to help the girls cover up the goods, and that
just hinders my getting the train till after seven, so that I am
not home till eight. . . . I told him that the girls at my counter
would be glad to cover my goods, and if he would only let me
go at six it would give me a little more time for mother.[5]

The investigator could scarcely credit this tale and so verified it
with the management. She found it to be "true in every detail and
also that she was a valuable assistant, one of the best among a
hundred or so employed." Moreover, the young lady had offered to
exchange her lunch hour for these seven minutes, but had met
only a stone wall of refusal; "she dared not speak again for fear of
losing her place." The firm, ironically, gave "largely to charitable
objects."[6]

Not many immigrants accepted these conditions. The language
barrier prevented the newly arrived from working in stores, but
those who learned English, as well as English-speaking immigrants, stayed away. Store employees were largely Americans who
were willing to accept these poor working conditions because an
American from a middle-class family would lose status by working
in a factory. To most immigrants, all work was honorable and that
which paid best was the one to choose. The immigrants employed
in stores were usually either young and inexperienced in the labor
market or, less frequently, attempting to emulate the Americans.

———

One serious problem for women in getting and keeping jobs was
a demand for sexual favors. While many factories strictly segregated the sexes with only female bosses over women, in others,
especially ghetto sweatshops, there was closer contact. Even children were not exempt. Rose Cohen was just twelve when she began work in a Jewish tailor shop that was all male except for herself
and one other girl. Though her father worked there, he could not
prevent the men from telling vulgar stories in her presence, and
the other girl assured her, "What you hear in this shop is nothing
compared with what you will hear in other shops."[7] Rose also had
an experience with a kindly-appearing boss who invited her to his

house to collect her wages, and made it plain on her arrival that he had something else in mind.

Elizabeth Hasanovitz lost two good jobs because her bosses could not control themselves. At the first the boss's wife fired her because the old man kept hanging around her. At the second, she had gone to the office to collect her pay. "I noticed how he was measuring me with his eyes while he spoke. I felt what that glance . . . meant. It was quiet in the shop, everybody had left. . . . He grasped me in his arms. I screamed, and with superhuman strength threw him from me and ran into the hall. Luckily, the elevator stopped at the same moment. . . . I ran into it."[8]

Elizabeth pretended she had lost her pay rather than explain why she did not have it. Most women were ashamed to tell anyone of these experiences and were tortured by the thought that somehow it was their fault. To complain was to risk one's job. Sociologists testified that sometimes when women asked for raises, employers encouraged them to sell their bodies instead. In the 1880s the Working Women's Society of New York said, "It is a known fact that men's wages cannot fall below a limit upon which they can exist, but women's wages have no limit, since the paths of shame are always open to her."[9] Yet, as Jacob Riis commented, "To the everlasting credit of New York's working-girl let it be said that, rough though her road may be, all but hopeless her battle with life, only in the rarest instances does she go astray. . . . New York's army of profligate women is not . . . recruited from her ranks."[10] If a job came with sexual strings attached, even women in dire need gave it up and searched for another.

All jobs were not a running battle. The laundry where Cornelia Parker worked was a sunny, cheerful place even if the work was hard. The women sang as they ironed, with the Italians offering bits of opera and all singing standard hymns. She also worked in a rural New York bleachery, which employed immigrants as well as Americans. "There was never the least 'factory atmosphere' about the place," she reported, and this company showed that contented attitudes increased production. There was always laughter. "Nor was the laughter the giggling kind, indulged in when the forelady was not looking. . . . Like as not the forelady was laughing with the rest. . . . It is significant that with all the fun, the standard of efficiency and production in our bleachery was such that out of eighteen like industries in the country, we were one of the only two running full-time."[11]

Dorothy Richardson reported of a flower factory employing many foreign women that a child took each worker's grocery order before noon, and when lunchtime came:

> The pincers and tongs of the rose-makers, and the pressing molds of the leaf workers, were taken off the fires, and in their place appeared stew pans and spiders, and pots and kettles. Bacon and chops sputtered, steak sizzled; potatoes, beans, and corn stewed merrily. . . . It was like a school girls' picnic. . . . We ate our luncheon at leisure, and with the luxury of snowy-white tablecloths and napkins of tissue paper.[12]

The psychological environment mattered a great deal. Immigrants were prone to suffer mental distress, for they often felt exclusion and alienation and were sometimes the direct object of insults. Strict segregation of ethnic groups was common. Situations were like that of a Pittsburgh hinge factory where the Slavic women were "kept sedulously apart from the Americans; they are paid at different times, and work in different parts of the room. Whether they are making less than the American girls or not they do not know."[13] Foreigners were almost invariably given the dirtiest, least-rewarding tasks. One sociologist testified:

> Although Italians, Russians, Irish, Polish, Germans, Americans and Swedes are employed in New York laundries, . . . the Irish receive the higher prices, the Italians the lower prices. The best-paid work, the hand starching . . . and hand ironing, is done by Irish women. . . . The actual process of hand starching may be learned in less than one hour. . . . On the other hand, to learn the nicer processes of the ill-paid work of feeding at the mangle . . . requires from thirteen to fifteen days. The reason for the low wages listed for mangle work seems to lie only in nationality.[14]

There were sharply differentiated social castes on the job. Workers doing the superior tasks scorned those assigned to the more menial. When Cornelia Parker began laundry work, she sat down at the "wrong" table at lunch, and no one spoke to her the entire time. Foreladies could make life rough for immigrants. Many of them fondly recalled the "good old days" when there was none of the riffraff that emigrated now from Europe. Miss Parker found that she was promised favorable treatment even before she began work simply because she was not "Eyetalian."

Immigrants could avoid some of this unpleasantness by staying in the ghetto sweatshops of their own nationality. Here there might be security among co-workers sharing a common background, but it certainly did not assure agreeable working conditions. The small shops of the newly arrived were more crowded, unsafe, and ill-lit; hours were apt to be longer and wages lower. Often the most exploitative employers were those who were cheating their own compatriots. Yet the comfort of being among one's own kind had great appeal. A study of the men's garment industry in Chicago in 1912 showed as many as 91 percent of German, 88 percent of Bohemian, and 85 percent of Polish women worked in shops where the employer was of their nationality.[15] They evidently preferred working together to American industry where one ethnic group was often played against another.

Early in the morning and full of anticipation I made for the bindery. . . . It must be where that crowd was on the sidewalk ahead, some thirty girls and as many men and boys. . . . Rather too many wanted the same job, but there were no worries to speak of. . . . Finally the prettiest and brightest of the lot peered in. . . . "Say, w'at d'ye know? I see a bunch inside! Come on!"

In we shoved our way, and there in the dismal basement-like first floor waited as many girls and men as on the sidewalk. . . . The pretty and smart one was not for such tactics long. "W'at d'ye say we go up to where the firm is". . . . We tore up the iron stairs. . . . Up seven flights we puffed. . . . The bright one opened the door and our group of nine surged in. There stood as many girls and men as were down on the first floor and out on the sidewalk. "My Gawd!" There was nothing else to say.[16]

Of this horde of job-seekers, only two women—who had been promised jobs the previous week—were hired. Over a hundred women and an equal number of men had applied for just two jobs. Nor could one easily go on, for "it is something of a catastrophe if you do not land the first job you apply for Monday morning." By the time one reached a second prospect, those places were usually taken. "The third chance is slimmer still by far, and if you keep on until 10 or 11 it is mostly just plain useless. And if you do not land a job on Monday, that whole week is as good as lost."[17]

These fearful Monday mornings would be much worse for the unassimilated worker, who was usually unfamiliar with cities in general, to say nothing of the geography of this particular city; unfamiliar with the subway system; unabled to read signs; unable to ask questions. How difficult it would be for her to hurry and to make a good impression at the much-wanted-yet-dreaded interview.

Most immigrant women depended on rumor and pavement pounding in their job searches. Rose Cohen had been in America for six years when "I learned to find a job it was not necessary to go from factory to factory. Instead you read the advertisements in the newspapers."[18] A Boston study of 266 newly arrived women at the turn of the century found that only two made use of advertisements to seek work.[19] In a YWCA study of over 600 Italian women, just three obtained their jobs through ads.[20]

Nonetheless, foreigners in the earliest days showed a willingness to use employment agencies where they existed. In 1850, the Boston Society for the Prevention of Pauperism reported that "their office . . . received, during the last five years, applications for employment from 15,697 females, of whom 14,044 or 90 percent were foreigners."[21] But not all agencies were reputable. In 1903 sociologist Frances Kellor did a detailed study with nine incognito investigators in several cities. They found that the vast majority of these firms did not live up to minimal standards. In some, women applicants were assaulted when they resisted paying fees; in others, they were directed to brothels as potential employment. Virtually all of these agencies, however, specialized in domestic servants, so that their effect on the industrial scene was insignificant.[22]

Friends were by far the most often used means to obtain employment. Over three-fourths of a large group of Italian women questioned had gotten their jobs through relatives or friends.[23] Rose Gorgoni, for instance, waited for the neighborhood network to come up with a job for her, taking no action herself "as she had no jobless friend to go around with and was 'ashamed' to go alone."[24] Responses to inquiries about job-seeking show both persistence and a lack of system:

> "I was all over asking."
> "I went all over the places, nothings, nothings."
> "Walking and walking, I wore my feet out."
> "I walked all over, five or six weeks, and ask if she need a woman; I look, I look, came back and next day go again. They all say, 'too late,' 'call again,' 'will let you know.' "

"When I first here I so foolish, I go out, I make chalk marks so I find my way home again; that how dumb I was. I was in the street and I saw a factory. I was coming in to ask for a job and they give me."[25]

No thought was given to aptitude. Often a woman ended up in the trade where friends secured her first employment and stayed there unhappily for years. Their fatalistic attitude can be summed up by the Sicilian who said bleakly, "I would like to be in another trade, but I never had any friend to take me into any other trade." Even when one had her niche in the labor market, seasonal employment plagued the best of workers. Fewer than 5 percent in one study had drawn full pay for an entire year; almost half were jobless for eight weeks or more. Only 12 percent of these women were unemployed because they quit their jobs; only 17 percent took any vacation.[26] And, as the investigator, added:

It is a matter for comment that three-fourths of the women had lost no time on account of illness. . . . Many had always been accustomed to a low standard of vitality, so that they continued at work when others of different health standards would feel fully justified in remaining at home. . . . The fact of long periods of enforced unemployement accounts for their determination to stick on as long as work is to be had.[27]

Workers were forced to drift from job to job, always hoping to get something better, never building up skills or seniority or bargaining power. Since employers had to pay neither mandatory overtime nor unemployment compensation, there was no incentive for them to smooth out their seasons and keep people on regularly.

These problems existed even in prosperous years, but when the economic cycle went on a downward trend the continual scrambling for a job became even more futile. Rosa Cavalleri tells how she and her children suffered during the Depression of 1893. Her husband had gone logging in Wisconsin and sent no money home. Pregnant Rosa tried to support the family alone.

In that time I was scrubbing the saloon—all the floors . . . for 50 cents. But then I didn't get the 50 cents; the man he kept that for my rent. . . . The city hall was giving food to the people. The people were standing in line. . . . Us poor women were frozen to death; we didn't have the warm clothes, and there was such a storm with the snow and the wind! Eight o'clock, when the door opened, all the people were pushing to get in. There came the police with their clubs and they were yelling like we were animals. Then one of those police hit the woman next to me on the head with his club. . . . When I saw that, I said to myself, "Better I starve before I let that police-man hit me!" And I ran home from that line. And I never, never went there again.[28]

Rosa, like millions of others, came to work; they wanted to work, but the economic system kept them idle and hungry. Even in good times one seldom escaped periodic unemployment, and even an extremely capable and valued employee found that she had no assurance of steady pay and promotion in the whimsical business system of that era. Often any job at all was a blessing.

Elena and Gerda Nakov were, according to others, two beautiful and healthy girls when they came from Russia. After thirteen years, "these young women's strength is simply worn out from years of overwork and strain and poor and scanty food," their doctor said, and "they can never again be really well."[29] It was nervous strain as well as the heaviness of work and the long hours that wore them out. Cornelia Parker, the incognito sociologist who worked in various factory jobs, incessantly complained of being exhausted by factory work. Yet she was a strong, athletic person. In addition to not being under emotional pressure, she had the advantages of a balanced diet, medical care and vacations. But her fatigue was real; she wrote if this work "taxes my strength who seldom has known what it is to be weary, what can it do to the average factory worker, often without even a fighting physical chance from birth on?"[30]

In one comparison of working and nonworking women, the workers had fewer health complaints. Of over 700 employed moth-ers, 44 percent reported illness in the last year, but housewives were sick in greater number—63 percent having been ill. The so-ciologist concluded that women who entered industry were stronger and that "they have less time to think about their health."[31] Of course, housewives would include those women who had in fact worked earlier in life and may have literally given their best years to the industrial machine.

Safety regulations throughout most of the immigrant era were either nonexistent or ill-enforced. Dangerous machinery was un-

guarded; floors were often wet or slippery; aisles were filled with
obstructions; haphazardly constructed buildings and unsanitary
practices that allowed oil, rags, and lint to accumulate made these
usually wooden structures into firetraps.

The dress code of that day promoted accidents as long skirts and
uncut hair brushed against whirring machines. A Polish girl in a
Lawrence mill let her hair get too close to her machine. She, "sec-
onds later, lay writhing on the floor with part of her scalp torn off.
After placing her scalp carefully in a paper bag, her friends carried
her to a doctor, and . . . she survived."[32]

Too often the situation was like that of the manufacturer who
considered his duty done when he posted a sign saying, "Girls must
not work at any machine without board over shaft." That many
machines were without them and had to be used was no conern
of his.[33] Factories felt so little reponsibility for safety, reported one
sociologist, that elevators were "frequently decorated with the
signs, 'You travel on this elevator at your own risk.' "[34]

Besides unsafe machines, the buildings that housed them were
often inadequate. In the early part of the era, industrial engineering was still too new for architects to realize what safe standards
were. The Pemberton Mill of Lawrence was a source of local pride
in 1860, but it proved a deathtrap. The mill stood five stories high
and had six-inch solid oak floors and wide windows. But the windows were too wide, the floors too heavy, and the supporting pillars
too weak. The top floor collapsed and within a minute the entire
building was on the ground. Townspeople worked for hours to free
victims from the wreckage. Near midnight a fire broke out. "The
moans of pain became screams of panic" as the trapped workers
were burned alive. One hundred and sixteen people were seriously
injured and eighty-eight perished.[35]

In this case the management was trying to do right, but simply
was uninformed or careless about engineering. Too frequently, the
evidence is that management was deliberately callous in regard to
safety. The unquestioned discipline of the era led to the policy of
locking factory doors after starting time to prevent unnoticed late
arrivals or the possibility that someone might slip out for a break.
A Providence newspaper reported in 1866:

> When the fire occurred, there were about two hundred opera-
> tives in the mill. From what we could learn last night, it ap-
> pears that the doors were locked and the lower windows nailed
> down. As a consequence, a terrible panic prevailed among the

operatives, very many of whom were females, and as the watchman refused to open the doors, they leaped from the second and third story windows to save themselves from death by flame or suffocation.[36]

In 1911 some factory doors were still being locked. The Triangle fire was burned into the memories of immigrants who lived in lower Manhattan. Triangle was a dress manufacturing company known for its shabby treatment of workers. They "always tried to get in newly arrived immigrants . . . who lived at the mercy of the bosses."[37] In the great garment strike of 1909, Triangle had been adamant in its refusal to improve conditions and by 1911, the activists had left or been fired. Those remaining were mostly Italians and Jews willing to work in a nonunion shop.

It was late on a Saturday afternoon and the rest of the building was empty. Only the employees of the Triangle factory on the top floors worked on. Evidently one of the few male employees lit a cigarette and dropped a match into waste cloth near oil cans. The flammable fabric and sewing machine oil spread the fire quickly. Those who were not lucky enough to get to the elevators while they still functioned, crowded about the windows, but the fire department's ladders stopped two stories short. "Five girls who stood together at a window close to the Green Street corner held their places while a fire ladder was worked toward them, but which stopped at its full length two stories lower down. They leaped together, clinging to each other, with fire streaming back from their hair and dresses."[38]

Survivors testified that many girls had not jumped, but were pushed out the windows by those behind them, the fire at their backs. After the first girl jumped and broke her body "into a thousand pieces," the crowd yelled: " 'Don't jump!' but it was jump or be burned—the proof of which is found in the fact that fifty burned bodies were taken from the ninth floor alone. They jumped, they crashed through broken glass, they crushed themselves to death on the sidewalk. . . . A heap of corpses lay on the sidewalk. . . ."[39]

There was controversy about whether or not the doors were locked. One of the owners rushed to deny that they were immediately after the fire, even before the charge was made. The evidence seemed to prove that at least some were locked. Labor leaders did not expect these newly arrived immigrants to be brave enough to publicly challenge the owners, so they published a list of persons to whom this information could secretly be given. The district attorney soon had sufficient facts turned over to him to "show that doors . . . had been kept locked."[40] Two doors were intact after the fire, and they were locked. Over fifty bodies were found piled behind them.

By December when the trial of owners Harris and Blanck was held, public outrage had dimmed. At one point the jury was evenly divided, but after two hours they issued an acquittal. They apparently agreed with one who said, "I think that the girls, who undoubtedly have not as much intelligence as others might have in other walks of life, were inclined to fly into a panic."[41]

Thus the deaths of 146 people went unpunished. "Most of them," reported the *Times*, "could barely speak English. . . . Almost all were the main support of their hard-working families."[42] Many had emigrated alone and had no family here. While some mourners searched the morgue in a vain attempt to determine which of over fifty unrecognizably charred bodies was their loved one, other bodies went unclaimed. Quite probably their families were in Europe, and long would be unaware of the calamity that had befallen their daughters.

The immigrant ghetto did not forget. The 25th of March was memorialized for years afterward by garment workers. Within a few days of the fire, a factory safety committee received over a thousand reports of dangerous conditions similar to those at Triangle. By drawing attention to these abuses, the deaths were not in vain. Eventually safety standards were upgraded and laws enforced—although just days after the fire, Harris and Blanck shamelessly ran an advertisement of their new location. For them it was business as usual.

"I knew nothing about trade unions or strikes," said Rose Schneiderman as a capmaker earning six dollars a week, "and like other young people, I was likely to look upon strikebreakers as heroic figures because they wanted to work and were willing to risk everything for it."[43] But Rose would be a nationally known labor leader one day. Like thousands of the individualistic women who emigrated alone, Rose would see that the working conditions in America were not what she had envisioned and would come to understand that in union there is strength.

Not all immigrants were newcomers to unionism. British women had been accustomed to a working-class consciousness. Holyoke mills were disappointed to find that the Scottish female weavers they imported were "not sufficiently docile."[44] Bohemian women cigarmakers were early unionists, much in advance of the American women who broke their 1877 strike and the American male-run unions that refused cooperation. In 1859 German female shoemakers organized a union and affiliated themselves with the New York City General Labor Union.[45] Later many of the Jewish newcomers would bring with them a leftist philosophy that included support of unions.

The immigrant was caught in the middle on the subject of labor disputes. If she did not strike, she was accused of lowering American wage standards. If she did, there were others ready to accuse her of being a foreign radical, an agitating Communist. The views of the women themselves were sometimes equally inconsistent; they held the same ambivalence on this that they had in many other areas. Even those who had thought things through to the point of joining a union had periods of ambivalence when jobs were hard to get and a worker had to disavow her unionism. When one middle-aged woman cited her years of experience in a job interview, the employer immediately pounced on her: "You belong to the union, don't you?" She admitted that she did, but hurried to add, "That makes no difference. I'm perfectly willing to work with nonunion girls. I'm a good worker and I don't see what difference it should make."[46]

Cornelia Parker asked a co-worker if she had ever worked in a union shop and if it was any different, and the woman replied: "Different? You bet it's different. Boss wouldn't dare treat you the way you get treated here. . . . They sure treat you like dogs here!" Despite the woman's vociferousness, Parker adds, "The papers were full of a strike to be called next week throughout the city. . . . It might as well have been in London. Not an echo of interest in it reached our factory."[47]

A leader was essential, but an avowed union member often found herself without a job. When she did get one, she frequently was punished for her beliefs by being given the least profitable piece work. Even in a well-organized shop, being a labor leader called for personal sacrifice, for the union representative had to attend to the complaints of others at her own loss. Elizabeth Hasanovitz, an elected chairlady in her shop, had 200 workers whose grievances had to be looked after:

A complaint now came from an ironer who did not receive the scale [minimum wage], now a girl came late and she was sent away, now a girl was discharged for spoiling something unintentionally. I, as shop representative, had to take up every grievance with the boss. If I failed to settle the matter, I had to report and complain to the union. All of that required a great deal of time, and I was too often distracted from my machine. In the busiest weeks, when the workers were making more money, I was kept busy straightening out difficulties for them.[48]

These shop leaders, though insignificant to the public, were the backbone of trade unions. They endured the hatred and ridicule of their bosses. Anna Klotin, for example, was employed by a garment factory that was one of a handful that did not settle with the union in the 1909 garment strike. Her factory offered twenty of the more skilled women union terms, but refused to do anything for the majority of their employees. Anna was one of the twenty, but she refused to separate from her fellow strikers. This solidarity could be measured in dollars, for after that Anna earned only six and eight dollars weekly instead of her prestrike twelve dollars.[49]

A half-century earlier Irish newcomers had shown their solidarity when Holyoke mills promised to bring their pay up to that of nearby towns sometime in the future. They found, "instead of the grateful reception anticipated, nearly one hundred Irish girls demanded at once a flat rate of sixteen dollars a month, walked out at noon, and were joined the next day by others."[50] As the Massachusetts Irish became more assimilated, their identification with the working-class lessened. In the 1850s the Irish were united as workers, but by the 1882 strike, Irish were to be found on both sides, and when the violent 1912 strike occurred, the Irish generally supported the owners.

Sometimes newcomers showed initiative in organizing even without support from existing unions. Scandinavian women in Chicago's clothing industry in 1897 asked the United Garment Workers to help them organize, but were given no response. They proceeded independently and set up an effective union. "The women," says a government report, "were thus in a large majority and soon came to have control." A ten-hour day and closed shops were obtained, as well as wage increases that for some were 80 percent. The Swedish women insisted on the inclusion of the ill-paid Italians in their union, and they "lived well, maintained good homes and aspired to general education and culture."[51] Eventually the American United Garment Workers moved in and took over the union that these immigrant women had managed so admirably alone.

The apathy and opposition of male unions to the addition of females to their ranks is one of the chief causes of the low wages that women received. Repeatedly men engaged in futile efforts to keep women out of the trades. Instead of demanding equal pay for women and thus maintaining a high pay rate, they vainly attempted to keep women from working at all. Such action only encouraged employers to hire women, who would work as hard and more docilely and dependably for less money.

The men in Rose Cohen's tailor shop joined a union, but neither invited the women nor informed them of their action. The women found out only by observing their strange behavior—they did not start work until seven o'clock, they quit promptly at noon, and did not start again until one. They left on the dot of seven. "We girls watched them go enviously. . . ." As their discontent increased, the women acted without the encouragement of the men. Rose went to a garment workers' meeting and organized the others. Since she was just thirteen or fourteen at the time, she had a right to take pride in her achievement. "Now," she wrote, "our shop was a 'strictly union shop.' I'll always remember how proud I felt when the first evening at seven o'clock the presser blew the whistle and I with the other girls stood up with the men."[52]

Throughout the era men preferred to promote the myth that women could not be unionized rather than to accept them as equals. Yet there were many cases where women proved their willingness to organize and strike. In the Fall River cotton mills, where 97 percent of the employees were of foreign birth or foreign parentage, it was the women who provided the strike leadership: "In 1874 the men weavers had met without the women and voted to accept a marked reduction of wages; but the women at a meeting of their own . . . decided to strike."[53]

Men chose not to recognize that these people they excluded from their unions were, in general terms, their own wives or sisters or daughters. The sexes battled each other to the victory of the owning class, and women were left in the weakest position of the three.

When the 1909 garment strike began in New York, Natalya Urosova and the women in her shop were unsure what to do. At last
they arose in fear and trepidation and left the shop. Arriving on
the street, they were shown immediately the serious consequences
of their decision; policemen lined the sidewalk and one greeted
them, "If you don't behave, you'll get this on your head," shaking
his club threateningly. "We hardly knew, said Natalya, "where to
go—what to do next. But one of the American girls, who knew
how to telephone, called up the Women's Trade Union
League. . . ."[54]

The strike lasted from November to February and involved
30,000 to 40,000 workers, the majority of them immigrant women,
mainly Jewish. Thousands of these women had emigrated alone
and had no family or savings to support them. The strike meant
weeks of hunger for them. It could also mean violence and im-
prisonment. Police were more than ready to arrest women, something that was proven by cases of mistaken arrests of women who
happened to be in the area. One upper-class woman appeared at
the offices of the *New York Times* to show them her coat that had
been ripped by attacking police. "While I am not a striker myself,"
she said, "I am deeply interested in the girl workers of the East
Side." She continued, "Between twenty and thirty special policemen . . . hurled themselves upon us and threw us off the sidewalk
onto the pavement. . . . They shoved, elbowed and even kicked. . . .
I narrowly missed having my skull fractured. . . . They called me
the most vile and insulting names, and finally dragged me. . . . I
believe I should have been badly injured if a crowd had not gathered and shamed the men."[55]

Similarly, Mary Drier, "a woman of large independent means,
socially well-known throughout New York" was arrested when "she
entered into a quiet conversation with one of the strike breakers."
She was taken to the police station, but "when the sergeant recognized her . . . , he at once discharged her case, reprimanded the
officer, and assured Miss Drier that she would never have been
arrested if they had known who she was."[56]

Poor and foreign strikers found that they were not allowed to
inform anyone of their peremptory arrests; Natalya and her friend
were arrested, tried and carried to the Tombs in a day. The food
there "smelled so bad it made you sick" and they had only iron
springs for sleeping. Worse, though, was the attitude of their fellow
prisoners. Prostitutes ridiculed Natalya and told her how much
better off she was as a prisoner in America than free in Russia.

This 1909 strike was unusual in that upper-class women went to the support of their needy sisters. The Women's Trade Union League included both working and nonworking women. Support of the working class became—briefly—quite the thing to do, as even such women as the daughter of J. P. Morgan and Mrs. O. H. P. Belmont participated. There was considerable ambivalence among strikers on the matter of these eminent capitalist helpers. Some resented going before the wealthy women in the role of beggars instead of independently making their own way as they were accustomed. In return for humbling themselves they received sums that, in comparison with the wealth of these ladies, were miniscule. Labor leaders also were annoyed by the injection of the suffrage issue into the strike, for while most did believe in political equality, suffrage added another controversial element that was extraneous to their issues.

Nonetheless, the money donated was more than they could hope for elsewhere, and it made a vital difference. More important was the influence, for employers apparently decided that they could not battle both their employees and their customers. To the credit of all of these women, the strike was largely successful.

Three years later there was another and more violent strike of immigrant women, though this time more men were involved. The textile workers of Lawrence, Massachusetts struck in response to a pay reduction. This strike was extraordinary in view of the motley nature of that town in 1912: "No less than forty-five tongues are spoken by employees of Lawrence mills."[57] An Italian woman, Annie LoPezzi, was killed in this strike, and her death became a *cause célèbre* as the town's officials without any reasonable justification tried to convict the strike leader of responsibility.[58] Women also proved their loyalty to the cause by sending 300 children to be cared for by New York Socialists when hunger began to be a factor. The city government accused them of using their children as pawns, but sending their children to stay with strangers shows how seriously the strike was taken by these immigrant mothers. A reporter for a national magazine testified:

> I saw with my own eyes, under the gray light that precedes dawn . . . , a little group of twenty-five women shivering in the cold.
> . . . I saw them pull their shawls over their heads as they laughed and chatted in low tones. . . . I knew this was "picketing," which even when peaceful, is unlawful in the Commonwealth.

I saw them stamp their feet because they were cold.

I saw a detail of men come down the street clad in police uniforms, with badges gleaming as they passed under the arc light. . . . I heard horses' hoofs upon the pavement. . . . A detachment of cavalry was coming. . . .

I saw the patrolmen surround the twenty-five women who had huddled and flattened like hens as the shadow of the hawk falls. I heard the voices of men, but no answer from the frightened women. . . .

I saw the women at the command of the policemen move forward. I heard a rough voice call upon God to damn them.

I saw the night sticks driven hard against the women's ribs. I heard their low cries as they hurried away.

I saw one who passed me.

"Listen," she called to a friend. "I go home, I nurse the little one. I be back yet."[59]

In the great Homestead steel strike of 1892, women as well as men rushed to the barricades. Women were machine-gunned to death in the 1914 Ludlow strike in Colorado. During a 1913 strike in Michigan copper mines, women were the employers of violence instead of the victims. An aide to the state governor complained:

Women continually resort to rock throwing. . . . At Trimountain the soldiers were rotten egged and were assaulted by women with brooms, which brooms had been dipped with human excrement. . . . It is a very difficult thing to deal with women who resort to these tactics, and who are physically nearly the equal of an average man. Many of them profess to be unable to understand our tongue, and of course are excitable and impulsive, as is somewhat characteristic of the entire sex.[60]

Some women organized and used violence outside the usual realm of unionism. Jewish women in the West End of Boston, angered over high meat prices, managed to close down the kosher butcher shops. "Any person carrying a parcel bearing the slightest resemblance to meat was set upon by mobs of women, the bundle taken away and its contents broadcast," reported a newspaper. Women were completely in charge of the boycott, presiding over the meetings and doing picket duty; "women were beaten with clubs by the police and seven arrests were made."[61]

However, not everyone was brave. While union leadership and male co-workers must accept some of the blame, ultimately the disorganized state of female workers must be the reponsibility of the women themselves. A sociologist studying artificial flower-makers found that most of these Italian women were apathetic: "an attempt on the part of the Jewish girls to organize a trade union . . . failed so signally that not [for] . . . several months did we find any girls who had ever heard of such an effort."[62] A study of 370 working mothers found only four union members.[63]

But statistics on union membership may not tell the whole story. Often when there was a point to be gained, women rallied, supported the unions, and walked the picket lines. When they achieved their aim—or sometimes, decided it was futile—they disbanded. A few leaders kept together a skeleton organization to have a base for the next struggle. Many leaders accepted this as necessary, given the cirumstances of women's lives.

Not everyone was brave, but many were, and some were extraordinarily so. On the whole, immigrant women understood better than their American sisters the need for workers to unite.

One Friday Cornelia Parker asked her co-workers in a dress factory, most of whom were immigrants, if they weren't glad the next day was Saturday and they had the afternoon off. To her surprise, most of them weren't glad at all, because they had to go home and clean house: "Gee, don't you hate work 'round the house?' and 'Ever try workin' at home? Ain't it just awful?"[64] Several sociologists reported that many women—although they worked primarily because of need—were glad to have the opportunity to be out of the house.

Some felt that work outside the home improved their mental health. Mrs. Pagano, for example, stayed home all her life, but when her son was killed she discovered the therapeutic effects of joining her husband at his produce business and insisted over his objections that she be allowed to work there. Widows interviewed in one extensive study several times expressed the opinion that working eased their grief and anxiety.[65] Cases were not unheard of where widows gave up charity aid in order to work rather than stay home as the philanthropists dictated.

An English philosopher, Graham Wallas, while visiting Boston in 1910 determined to inquire whether working women "were happy." The answers surprised Mr. Wallas. "I expected to hear those complaints about bad wages, hard conditions, and arbitrary discipline, which a body of men . . . would certainly have put for-

ward. But it was obvious that the question, 'Are you happy?' meant
to the girls, 'Are you happier than you would have been if you had
stayed home instead of going to work?' And almost everyone answered 'Yes.' "[66]

Yet an analysis of the comments Mr. Wallas cites indicates that
many of the women were not genuinely happy at all, but rather
viewed their work as an escape mechanism that allowed them to
ignore their fundamental depression. Some Irish laundresses "answered empathically yes" when asked if they were happy, but went
on to explain "that work 'took up her mind' " and that it "leaves
me no time to think."[67] Their view of work was stoical and fatalistic
as conveyed by responses to similar questions posed twenty years
later: " 'I must like, I make a living.' 'My business to like it.' 'Sure,
I have to like it.' 'So much baby, if I no work, I no eat.' "[68]

Most immigrant women worked because they had to. Yet they
did not feel that life had treated them unfairly. They did not generally believe, as did most Americans of that era, that work was a
male obligation. They had been reared under a system where the
family was an economic unit and all members had a part. The
thinking of Americans that women should be supported solely by
their husbands was foreign to many of them. Some clearly said
they wanted to pay their own way, as the Irish girl who said that
working "made her feel she was worth something."[69]

The earliest immigrants to America, the Puritans, thought
women and children should work, believing that idleness promoted
the devil's work. It was only later, about the time of the Irish influx,
when Americans became wealthier, that women were elevated to
a nonworking pedestal. Even then, many women did more work
than the public acknowledged, but the platitude became that respectable ladies should be supported by men.

Enforced leisure, like enforced labor, is a kind of slavery that
only a rich society can afford, but the immigrants came from quite
another background. Their values were closer to those of the Puritans, and productive work was seen as good no matter who did
it. At the same time Americans began to look down on work—
especially work done by women—as something suitable only for
blacks, foreigners, and occasional poor whites. For a while the immigrants kept a different value system, but in time they aped that
of the Americans. Woman's work was not recognized as valuable,
but as a source of shame. Her husband began pressuring her to
stop being productive when he saw that in American eyes, he was

inadequate in "allowing" her to work. Women who "hated workin'
round the house," would be bound to their homes when their families could afford this luxury.

F O R E I G N
D O M E S T I C S

T HE most traditional work for women was housework. If
a woman was not fortunate enough to be the mistress of
her own home, then her proper place was often seen as
a worker in someone else's. From the beginning to the
end of the immigrant era, millions of women assumed this role.

There were some advantages to domestic work, not the least of
which was its constant availability. While factory women wore out
their soles searching for a job, household positions continually
went vacant. The advice of an 1869 correspondent was valid
throughout the era: "America is an excellent country for capable
and moral servant girls. . . . People are constantly looking for . . .
servant girls; and as they are treated very well, especially in Yankee
families, there is no one whom I can so safely advise to emigrate."[1]

Women willing to work as domestics could find jobs even when
men could not. Wisconsin in the 1850s was still inhabited by Indians, yet a Norwegian pastor asserted that those most likely to
find work were servant women. An 1841 writer speaking of widespread unemployment added that this "applies to men. Women,
especially young girls, will be able to do relatively better."[2] In the
Far West opportunities for women were always plentiful; when
eastern domestics earned nine or ten dollars a month, the West
offered twenty to twenty-five dollars.[3]

A multitude of women took this advice; an 1895 Boston study
showed that 80 percent of that town's servants were foreign-born.[4]
In Chicago at the turn of the century there were "many" employment agencies "entirely for foreign women," while New York City
had "169 agencies run for the purpose of distributing immigrant
houseworkers, chiefly women."[5] And while it may be that they
lacked the knowledge for any other response, a remarkable 84 per-

cent of women entering the port of New York in 1905 gave domestic service as their occupation.[6]

The demand for domestics continued to exceed the supply. In the period between the Civil War and World War I, every respectable household had at least one maid. Middle-class men did not feel that they could marry unless they could afford to provide their brides with this surrogate housekeeper. The Victorian lady could not possibly keep her social position in the community if she did her own housework.

The Irish filled this need from the 1840s on. Practically every affluent home in the northeast had its Bridget, and even as late as 1920, the Irish accounted for forty-three percent of all domestic servants.[7] The willingness of young Irish women to accept the most menial labor to help their families was lauded by many:

> The great ambition of the Irish girl is to send "something" to her people as soon as possible after she has landed in America. . . . She will . . . risk the danger of insufficient clothing, or boots not proof against the rain or snow, rather than diminish the amount of the little hoard. . . . They regard the sacrifice they make as the most ordinary matter in the world. . . . To keep her place . . . , what will she not endure:— sneers at her nationality, mockery of her peculiarities, even ridicule of her faith. . . . In populous cities the women send home more money than the men.[8]

Nevertheless, there existed significant prejudice against Irish servants. Advertisements appeared in New York newspapers such as, "None need apply without recommendation from their last place. IRISH PEOPLE need not apply" or "Woman wanted—To do general housework. . . . English, Scotch, Welsh or German, or any country or color except Irish."[9] As late as 1870, Her Majesty's Vice-Consul at New York wrote, "Women household servants are always in demand, but in this, as in most cases, preference is given to all other nationalities before the Irish."[10]

Prejudice against the Irish was based in part on their religion. Some mistresses harbored hysterical fears that nursemaids would secretly baptize children into the Catholic faith and that maids acted as spies for the Jesuits. Other negativism was based on Irish inexperience with American housework. One household advice writer tried to break through the American woman's attitude that all her troubles were imported from Ireland when she wrote:

Do mop and broom in her hands do their task slightingly? . . .
If you reflect that her floors at home were earthen ones, you
will think it remarkable that she has learned to use such im-
plements with half the skill she does. . . . Does she nick the
edges of your cut glass, and break more than the value of her
wages? Perhaps if you yourself had done no more dainty work
all your life than the farm-work of the fields . . . then china
would slip through your fingers, too.[11]

Irish dominance of the field was by default—they got the jobs
because few others would take them. Jewish and Italian females
avoided domestic service entirely. What few Jews did do this work
accepted employment only in Jewish homes, for to enter the non-
kosher kitchens of American Christians would have been anathema to them. One historian of New York City reports that in his
census searches, he found "no recognizably Jewish names among
immigrant servants living in what seemed to be Christian
homes."[12]

Italian women avoided it because their cultural mores did not
allow females to live outside the family circle. Married Italian
women might sometimes do "day's work" as general houseworkers,
but for an unmarried Italian woman to "live in," as most domestics
did, was unacceptable.

Yet getting inside an American home was one of the fastest ways
to learn about the country. It is not surprising that we find a correlation between rapid acculturation and those groups whose
women adopted domestic work. The Irish, German, and Scandinavian, whose women were often domestics, were easily assimilated while those whose women did not go into domestic service—
Italians and Jews—remained longer outside the mainstream of
American life.

───────

It was easy in American homes to pick up the language and the
culture; a woman then married, taught her husband and children
what she had learned, and ran her household according to the
American example. A 1905 study reported that domestic workers
learned English faster than either housewives or women employed
in jobs outside the home.[13] Undoubtedly the nature of the work
forced one to use a larger vocabulary than required in factory labor.
Kyra Goritzina, a fallen Russian aristocrat, did not know much
about cooking when she first began as a cook in Park Avenue

homes, and she certainly knew little about American foods and methods. "I had to bring down my English-Russian dictionary," she said, "and translate the whole recipe word for word, put it down in my notebook and then figure out the right way to follow it. For many months the dictionary was my inseparable and inestimable companion."[14]

Just as important as learning the language was acquiring skills. The diary of midwesterner Kjersti Raaen shows her gratitude for this experience:

> It is a big house full of beautiful things. When I told Mor about the rugs and carpets on the floor she wouldn't believe me. The food is all different, too. I didn't think I could learn so many new things, but Mrs. Hoyt worked right with me the first three weeks. Yesterday I made a cake; it did not turn out right. When Mrs. Hoyt saw that I felt unhappy about it, she said, "You are clean, orderly and careful, and that is worth much more than being able to make cake." ... I get two dollars a week; as soon as I can do everything alone she will pay me two dollars and a half. ... I wonder if I have done enough work for all this money![15]

During trips home, Kjersti made the first pie and cookies her family ever tasted. She also bought a used coat from her employer, giving her mother a replacement for the plaid shawl she had worn all her adult life. Kjersti's sister Aagot worked for an attorney's wife, and there learned to make the first Christmas presents the family ever received.

Women who had done domestic work both in Europe and America preferred it here. Rosa Cavalleri did not work as a domestic in Italy; however, her boyfriend, who was employed by a count, found it necessary to flee to France when he accidentally shattered the contents of a china-laden cart. Naturally, Rosa was frightened when she first broke something as a cleaning woman:

> One day. . . . That lamp fell over. I heard the crash and . . . when I saw that beautiful pink glass lamp shade in a million pieces on the floor I fell over in a faint. I thought I would be put in jail! I thought I would be killed! Miss May and one other . . . they came running in to see what had happened. When they saw me there on the floor without my senses they woke me up and carried me into the kitchen and made me drink hot tea with sugar in it. "Rosa, Rosa," they said. "Where are you hurt? Where did it hit you?" And when they learned

that I had only fainted from scare because I had broken the
pink glass lamp they started to laugh. . . . How can I *not* love
America! In the old country I would have been killed for
breaking a lamp like that![16]

A German girl who came to New York as a domestic thought
her $14.00 monthly earnings a fantastic fortune, for in Berlin she
had received $8.25 a *year*.[17] The reputation of America as an Eden
for servants was early established as letters reached Europe such
as this one written in 1853 by pastor's wife Emilie Koenig:

The servant girls in the church presented us with a beautiful
rug. . . . You are probably wondering about such an expensive
gift from servant girls. They really have it very good here in
America. They earn very much money . . . and are treated almost like daughters in the house. . . . The housewife dare not
tell them anything. They arrange the work the way they wish
it, and they are never asked to do anything that the housewife
herself thinks is beneath her. . . . They are dressed like the
grandest ladies when they come to church. . . . They really
behave like genteel ladies.[18]

Servants in America expected and received treatment much superior to that of their European counterparts. One student of immigration, speaking of people who returned to their native land,
said:

Most blessed are the girls who have been in service in American families. They have learned English well, and also the
ways of the American household. They have tasted of the spirit
of Democracy which permeates our serving class, and when
such a one returns to her native village she unsettles the relations of servant and mistress. Therefore, her coming is
dreaded by the "Housefrau" who has had one servant-girl
through the years, paying her fifteen dollars a year and treating her like a beast. Shall I quote one of those mistresses?
"What kind of country is that anyway, that America? These
servant girls come back with gold teeth in their mouths, and
with long dresses which sweep the streets, and with unbear-
able manners."[19]

Besides dependable employment and generally considerate treatment, one important advantage in domestic work was the opportunity to save. Since she had practically no expenses a woman

could save virtually all of her earnings, and to immigrants who wanted to pay passages and fulfill family obligations, this was a tremendously important reason for choosing domestic work. Many women agreed with one who preferred the work because, "I can make more. I have put $100 in the savings bank in a year and a half."[20]

Other immigrants chose service because it gave them the security of a family-like situation in this new land:

"I came to a strange city and chose housework because it afforded me a home."
"When I came . . . and saw the looks of the girls in the large stores and the familiarity of the young men, I preferred to go into a respectable family where I could have a home."
You can have better cooked food and a better room than most shopgirls."[21]

Sometimes life in a large, wealthy household could be almost idyllic in comparison to factory routine. Agnes was a German girl who had considerable ability as a milliner and dressmaker, but she resented the long hours required in that work. She decided to care for children. "These people had a fine place down on Long Island to which we all went in the summer, and there I had to ramble around with the children, boating, bathing, crabbing, fishing and playing all their games. It was good fun, and I grew healthy and strong."[22]

Similarly, Bridget Fitzgerald, who came from Ireland in 1921, found a job as a "useful girl" on a large estate where fifty people worked for one woman. "I had my own bedroom . . . a bathroom to each two girls. They'd give you a clean uniform every day. . . . There were three cooks for the servants. The food was out of this world. . . . There was a chauffeur to drive you to church if you wanted."[23]

Many domestics worked in households where there were other servants. One survey sent to alumnae of women's colleges and to members of "various women's clubs" found that the average household employed two servants. One family in seven had as many or more servants as there were members of the family, "while in the average family one servant renders service to every two persons."[24] Admittedly this sample had an upper-class bias, but nonetheless, many servants did work in places where they had the friendship of equals and were not socially isolated. In fact, no factory worker could claim to have more fun than Agnes. She had an abundance of friends with whom she went to the beach, dances, and so forth on her days off. Moreover, she could spend her money on recreation without worry, for food, clothing, and housing all came with her job.

———————

To some social thinkers, domestic work was ideal employment for young women because of the good preparation it gave them for marriage. In the writings of sociologists and interested laypersons this attitude frequently comes through: marriage was the chief goal or inevitable destiny of women, thus their premarital occupation should be designed to groom them for their "real job." Yet the evidence indicates that it was debatable whether or not domestic employment accomplished this purpose. One sociologist confessed that the facts did not coincide with the theory:

> To my surprise also I found that in some instances domestic service was ... no ... satisfactory preparation for housekeeping. I remember a kitchen where all was wretched, the children unwashed, the woman untidy, the room unswept. Though the man earned $3.20 a day, his wife, trained as a servant in a wealthy home, had learned extravagant ways, and realized helplessly that she could not "get caught up" with her bills, manage her home effectively, or train her children.[25]

However, another sociologist asserted that in "some families [where] the woman was a servant before her marriage, ... the care these women take of their children's diet and health presents a striking illustration of the superiority of domestic service over factory training for developing intelligent homemakers."[26]

Far more important than preparation for marriage was the excellent opportunity to save money that service afforded. One sociologist did an extensive comparison between domestics' wages and teachers' salaries in the 1880s, and determined that domestics could save more. Bank clerks questioned in small cities, where the occupation of customers was generally known, also bore out this impression. In one small town of about 2,000 factory employees, a domestic had the biggest savings account among the women workers.[27]

Foreign-born domestics, unlike industry employees, were better paid than natives. "This was found to be true in every class of occupations [cooks, parlor maids, chambermaids, etc.] in every section, in the case of both men and women, and in the [survey] returns made by both employer and employees."[28] There are various explanations for this phenomenon, including the fact that the wages of blacks lowered the average native pay, and that foreigners were concentrated in cities where wages were higher. Many employers did in fact genuinely appreciate their servants and made it evident in the paycheck. Nor was the paycheck the only benefit. Family-like situations where personal problems were shared and consideration was real were far more common in domestic work than in industry.

While conditions for servants were better in America, there were cases of mistreatment and unscrupulous practices by employers as well. It was not uncommon for domestics to be accused of theft or damage to household goods as justification for withholding wages. An expert on the legal problems of immigrants reported:

> Many cases are brought to the legal aid societies, giving evidence of a deliberate plan on the part of the employer to let wages accumulate in his hands, and finally refuse to pay. This often happens in the case of domestic servants. The Educational Alliance of New York in a recent report on their legal aid work, asks, "Have you any idea of the number of immigrant young women employed as servants, who, when their wages became due, are thrown out bodily?"[29]

Anzia Yezierska had such an experience; her first job was in the home of an Americanized Russian-Jewish family. She began work without a definite arrangement in regard to wages and, with a heart full of trust, expected payment at the end of the month. "Before dawn I rose. I shined up the house like a jewel box. I prepared breakfast and waited with my heart in my mouth for my lady and gentleman to rise." Breakfast passed. Lunch passed. Finally she could stand it no longer and blurted out an inquiry about her wages. " 'Wages? Money?' The four eyes turned into hard stone. . . . 'Haven't you a comfortable bed to sleep in and three good meals a day? . . . You should be glad we keep you here. It's like a vacation for you.' "[30] Anzia left, never to return to domestic service.

While there was general agreement that servants were fed better in America than in Europe, there were employers who ate well while the serving members of their household were malnourished. A woman who worked for a family of four reported that when chops were on the menu, "the lady of the house ordered just four, which meant she who cooked the chops got none."[31] Rose Cohen did heavy domestic work when still a growing girl and was constantly hungry. Her employer "always doled out the food on my plate. It was usually the tail of the fish, the feet and the gizzard of the chicken, the bun to which some mishap had occurred. And she would look through the whole bowl of apples to find for me a spotted one. She rarely failed to remark at meals, 'What an enormous appetite you have!' "[32]

The majority of these insensitive employers, like Rose's and Anzia's, seem to have been of foreign origin themselves. Remembering their own famine days, they rationalized mistreatment of their servants, convincing themselves that the servant "ought to be grateful for the chance." By European standards they were guilty of no particular wrong and in this area, they were reluctant to adopt the American norm.

Many employers were so suspicious of their servants that the home became the scene of an undeclared war. Mistresses counted silver and linens and snooped in maid's rooms. Should something be lost, servants were accused of theft. Once in a while employers' fears were justified. Cooks who ordered household groceries were in an especially good position to cheat employers, both by padding accounts and by getting rebates from certain merchants if the sum of the household purchases was sufficiently high. A former cook casually said without guilt that "one could make a lot on the side" and that her sister, presently cooking, "made over $100 a month, counting what she got off tradespeople."[33]

The chief complaints about domestic service were its long hours, isolation, and social status. Domestics were expected to rise in the dark to light the family fires, heat water, and prepare breakfast, and their day did not end until the fire had been put out at night. Kyra Goritzina said of one of her first jobs that she and her butler husband "never had enough rest." "We spent whole days working or sitting in our dark and overheated basement and I still wonder how we lived all those months without falling ill . . . from lack of fresh air and proper relaxation. Having no friends among domestic workers we did not know about the general rule of regular days off for servants, and evidently our employer was taking advantage of our inexperience."[34]

Since most domestic workers were single, the social isolation, especially in small households and for young women, was a genuine problem. It was difficult for her to meet people of her own age and class to say nothing of nationality, and young women who wished to marry correctly viewed domestic work as a trap into spinsterhood.

Of these three complaints, the most frequently expressed was the reduction in social status that domestic service implied. A servant in the eyes of many was not a person but an automaton, as one sociologist wrote:

> The domestic employee receives and gives no word of recognition on the street except in meeting those of her own class; she is seldom introduced to the guests of the house, whom she may faithfully serve during a prolonged visit; she speaks only when addressed, obeys without murmur orders which her judgment tells her are absurd, is not expected to smile under any circumstances, and ministers without protest to the whims and obeys implicitly the commands of children.[35]

Even outside her "place" she was viewed as something less than a complete person because of her occupation. A maid had to have a note from her employer, for example, to obtain library books in some towns while other women, employed or not, could freely obtain them.[36] The customs of domestic service were such that the worker was constantly, subtly reminded of her inferiority. In fact it was this comparison with other kinds of work and the greater respect given those workers that drove people from domestic occupations. Even though her job might be satisfying and the wages good, a woman could not avoid realizing that her occupation lowered her socially. Sociologists who made comparisons of the two general classifications of employment found that most women preferred work in industry.

A YWCA Commission on Household Employment, for example, interviewed over a hundred young domestics and a similar number of factory workers on the relative merits of their jobs. Even though the questionnaire was loaded to solicit favorable responses for domestic employment, the commission found that the workers refused to agree. It was forced to conclude: "Domestic workers themselves are not enthusiastic about advising other young women to enter their occupation, the advantages of health, wages, preparation for the future, not counterbalancing the present disadvantages of long hours, lack of place to entertain, dearth of social life and recreation, no opportunity for self-direction and self-development."[37]

For some the choice was clear. Rose Cohen had tried both and she reasoned:

> Though in the shop I had been driven, at least there I had not been alone. I had been a worker among other workers who looked upon me as an equal and a companion. . . . The evening was mine and I was at home with my own people . . . while as a servant my home was a few hard chairs and two soiled quilts. My every hour was sold, night and day. I felt that being constantly with people who looked down upon me as an inferior, I was, or soon would be an inferior.[38]

Therefore, the goal of aspiring young women was to work their way out of the serving class and into what they thought of as the "real America." Kate Bond, an Englishwoman who praised the Connecticut "master" who employed her and her husband in 1870, later moved to a Kansas farm. She acknowledged that they had "very poor crops," but added, "it was still better than working for another."[39] This mental transition seems to be a key to Americanization. In time independence became more important than security.

It was part of the change from European fatalism to American optimism. The European woman and her forebears had the notion of "place" bred into their bones—where one was born was where one stayed. One might not be as comfortable physically as one's masters, but there was a certain mental comfort, a sense of safety and security, in "knowing your place." Those Europeans who questioned the wisdom of this attitude took their first risk with emigration; in America they would slowly begin to question more, to take more risks, and so evolve from fatalism into the American creeds of progress and faith in the future.

Those who were looking to European immigration for the establishment of a permanent serving class were bound to be disappointed. American households would train the green immigrant and she would reward them with her dutiful service for a time, but she hoped for something better in the long run.

HOMES ON
THE RANGE

I T must have seemed to the women who settled the Midwest that nature's behavior there expressed God's displeasure that they had left their homes. Never in Europe had there been anything comparable to the power of midwestern thunderstorms; the capriciousness of locusts descending from heaven; the mysteriously started prairie fires that looked as if they had been sent from hell. Gro Svendsen wrote of the enigmatic landscape:

> The thunderstorms are so violent that one might think it was the end of the world. The whole sky is aflame with lightening. . . . Then there is the prairie fire. . . . This is terrifying. . . . It is a strange and terrible sight to see all the fields a sea of fire. . . . No one dares to travel without carrying matches so that if there is a fire he can fight it by building another and in this way save his life.[1]

Life on the frontier was indeed precarious. Women there were charged with the obligation of preserving human culture against the threats of a wilderness. They settled, they civilized, they contributed very directly to the growth of a nation. They generally did it in partnership with a man, but if no men were available, it was a woman's duty to unhesitatingly meet the enemies that appeared so suddenly there.

Norwegian Mrs. Brandt was alone one day in her North Dakota home when she noticed a fire advancing on their newly planted grove. "I immediately ran out," she said, "to see what I could do to save the trees. Slipping off my petticoat, I set to work to beat out the flames. A passer-by stopped to help me, and between us we saved the trees."[2] Mary Sandoz, a Swiss settler in Nebraska, was even more vigorous in meeting the threat. When fire was sighted near the cattle range:

> Mary ran out with an armful of empty gunny sacks, dropped them before the men, and was gone, her blue dress a streak through the orchard toward the river. With a sack apiece the four [men] followed, but not even the leggy Andrew caught up with her in the two-mile run. To them it was an unpleasant turn of events. To Mary it meant the range feeding the cattle had in summer—the money for their winter clothing.[3]

Even stranger than the inexplicable fires were the swarms of locusts that came from nowhere. After having escaped frost and flood in spring, drought and disease in summer, people anticipating reward for their labor found in a moment their crops vanished. Swiss Elise Isely, a Kansas settler, was chatting with a friend when:

> Suddenly to the west we saw what seemed to be a glistening white cloud . . . only it came faster than a thunderhead. Taking short leave of Mrs. Hatfield, I hurried for my own home, three quarters of a mile away. Soon I realized that I could not reach home before the storm struck, and I was worried about my baby whom I was carrying in my arms. Racing toward me, the cloud obscured the sun. . . . I had not quite reached home when it suddenly descended to the earth, . . . It fell about me . . . not a storm, but a plague such as ravaged Mosaic Egypt . . . millions of grasshoppers lit all around. . . . In a few hours our prospects for a bountiful crop were gone. . . . Trees stood under the August sun as naked as in the winter.[4]

Elise Waerenskjold sadly recorded the damage done by unpredictable weather changes: "In the evening it was still so warm that it was uncomfortable to use a blanket; in the morning, cabbage, wheat, turnips, fruit trees and the like were frozen."[5] Such a capricious climate was far different from that of her native Norway.

Sudden weather changes meant not only loss of crops, but also of life. With no forecasts to guide them, unaware travelers were caught by blizzards. The husband of one Scandinavian woman had gone to town in the morning:

> In the afternoon the blizzard struck. Hours passed and no husband appeared. Finally Mrs. Jacobsen acted on a sudden impulse. Grabbing the dishpan and a mallet she went outside and banged away with all her might. The husband who had just passed the house and was headed for an unsettled stretch south of his home, heard the noise of the dishpan, turned his horse back and steered for the sound. He was saved. "It was God's finger," said Ole Jacobsen, "that moved my wife to act as she did that night."[6]

One pleasant winter afternoon Mrs. Brandt was watering the stock with her husband. "When we finished and started up the incline toward the house we were suddenly met by . . . a wall of snow and wind. It almost carried us off our feet." Unfortunately Grandfather Brandt had left for the post office just earlier. Anxious about his safety, her husband determined that he must take his compass and go search. Mrs. Brandt recalled, "It was a long night. I busied myself as much as possible. About midnight I had a nervous chill and began to tremble all over. But I took myself to task and told myself, 'We must do what is right, and leave the rest to the Lord.' "[7] Her husband had in fact made it safely to the store, as had the grandfather, and they and some other men spent the night there, while their wives fearfully waited at home.

Women new to the prairie could not suppress all of their anxieties and revulsion against some of its untamed aspects. The cultured Elisabeth Koren wrote in disgust: "This is really too much! . . . A snake in the house! That is what we had here today. . . . It was probably one of those harmless grass snakes, but it was at least two feet long, and it is horrid that such visitors can get into the house."[8]

But another Norwegian woman who had lived there longer "laughed heartily at our fright. . . . Grass snakes are almost domestic animals with them."[9] Yet all snakes were not laughable; Elise Isely wrote that breaking prairie sod "really was dangerous because of rattlesnakes. Every acre held two or three nests of them and it angered them to be disturbed in the home which they and their kind had occupied since the Ice Age." Sympathetic though she was to the rattler's loss of a home, she agreed that they had to be killed, for their bite could be "deadly poison." "Their very combativeness undid them; for every time a pioneer plowed up a rattlesnake, he killed it."[10]

Nor were snakes the only wild things on the frontier; Elise Waerenskjold wrote from Texas:

> To be sure, quite a few beasts of prey are found here, for there are panthers (a kind of tiger, the size of a dog but shaped like a cat), bears, wolves, foxes, opossums, skunks, several kinds of snakes, and alligators in the lakes and rivers. But there is enough food for all these animals so they do not need to attack human beings. . . . On my travels I myself usually sleep out . . . I have felt no more fear out in the woods or on the prairie, though at times a couple of days' journey from people, than I did at home in Norway behind well-locked doors.
>
>   . . . But snakes can be a nuisance and may crawl clear up to the second story, especially a type called the chicken snake. . . . The reason for its intrusion into houses is that the

hens usually have their nests under the beds and up in the lofts. These snakes are harmless, however; but of course, such an uninvited guest can put a scare into newcomers.[11]

Elise considered the untamed beasts less dangerous than embarrassing. Newcomers, already unnerved by the presence of chickens in the house, were appalled when wild animals pursued the tame into the homes of ostensibly civilized people.

There were those people on the frontier who did not claim to be civilized, and immigrants agreed that certain native humans were more dangerous than any animals. Women who could empathize with snakes had no shred of sympathy for their fellow-human, the Indian. Gro Svendsen was sometimes excessively sentimental, but she had not a mite of compassion for Indians. When the Sioux in 1862 tried to retake the homelands they had occupied for aeons in southern Minnesota, Gro wrote from the relative safety of her Iowa home: "It isn't enough merely to subdue them. I think that not a single one who took part in the revolt should be permitted to live."[12] One writer portrayed that 1862 uprising which chilled the hearts of the German and Scandinavian settlers:

> They have already killed a great many people, and many are mutilated in the cruelest manner. . . . Children . . . are usually burned alive or hanged in the trees, . . . I believe that even if I described the horror in the strongest possible language, my description would fall short of reality. . . . Every day larger numbers of settlers come into St. Peter to protect their lives. . . . A few persons arrive almost naked, others wounded by bullets or other weapons, and some with their hands and feet burned off. . . . I will relate one of the most gruesome incidents in detail. The Indians had captured about thirty women whom they used to herd cattle that they had seized. Immediately a small detachment of a few soldiers we have here was dispatched to their rescue. But as soon as the Indians found out that they were being pursued, they crowded the women into a house, set it on fire, and let them burn to death alive.[13]

This particular Sioux uprising was in the heart of immigrant settlement and during the Civil War. Families who came from the peaceful countries of northern Europe found themselves with war on all sides. Men who wanted to be farmers, not soldiers, were faced with a draft in this new country (which had always abhorred conscription and preached individual liberty) to fight in a war between Americans, while they still felt themselves to be foreigners. Women were left alone to worry about husbands in battle; to try to care for the family and run a farm; to manage at the same time to defend themselves, their families, and property from hostile Indians. To more than one writer it was an incredible irony that men should be taken to fight in one war, while their families were left unprotected in another.

Fourteen-year-old Mary Schwandt saw her entire family atrociously killed by Sioux. Her pregnant sister's unborn baby was ripped from her womb and nailed to a tree. Mary was taken captive, and recalled some years later:

> I was sitting quietly and shrinkingly by a tepee, when he [Little Crow] came along in full chief's costume and looking very grand. Suddenly he jerked his tomahawk from his belt and sprang toward me with the weapon uplifted as if he meant to cleave my head in two. . . . He glared down at me so savagely, that I thought he would really kill me; but I looked up at him, without any care or fear about my fate, and gazed quietly into his face without so much as winking my tear-swollen eyes. He brandished his tomahawk over me a few times, then laughed, put it back in his belt and walked away, still laughing.[14]

Guri Endresen found the murder of her family so traumatic that it was four years before she could bring herself to give some of the details to her relatives in Norway:

> I myself wandered aimlessly around on my land with my youngest daughter, and I had to look on while they shot my precious husband dead, and in my sight my dear son Ole was shot. . . . We also found my oldest son Endre shot dead, but I did not see the firing of this death shot. For two days and nights I hovered about here with my little daughter, between fear and hope and almost crazy before I found my wounded son and a couple of other persons, unhurt, who helped us to get away to a place of greater security. To be an eye-witness to these things and to see many others wounded and killed was almost too much for a poor woman, but God be thanked, I kept my life and my sanity.[15]

While her suffering was acute, Guri understated her strength in meeting it. The facts are different from what she wrote. Her letter says that she found "a couple of other persons, unhurt, who helped us." In fact she found two men seriously wounded. According to them, she dressed their wounds, obtained bedding and other supplies, and drove unbroken oxen thirty miles to safety, staying awake at night to guard her charges.

Others remembered the hospitality of Indians in the very early days of settlement before they felt pressured by whites who were destroying their land. Mrs. Assur Groth wrote of Iowa Indians that "they were friendly and did us no harm." Her family gave visiting Indians bread "which made them glad and thankful."[16] Similarly, Cornelia Slag Schaddelee, a Dutchwoman who arrived in Michigan in 1847, recalled that "the Indians came nearly every day to buy something. They were . . . very honest . . . good-hearted people, and never molested any of us."[17]

Hospitality on both sides waned as whites insisted on plowing the prairie grass. Plains Indians were hunters; Europeans and Americans were farmers, and the cultures clashed. The natives fought to retain their land with methods that were indeed atrocious, but whites were equally willing to kill and even scalp Indian women and children. To immigrant women, a hostile Indian was no different from a rattlesnake: both represented deadly poison and both must be thoroughly eradicated. They had no doubt that what they were doing was right and good and justified, even sponsored, by God.

Gro Svendsen—though "terrified" by prairie fires, "horribly afraid" of snakes, and implacable in her hatred of the savages—never once expressed a desire to leave this land and return to her beloved Norway. She would not let her family in Europe think that she and her husband regretted the decision to emigrate. Part of their mission in creating a new home was to civilize the wild, to build churches and schools where the tall grass had blown free, to make farms and fences where the buffalo had grazed. Elise Waerenskjold talked of the "struggle between man and nature:" Nature was their foe, not their friend, and the purpose of civilization was to subdue her.

———————

"I have read in books," wrote Elise Isely, "that the people of the frontier kept moving ever westward to escape civilization:"

But if my experience counts for anything, such people were the exceptions. So eager were we to keep in touch with civilization that even when we could not afford a shotgun and ammunition to kill rabbits, we subscribed to newspapers and periodicals and bought books. I made it a rule, no matter how late at night it was or how tired I was, never to go to bed without reading a few minutes.[18]

But civilizing the West could not be accomplished by reading alone. Women plowed, planted, and reaped; they cared for cattle and hogs; they cut wood and cleared land. They were farmers in every sense. Immigrant women wrote detailed letters home of crops and farming methods, and most letters carried much more information about what went on outside the house than inside. They were more farmers than housewives, and livestock receives more attention in most letters than children. Ann Whittaker, an Englishwoman in Illinois at mid-century, was but one of many such letter-writers who proudly described their newly planted farms: "Our house stands at the top of a hill and we have bought 80 acres of land. We have got 10 acres of wheat which will be ready in August. . . . We have 2 cows, 4 calves, 2 horses, 24 pigs, 2 dogs and I cannot tell you the number of chickens. Before you get this letter we shall have more young pigs."[19]

Conditions after the Civil War were less pleasant; railroad and industrial monopolies tightened their hold on farmers while drought and blizzards complicated their woes. Yet most immigrants, who could not easily return home, resolved to stick it out. Kate Bond, writing during the calamitous 1880s, exemplifies their love-hate relationship with the land. "We have had two very bad years out here, but we have pulled through them and this year is better so far," she wrote with timid optimism, affirming clearly, "I like a Western life." But Kansas did not reward her faith and a few years later as bad weather and low farm prices continued, Mrs. Bond was more discouraged. "We left to better ourselves, but sometimes I thinck [sic] we should have done as well if we had stayed. We have our own home and our children are all with us, but there is a lot of care."[20]

Fredricka Bremer wrote of the harsh disappointment of Wisconsin Swedes in the early 1850s:

These Swedish gentry who thought of becoming here the cultivators and colonizers of the wilderness, had miscalculated their fitness and their powers of labor. . . . The first year's harvest fell short. Then succeeded a severe winter, with snow and tempests, and the ill-built houses afforded but inadequate shelter; on this followed sickness, misfortune, want of labor, want of money, wants of all kinds.[21]

She speaks of one sad woman whose husband had a broken leg, leaving her to do the farm work alone, and who "had seen her first-born little one frozen to death in its bed in the room, into which snow and rain found entrance."[22]

Yet when the wilderness was tamed, it yielded bountiful harvests with only casual care. Letters went back to Europe in which the writers expressed amazement that no manuring was necessary for luxuriant crops; that pasturage and hay were free for the taking on the prairie—for a decade or two. But the grass was soon overgrazed and the virgin soil eroded. Elise Waerenskjold wrote after fifteen years:

> Texas has changed considerably during the last years. Much of the grass has yielded to all sorts of weeds that animals cannot eat. In the winter of 1861–62 about 30 cattle died; the winter before last, 47; and last winter about 20. . . . We could have been rich if conditions had continued as they were a decade ago. As things are now, we would gladly move, but this cannot be done, since it is impossible to sell for money [due to the Civil War.][23]

Elise, like most Americans, did not see that it was partly her fault that Texas had changed. Instead of advising European methods of soil maintenance, her solution was to adopt the American way of moving on. Europeans built barns and tended their animals in winter; Elise had accepted the Texan method of allowing them to forage. She had a curious comment to make regarding these free-ranging animals: "despite the fact that cattle, horses, and pigs run about in the woods without any supervision and at times may be away for days or even weeks and months, it is a peculiar thing that most of the animals here are more amiable than those in Norway. I have not seen a single mad bull here, while most of those I saw in Norway were very fierce."[24]

Elisabeth Koren found free-running domestic animals less amiable. "These impudent hogs and cattle," she wrote, "I wish I had Vige [a dog] here; he would certainly keep them from licking the window panes! They did great damage in the summer kitchen one night; they drank up all the water and chewed the oven door and the teakettle cover to pieces."[25]

Despite their occasional impudence, the health and welfare of her animals formed a large part of the immigrant farmwife's letters. It was usually the woman who milked the cows, fed and watered them and the other stock, and it was invariably she who cared for the poultry—and slaughtered them when necessary. Though the animals provided food for the table, many women grew attached to them; they reported their names in letters and wanted to know the names of animals back home. "Don't read this part of the letter to anyone who would chide me for being so childish,"[26] Gro Svendsen cautioned, and then wrote a long paragraph on her animals. Elisabeth Koren complained that whenever neighbors gathered together for visiting, the women always "went out and looked at the calves and livestock, which are among their chief interests and positively have to be inspected wherever we are before we can leave."[27]

A wife's labor was essential to a farm. Single women were sought after and imported, and those with a reputation for hard work were those most highly recommended. Second to her own labor was the ability of a woman to provide children. For immigrants who had come here because land of this size and quality was beyond their hopes in Europe, no sacrifice was too great to make that dream come true. The lives and sanity of many—men and women, native and immigrant—were exhausted in building their farms, but to these people, few words were sweeter than "land."

Loneliness was a third reason why marriage seemed essential to farmers. The winter was long; weeks could go by when one could not travel and a congenial companion made life bearable. Some couples grew into inseparable partners through sharing of all aspects of work. One Norwegian man whose wife was away helping with their new grandchild found that, "he just could not get used to not having her with him. He cannot even stack his hay unless he has Guri in the wagon treading down the hay."[28]

With or without the aid of men, immigrant women were farmers. When Elise Waerenskjold's husband was murdered, the widow went right on farming as before. She and her adolescent sons raised twenty-two acres of cotton, fourteen of corn, six of rye, and seven of wheat plus 200 to 300 hogs, cattle, turkeys and oxen, and over 100 sheep. The weather, crops and farm prices are the main topics of this educated woman's letters. Countless other widows took the path followed by Elise and continued to farm after their partners' deaths. Gro Svendsen mentioned women who emigrated without husbands intending to farm as though she found nothing exceptional about this. Married and unmarried women alike filed for land under the Homestead Act, which required residence on the land claimed.

Even when they had dutiful husbands, farm women were often

alone. Husbands were gone for weeks hunting, trapping, and marketing farm goods, and wives were left to cope with the problems alone. Men who were ministers were gone more often than they were home. Linka Preus, who was accustomed to servants in her home in Norway, found that now "with Sina on my arm and Christian clinging to my skirts,"[29] she had to manage not only a parsonage, but a farm as well. Besides the routine work, sometimes there were unexpected crises. One day the chore boy rushed in to say a calf had slipped on the ice, knocked off the cover on the well and fallen in. Linka knew that she could not allow the calf to die and contaminate the well, and convinced the boy that she could safely lower him into the well and pull him and the calf out again. She did, but not without moments of gripping fear, which she controlled to meet this emergency. Her final comment was to hope that her absentee husband would now be serious about building the long-promised enclosure for the well.

The recognition that a farm woman received was symbolized by the "butter and egg money." Churning butter and tending the hens—these areas were her exclusive domain and if the husband was a decent sort, the proceeds were her own. She spent them on household needs, but they were also a measure of her success. Elise Isely found that Americans appreciated her Swiss cheese-making abilities and her product was regionally unrivaled. She also earned money selling butter:

> My butter was of extra quality, being firm and always sweet. . . . There grew up a local demand for butter, and my product sold at a premium. I molded butter into pound rolls, being careful to give full measure or a little more. I finished the roll by imprinting on the top and sides a scroll of oak leaves. The mold with which I did this had been sent to me by relatives from Switzerland. This was my trademark, for nobody else had a print exactly like mine.[30]

While the assumption is common that men had more opportunity for contact with natives than women, one writer speaking of a Czech community that was isolated from the mainstream of immigration in Virginia, said, "The only contacts many Virginians in the city have with Bohemians are through these women peddlers" of butter and eggs.[31] One of them acknowledged the importance

An old-time sweatshop in New York, 1910 or 1912. (Photograph by Lewis Hine; courtesy of the George Eastman House Collection.)

The box factory was a poorly paid industry that employed many newcomers. (Photograph by Frances Benjamin Johnston; courtesy of the Library of Congress.)

Immigrants often went to employment agencies for servants. The dress of the woman on the stairs suggests that she is an employer seeking new household help. (Courtesy of the Brown Brothers.)

The photographer, Lewis Hine, wrote, "Family making artificial flower wreaths in their tenement house. The little 3 year old on the left was actually helping, putting the center of the flower into the petal, and the family said she often worked irregularly until 8 P.M. The other children 9, 11, and 14 work until 10 P.M." (Photograph by Lewis Hine; courtesy of the George Eastman House Collection.)

A woman and her children shelling pecans. (Photograph by Underwood and Underwood; courtesy of the Library of Congress.)

Women vendors sold many products. This one, accompanied by her child in the early 1890s, is hawking stale bread. (Photograph by Jacob Riis; courtesy of the Library of Congress.)

These women are parading for improved working conditions. The photo was taken sometime around 1910–1914, during an era of great strikes and labor agitation. (Courtesy of the Brown Brothers.)

of his wife, who also bore and reared six children, in farming and marketing the produce, "Me and my wife worked very hard. She helped me clear the land . . . We . . . sell . . . cream and butter. Besides we have eggs and vegetables. Two times a week I hitched up the horse and my wife went to town to peddle. She took care of the cows and chickens and garden and kept the house that way. She always had steady customers."[32]

"She . . . kept the house that way": in other words, the woman earned most of the cash that supported this family as well as caring for "the cows and chickens and garden" that fed them. The earnings of women meant much more than pin money.

European women were accustomed to working in the fields; housebound American ladies thought this a disgrace. Women and children worked beside men in the truck gardens of southern New Jersey and western Massachusetts where Italians and Slavs produced food for New Yorkers and Bostonians:

> The women and girls . . . dress like men in overalls and without shoes or stockings. It is a familiar but picturesque sight, and one typically representative of their great patience, dogged perseverance and thrift, to see them, in blue jeans and huge straw hats, slowly crawling on their hands and knees up and down the long rows, astraddle the slender green onion tops, pulling out the tiny weeds. . . . They do not stop to rest even on the hottest days, and at noon the women go back to the house, prepare the meal, and bring it out to the men.[33]

As cooperative field work was a European tradition, so were the independent income-producing activities of farm women. While letters from America are filled with talk of the crops, animals, and weather, their homes generally receive less attention; Gro Svendsen, for example, wrote long letters detailing every aspect of farm life, but aside from once mentioning a new kitchen and some utensils, in fourteen years of letter-writing she gave no idea what her house looked like. She was not nearly so much a housekeeper as a farmer, yet doubtless if the census taker had asked her occupation, she would have unhesitatingly replied, "housewife." They did not question occupational stereotypes and did not completely break them, for women who did farm work also did the housework.

Compared to the city immigrant, a farming woman was much less independent. Though she worked from before dawn until after dark, she never really had a dime to call her own. While the city woman worked long hours, she was free from her job on Sunday and the pay envelope came with her name on it. A farm woman might keep her butter or egg money, but if she did, it was only through the largess of her husband and always the majority of her prodigious labor went unpaid. A woman was dependent on her husband for any small thing she wished to buy. She was put in the position of a dependent, nonearning child, when in fact she worked hard all day, every day. Yet the money was legally his, and if she ever wished to leave him, what then? She had no savings and no skills that were saleable for enough to support her children. The garden, the animals, the farm she poured herself into were not hers.

On the other hand, if the farmwoman had a good relationship with her husband and children when they emigrated, she was more likely to keep it than her city counterpart. The farming husband was less likely to squander the family's income in drinking and gambling, simply because such entertainments were not readily available to him. Then, too, a farming mother did not have to worry about her offspring as much as the woman in the city; she knew where they were and who they were with. Farm children were more likely to use the native language; less likely to look down upon their parents as ignorant greenhorns. Nor, in most cases, could they get a job and be independent until the parents were ready to give them land and set them up in farming, and meanwhile a mother's discipline over unruly sons was much more effective. There were compensations for the isolation and hard work. While all members of the family were less free, they were more secure and more apt to have a close relationship than city families where each went to his separate job and the tenement home was shared with many others.

Yet for a woman, all of this was dependent to a large extent on the goodness of her man. If he was a scoundrel the city woman could show him the door and get a job, but the farm woman often found no options available except insanity, suicide, or silent submission. Doubtless there were many who regretted that American-style farming placed neighbors widely apart, while in Europe they had lived together in the village and gone out in groups to work the fields.

But for most those regrets were ephemeral; more important was the fact that the family was rich in land, richer than they could ever have hoped to be in Europe. The family, the land, the farm— this was what mattered most. A woman would bury her sentimental longings and rejoice in the opportunity that America brought. And to make the most of that opportunity she, along with her sister immigrants in the city, would work. They poured themselves into the building of a country; they made their great unheralded contribution.

PART V

The Complexities of It All

STANDARDS AND DOUBLE STANDARDS

S ELDOM did the immigrant woman have more than a few years of education; often she was totally illiterate, yet somehow she dealt with problems that were surprisingly complex. Nineteenth-century bureaucracy had not yet reached the state of accomplishment that it has in the twentieth, but it was well on its way. Moreover, those early bureaucrats were commonly even more capricious and held even greater power. The grievance procedures and sensitivity training of today were inconceivable then, and the immigrant merely adapted as best she could to a legal system that was often arbitrary.

There was one government agency which struck fear in the heart of every alien: The United States Immigration Commission. It was omnipotent, sometimes literally holding a life-or-death power. Problems with the immigration bureaucracy could be very complicated and serious.

Potential emigrants had to battle their own government over the right to leave. While nativists had nightmares of hordes of paupers shipped to the United States by European governments anxious to lighten their welfare rolls, this was only occasionally true, and when it was true, the offenders were most likely to be local governments of enlightened countries like Britain and Germany. The autocratic governments of the more benighted countries of eastern and southern Europe were anxious to keep their peasants home, paying the heavy taxes and serving in the army. In the Austro-Hungarian Empire, priests were ordered to preach against emigration. Letters from America were opened and if they praised the new country, they were not delivered. Border guards arrested those attempting to go. Emigrating from czarist Russia was fraught with the same pitfalls faced by those trying to leave the USSR today. People used all sorts of devices to go to the promised land. They pretended to be going somewhere else; they hid from guards under wagons piled with hay; they agreed upon codes for letters; they poured out their savings in bribes.

Once they arrived, their troubles might begin all over again. As the years passed legislation increased and standards for entry became more rigorous. The legal net was aimed at catching not only criminals but also paupers, the "immoral," the insane or "feeble-minded," the sick, those "likely to become a public charge," those who had violated the Contract Labor Law, and even, ultimately, the unlearned.

Individual cases are bewildering and sad. Take for instance the vague charge of feeble-mindedness, and look at the conflicting reports of social workers on the intelligence of one Katie Schultz, a German-Hungarian who had been in the United States for nearly a year when she came to the attention of an investigator who, "became convinced that the girl was not moral and took her to Dr. X, of the Psychopathic Clinic, for an examination. He pronounced her feeble-minded to such a degree that she would be unable to protect herself; and as she is a pretty girl, it seems extremely dangerous for her to be at large."[1] Katie was deported. Social workers in Budapest, however, had an entirely different view of her mental state. ". . . She learns Hungarian so quickly that she will be able to speak it quite well in two or three months. She likes her work, is very diligent. . . . His Excellency says that neither he nor anyone else could find why one would call her feebleminded; she is quite bright. . . . She must have been shy and . . . did not speak sufficient English."[2]

Rachel Rosenbaum's husband died shortly after their arrival at Ellis Island. Mrs. Rosenbaum was beside herself with grief and anxiety, which the officials interpreted as evidence of a weak mind. Her prosperous family was already established in America, capable of and willing to support her, and even had a Congressman working in their behalf, yet she was deported. Since she had no family remaining in Europe, her life there would be lonely and sad.[3]

Many exclusions, while legally justifiable, appeared totally arbitrary. Complications arising from the Contract Labor Law were probably the most baffling. This law had been passed in 1885 at the urging of American labor unions to prevent employers from importing foreigners to serve as scab laborers in breaking up strikes. It had, however, the paradoxical effect of putting immigrants into a hopeless dilemma: on the one hand, they had to prove that they would not become public charges; on the other hand, if they had contracted for a job in advance of arrival, they had violated the Contract Labor Law and were subject to deportation. One Mrs. George Pearson, a British citizen living in Nova Scotia, wrote to a company in Connecticut and asked if work was available. When they replied in the affirmative, her family emigrated, but the government promptly produced a charge of violation of the Contract Labor Law.[4] Naturally immigrants wanted to know about the availability of work before they risked their jobs and savings in moving. It must have seemed very strange that the government which expected them to prove they were self-supporting would also forbid them from making such inquiries.

It was an incredibly complicated business. For example, take the unexceptional case of one Mrs. Kapolo. Like millions of others, her husband had preceded the family to America, leaving the woman to shepherd her brood of children halfway around the world alone. Eight-year-old daughter Mary had a severe case of measles en route which developed into nephritis, detaining them all at Ellis Island. If it became necessary for little Mary to be deported for failing the medical exam, the immigration officials insisted that her mother would also have to go back to Poland with the child.[5] Imagine then the predicament of that woman—herself and the sickly daughter in Poland, her husband and other children in Chicago, and years of hard-earned savings wasted on the trip, with no apparent hope of being reunited with her family. It took tremendous courage for these women to deal alone with such complicated, costly problems which were often beyond their control. The process involved bonds, deposits, affidavits, appeals to boards and Congressmen. Apart from the tremendous cost, the process itself must have been incomprehensible to the distraught and often illiterate alien.

Katerina Kosice, a twenty-one-year-old Slovak woman, exemplifies the staggering amount of red tape that could endanger one's trip and cost one's savings. Katerina attempted three times to emigrate. On her first arrival at a port of debarkation, the steamship doctor sent her back for treatment of trachoma. She returned home and was under a doctor's care for four months. He pronounced her cured and she traveled to Prague for a visa, but found the Czecho-Slovak quota for immigrants filled. She was forced to return home again. The next year she finally got her visa, said her goodbyes once more, and made it to New York. The trachoma scars were detected at Ellis Island, the doctor there decided she was subject to relapse, and Katerina was deported.[6]

Like any bureaucratic procedure, these medical examinations were unpredictable. By the height of the immigrant era the newcomers were well aware of the chanciness of it all, but considered it a risk worth taking. A young Italian girl who, like Katerina Kosice, emigrated alone, found herself similarly detained by an eye infection. She got a room in Naples, saw a doctor for twelve days, and went back to reapply. This time the government doctor did not even examine her, but merely waved her on. "All that time and money wasted!" she lamented.[7]

Disturbances like World War I meant additional years of separation and loneliness for millions of immigrants and their loved ones in Europe. However, even in peace time, for a political or racial minority, exclusion from America could literally be a sentence of death. The friends of a Jewish widow wrote to the *Jewish Daily Forward*:

> This is about a family from Yekaterinaslav, Russia, who suffered greatly from the pogroms. The father and a child were murdered, the mother crippled, a twenty-year-old boy had his head split open. . . . The survivors of the family, the mother and three children, came to America. . . . The older boy, whose head had been split by the hoodlums, had a recurrence of the effects of the blow and was taken into government hospital . . . Then the authorities decided that he had to be sent back to Russia—to the city where his father and brother had been murdered. His crippled mother intends to go with him, but she is desolate because she has to leave the other children behind.[8]

After World War I and the Russian Revolution there was even less chance for people to move about freely. The years of nativist fear of foreigners together with panic over the Communist revolution combined to bring xenophobia in America to its height. In the 1920s, immigration quotas for each ethnic group were set up. The quota system was biased to favor the countries of northwestern Europe—which sent few immigrants in the twentieth century— and against those of southeastern Europe, where many still desired to join their compatriots in the United States.

The quota system made immigration a nightmare. Steamship companies were not to allow emigrating passengers in excess of the quota, but enforcement was difficult and the companies would profit from women attempting to join their husbands. One Joseph Reverez spent $1,000 to pay passage and furnish a home in anticipation of the arrival of his wife and children, but they were immediately sent back to Yugoslavia because the quota was full.[9] The steamship company had to bear the expense of return passage, but Mrs. Reverez would have to buy another set of tickets if they came again. Aside from the tremendous disappointment they would feel, these women now had to make their way from the port city back home, where their property had been sold and their jobs abandoned—where they actually had no home at all. Yet immigration officials said that they had a hundred appeals similar to the Reverez case from Yugoslavia alone.

Even before war and the quota system, the evidence seems to be that women encountered more legal difficulties in immigrating than men. The law provided for exclusion of the "immoral" and immigration officials set themselves up as arbiters of morality. Appropriate to the Victorian thought which dominated the era, they were much more concerned with the morality of women than of men.

Where a woman intended to live was a matter of vital concern to them. A man's abode could be anything from a park bench to a freight car—the officials did not bother to ask—but a woman's intended residence could be inspected. One nineteen-year-old Russian woman who gave her uncle's address as an intended residence was refused entrance largely because there were empty beer bottles in the apartment when it was inspected.[10] There were many such cases: a German girl coming to join an elderly male cousin was not allowed to enter because, "The Board thinks it strange that a young girl should permit a man . . . to support her." Yet they contradicted their own moral rectitude, officially excluding her as "a person likely to become a public charge."[11] A woman was damned if she let a man support her and damned if she didn't.

Eighteen-year-old Maryana Rosorzki was detained at port because the inspector in Chicago thought the house which she gave as her intended residence was too crowded and unsanitary.[12] It must have seemed strange indeed to a woman like Maryana when immigration officials asserted that she was excluded for her own welfare, when she probably was accustomed to similar living conditions at home. Added to the frustration was the fact that she had little possibility of changing any of this without being allowed to try her wings in America.

Ironically, many of those most active in this movement to "protect" immigrant girls were women and feminists. Their fear of white slavery was disproportionate to its danger, and the effect of their protectionist efforts was to make women more dependent on men. One "protectionist" wrote proudly of the progress that had been made in placing restraints on the free movement of women:

> Unprotected women and children are detained until their friends or family are telegraphed for. On no occasion is a woman or child allowed to enter New York alone. . . . When a young woman comes to be married, if she is not chaperoned or cannot guarantee the observance of all the properties, she is married at Ellis Island. There is hardly a day without a wedding. In October there were forty-four.[13]

To a European girl these drab Ellis Island weddings in a language she did not even understand must have seemed a sham. Nor could the American reformers see that their limitations on a woman's freedom might sometimes have the very effect they wished to avoid: the enforced slavery of a gullible woman to a devious man. One hapless girl wrote to the *Jewish Daily Forward* of her government-imposed "wedding:"

Dear Mr. Editor:

   I have been in the country only two months, and I find myself in such terrible circumstances that I need your advice. . . . My mother was married a second time to a man who had a son. . . . When the son went to America my mother and stepfather decided I should marry him but didn't find it necessary to tell me about it.

   Mother wrote to my stepbrother about the decision, and since he liked the idea, he sent me a steamship ticket. Still nothing was said to me about marriage. . . . Before I left, Mother told me that when my stepbrother came to take me from the ship I should say he was my bridegroom, otherwise they would not let me into the country.

   At the age of seventeen I left home, and when my stepbrother met me on my arrival in Castle Garden, I repeated what I had been told to say. Then they asked me and my stepbrother to hold up two fingers, a man said something, they told us to kiss each other, and they let me out.

   . . . He took me to a room where he had his own belongings. I looked around in wonder and asked him, "Are you going to live here with me?" Then he answered that I was . . . his wife. . . .

Two months have passed, and there hasn't been a day that we haven't had bitter fights. He shouts that he married me legally at Castle Garden. He's willing to go to the rabbi with me too, and threatens that he can have me arrested. I scream that he is not my husband and that I will pay him for the steamship ticket. I am working . . . and I am willing to pay him a dollar a week, but he doesn't listen. . . . It's impossible to live in the same room with him, because I have no more strength to fight him off.[14]

Paradoxically, while sometimes immigration agents insisted upon unwanted weddings, at other times they tried to prevent marriages that the people involved wanted. For many years some women came to enter into arranged marriages with partners whom they had not met. In the post World War I crackdown, immigration authorities attempted to put an end to this un-American practice. One Rachel Badad arrived to marry David Solomon, an American-born man who had served his country in the Great War. Their parents had arranged the marriage, but the Immigration Board disapproved of this Old World custom and attempted to exclude Rachel as "a person likely to become a poublic charge"—a ridiculous statement in view of the fact that the Solomons owned their home, had savings of $12,000, and the potential groom was employed at $50 a week. Apparently their wealth was eventually persuasive, though Rachel was not released to them, but to the custody of a great-aunt who had to journey to New York for the purpose. Undoubtedly, a poor couple trying to marry in accordance with their parents' wishes would have met with less success.

Sometimes foreign women were deported even after very long residence. A woman who had been here since childhood—but who had neglected to become a citizen—was ordered deported because after reaching adulthood she had "become immoral."[15] Certainly this was not in the interest of her rehabilitation, for it is unlikely that she could earn an honest living in a strange country with no friends or family.

Even if one was spared deportation, the threat of such was disturbing. One Mrs. Banir appears to have been the object of constant surveillance by the authorities; her social worker's report in 1921 read, "Charge immorality. Evidence against her is strong. Her house has been raided twice by police because of immoral conditions there. Inspector was very unfavorably impressed by her. He said, 'She looked the part.' "[16] Four days later when the deportation hearing was held the "strong evidence" had evaporated, and it was concluded that "there is really no evidence indicating immorality."[17] Yet Mrs. Banir, her husband, sister and four children had been harassed and twice raided by police.

In conclusion, then, it seems that women did have more difficulty gaining entrance to the United States than men for several reasons: (1) They weren't properly married, were pregnant and unwed, had illegitimate children, or even because the admitting agent didn't like their looks. (2) Inspectors made it their business to approve a woman's intended abode, which never happened to men. (3) Mothers with ill or handicapped children were more likely to be excluded. (4) Women were more likely to be illiterate, girls having had less chance for education in most of Europe. (5) To immigration agents conditioned to think of women as economically dependent, they seemed more likely to become a public charge. (6) To some extent the fact that women came later, following the men, was a disadvantage, for they were more likely to encounter the post-World War I xenophobia.

The one area where men faced more discrimination was in the likelihood that they would be suspected of political radicalism. After the Russian Revolution, an irrational fear of foreigners and dissident ideas gripped the country, and people were deported without the opportunity to defend themselves. Most of these deportees were male, but their departures caused serious suffering for wives left behind in America:

> Mrs. B—— read of her husband's arrest in the newspapers, and went to buy him some clothes. On Monday morning she called at the Barge Office at South Ferry, hoping to be allowed to take the clothes to him herself. The officials then told her that her husband had sailed on the *Buford* the day before. The official, she said, laughed at her. Angered by her own loss and his unconcern, she broke a window in the Barge Office. The act, committed in the presence of other wives, was distorted by the newspapers into a large-sized raid on the Barge Office. Mrs. B—— was arrested and spent five days in jail. There, she says, the other women prisoners—prostitutes, pickpockets, and so forth—jeered at her, calling her the wife of a "Bolshevik." She cried when she was telling this part of her story. . . . "I can't express my feelings so good in English," said Mrs. B———, "but maybe it ain't necessary. You understand. Anybody would feel terrible to have a friend taken away without saying good-by, but I am his wife."[18]

Washington officials claimed that they had given orders "to prevent the separation of families, and the possible dependence and destitution of wives and children if the deportee was married," but "due to some unaccountable oversight," the directive was ignored.[19] There were several instances where these men had deposited money in banks, but the distressed wife could not withdraw it because it was in his name.

Immigration agents refused to believe women were capable of entertaining dissident political thought. In a raid during a concert at the Ukrainian People's Home in Newark, forty agents blocked all exits while detectives stopped the music and ordered women to depart. "The women protested and did not want to leave their husbands, but were thrown out from the hall."[20] Despite the fact that females shared the same harsh—and often worse—working conditions that radicalized males, the police apparently believed that none of these women shared her husband's objections to capitalism. Women were looked upon so wholly as sexual beings that no one would accuse them of thinking.

Political deportations that victimized men happened for only a few years at the end of the immigrant era. But for decades, women were subject to a double standard that inclined admission agents to wave a man on as presumably strong and able to take care of himself, while a woman was carefully checked. Emigration for her was a bigger gamble, a more complicated undertaking.

TRAVAILS OF TRAVEL

MOST of the millions of immigrants had never seen the sea before they crossed it. This crossing could be a terrifying experience. Traveling on an 1855 sailing ship, Swiss Elise Isely described a storm "turned our vessel over on its beam end so far that . . . those on the upper side clung to their bunks, fearful of being hurled down. . . . Salt water was spurted in. . . . The breaking waves boomed like never-ending thunder."[1]

The large steamers that replaced these sailing vessels later in the century would be safer, but nonetheless there would be seasickness. Like others, Rose Cohen thought she was dying. The first three days of her trip, "I was conscious . . . only part of the time. . . . I heard voices screaming, entreating, praying. I thought we were drowning, but I did not care." On the fourth day she tried to get up to get water but the ship lurched and Rose fell. A man picked her up and carried her to the deck.

> I had heard that those who were very sick on the steamer and those who died were thrown into the ocean. There was no doubt in my mind, therefore, that that was where I was being carried. . . . He went away, to fetch a rope, I thought. He returned in a few minutes. But instead of a rope there was half an orange in his hand. . . . After a while Aunt Masha came creeping up the steps on all fours, hugging our little bag of zwieback. From that hour we improved quickly.[2]

Conditions on the early ships had been so bad, the voyage so long, the medical inspections so indifferent, that plagues of all sorts occurred; on some ships ravaged by epidemics almost as many died as lived. The much quicker crossing provided by steamers as well as required inspections and vaccinations improved conditions so that steerage deaths, which had been commonplace, became unlikely. Nonetheless, steerage sanitation left a lot to be desired. The report of a female government investigator who disguised herself as a peasant and made the crossing in 1911 is worth quoting at length:

> There was no hook on which to hang a garment, no receptacle for refuse, . . . no cans for use in case of seasickness. . . . The first morning out I took special care to inquire for the women's washroom. One of the crew directed me to a door bearing the sign, "Washroom for men." Within were both men and women. Thinking I had been misdirected, I proceeded to the other washroom. This bore no label and was likewise being used by both sexes. . . .
>   The . . . same basin served as a dishpan for greasy tins, as a laundry tub for soiled handkerchiefs and clothing, and as a basin for shampoos and without receiving any special cleaning. It was the only receptacle to be found for use in case of seasickness. [Cold salt water was all that was available.]
>   . . . Steerage passengers may be filthy, as is often alleged, but considering the total absence of conveniences for keeping

clean, this uncleanliness seems but a natural consequence . . .
Many . . . make heroic efforts to keep clean. . . . It was forbidden to bring water for washing purposes into the sleeping
compartments. . . . On different occasions some of the women
rose early, brought drinking water in their soup pails and thus
tried to wash themselves effectively, but were driven out when
detected by a steward. . . .

The day of landing, when inspection was made by custom
officials who came on board, the toilets were clean, the
floors . . . were dry and the odor of disinfectant was noticeable.
All these were conditions that did not obtain during the
voyage. . . .[3]

A male passenger reported that on a ship in 1906 there were
seven lavatories to be shared by 2,200 steerage passengers—five
for men and only two for women. If one figures that 40 percent
of the passengers were women and children, then there would be
approximately 440 to a lavatory. The five male restrooms would
average about 260, or would be about half as crowded as the wom-
en's facilities. Since the male lavatories are described as "exceed-
ingly small and cramped, with the result that these places were
simply packed, jammed to the doors, an hour before breakfast,"
the situation in the women's restrooms must have been
impossible.[4]

In the early days, passengers brought their own food. This led
to shortages when winds failed and the trip was longer than anticipated. Some captains deceived travelers as to the length of the
journey so as to sell them provisions at a high price when they
ran out. "Eats were scant and not of the best," remembered one
Swedish passenger. "After the passengers fell away through illness,
then there was sometimes enough for all."[5] Steerage passengers
on the early ships did their own cooking, as Elise Isely reported:

Eight sheds, called kitchens, were assigned to the steerage.
These were on deck, sheltered from rain or snow by a roof,
but otherwise open on all sides to the weather. Under each
roof was a long iron trough and above each trough was an iron
rod from which kettles could be suspended. Fire was laid by
the seamen in the troughs, and when the billets of wood were
burned to redhot coals, the passengers were summoned to
cook. Woe to the passenger who did not respond immediately;
for the coals died down, and there would be no more fire until
the next meal! Woe to the passenger who spilled the water . . .
for water was rationed, and he could get no more![6]

Later food was served by the galley, but this too was unsatisfactory. The differing national tastes were ignored and food was served in an unappetizing manner, often within sight and smell of the seasick passengers. The incognito government investigator wrote:

> The white bread, potatoes and soup, when hot, were the only foods that were good. . . . The meats were generally old, tough, and bad smelling. . . . The vegetables were often a queer, unanalyzable mixture, and therefore avoided. The butter was rarely edible. . . . Breakfast cereals, a food foreign to most Europeans, were served in an abundance of water. . . . During the twelve days only about six meals were fair and gave satisfaction. More than half of the food was always thrown into the sea. . . . Many passengers made tea and lived on this and bread.[7]

Arriving twenty minutes after the bell meant no meal. Rose Cohen and her aunt, waiting in an embarkation station, discovered that "no sooner was the food put on the table than it was gone, and some of us were left with empty plates." Yet Rose wrote, "going hungry seemed easy in comparison with the shame we felt to put out our hands for the bread while there was such a struggle."[8] Immigrants soon were reduced to the base behavior that nativists loved to proclaim of them.

The saying, "the steerage pays the ship" was probably true. Steerage passage in 1906 was thirty to thirty-six dollars on the main passenger lines whereas the first class fare was seventy-five to ninety dollars, yet the difference in quality seems greater than the difference in price. For example, a Sunday dinner in steerage consisted of a choice of goulash or pasta with soup, potatoes, prunes and bread, while the first class menu offered flounder with shrimp sauce, lobster Newburg, turtle steaks, beef sirloin, lamb, corned beef, chicken, capon, roast beef, boiled ham, and roast turkey, plus assorted soups, vegetables, salads, and desserts. Moreover, the limited menu in steerage was not even wholesome; fat worms were found among the macaroni. On this ship there was again no provision in steerage for washing dishes; the harried passenger "scraped with my fingernails" to clean his plate, while first class passengers ate from china and linen that was cleaned by others.[9] A government investigator who traveled both steerage and third class said that though the fare differential was only $7.50, "the difference between accommodations is everything."[10]

Women frequently testified to the indignities they suffered at the hands of the crew. The following was a common situation in steerage:

> From the time we boarded the steamer until we landed, no woman . . . had a moment's privacy. One steward was always on duty in our compartment and others of the crew came and went continually. . . . The men who came may or may not have been sent there on some errand. This I could not ascertain, but I do know that regularly, during the hour or so preceding the breakfast bell and while we were rising and dressing, several men usually passed through and returned for no ostensible reasons.[11]

Elise Isely traveled on an English ship where because "we understood none of their words," passengers were treated like "dumb animals." One sailor was particularly mean and insulting to the women, but when they reached land, they had retaliation: "Two or three score women, each of whom had suffered all sorts of indignities aboard ship, rushed upon him, striking him."[12] It was dangerous to resist too much, though, before one had safely entered the United States, for to incur the anger of a ship official was to risk admission. A steamship agent in Hamburg succeeded in forcing his attentions on Rose Cohen's aunt for a week, since she believed he had the power to send them back.

Austrian Sylvia Bernstein said of her 1914 passage:

> The trip. . . I'll tell you. My mother was afraid, a girl alone. My mother said to me, "Don't talk to men, because if you talk to men you become pregnant. . . ."
>
> So I came on the boat, and I can't speak English. . . . There was a Russian from America, so I could talk to him a little. He says, "You want a cup of tea? There is the chef. Go over and ask him for a cup of tea." I says, "How do you ask in English?" He says, "Say to the chef, 'Give me a kiss.'" And I didn't know. I went over to the chef and I says, "Give me a kiss." He was an elderly man and the English are very polite and understanding. He looked at me and I looked at him, and I knew something was wrong.[13]

While some male passengers might mistreat unaccompanied females, they too were abused by the immigration system. Elizabeth Hasanovitz raged:

Immigrants were treated worse than prisoners. . . . In London, our baggage was opened, our clothes thrown carelessly together with those of other passengers to be disinfected by steam, then replaced in our trunks, all rolled up and wet. My things were so mussed that I had not even a clean shirt-waist fit to wear on the voyage. The food in the immigration houses was not fit for animals, but we were only immigrants.[14]

Jews were singled out for worse treatment by many steamship authorities. They were commonly segregated from other immigrants, and while to some extent this was justified by their need for kosher food, anti-Semitism was rife among crew members. Jewish baggage was disinfected while that of other nationalities was not.[15] Poor Rose Cohen worried over the money sewed into her underwaist which the authorities insisted upon steaming; luckily, the money came through unharmed, but her new shoes—the first good ones she had owned in her life—were ruined.

An appalling example of bureaucratic inhumanity was witnessed by Rosa Cavalleri at Le Havre: A departing ship took on one French girl, but "when the mother and sister tried to follow, that *marinaro* at the gate said, 'No more! Come on the next boat!' And that poor family was screaming and crying. But the *marinaro* wouldn't let the girl off and wouldn't let the mother and sister on."[16]

───────────

Reaching land brought other kinds of dangers. The Italian man who greeted Rosa Cavalleri and her companions was typical. His familiar tongue inspired confidence, so they believed him when he assured them there was no train for Missouri for three days. "He did put us on the train but he took all our money first, about $13 each one. He left us not even a crust of bread for our journey. And we didn't even guess that he was fooling us."[17] Rosa and her friends went from New York to Missouri without a bite, their leader being too proud to accept the charity offered by Americans, for they had learned to be wary of even seemingly generous strangers.

Sometimes the cheating began before one ever sailed. Bogus tickets were sold to the unsuspecting in America, who sent them to their dear ones in Europe. They in turn sold their goods, left their jobs, said their goodbyes—and when they arrived at the port city, found their tickets were no good. One 1908 writer estimated that over a half-million dollars had been lost by aliens in New York alone through the sale of these worthless tickets.[18]

Samuel Chotzinoff's Russian family found themselves stranded in London because of a ticket problem. His mother was the one to reason out a solution to this calamity:

> I heard my father and mother talking long and earnestly about our future. My father had little to suggest that was constructive. He spoke a good deal about "home". . . . But my mother, as usual, put her whole mind to . . . ameliorating our lot.
>
> . . . "Do we know anyone in London?" The query was obviously rhetorical . . . "Don't tell me *nobody*," she cried. . . . "There must have been somebody who went—*not* to America!"
>
> . . . My father said hesitatingly: "I seem to remember—I'm not sure—Aunt Rivka's son-in-law's brother. . . . He left Vitebsk about twenty-five years ago."
>
> "Did he go to London?" My father was not sure. "Well, did he go to America?" my mother persisted. On that point my father was certain. . . . "Well, then," my mother cried triumphantly, "if he did not go to America, where else *could* he have gone to?"
>
> My father ventured a suggestion: "Africa, maybe?"
>
> . . . "Well," my mother went on, "there can be no doubt about it, Rivka's cousin, or whatever he was, *must* have gone to London. The question is how to find him. What was his name?"[19]

After much remembering, he finally decided the name was Horowitz and she pushed him into a plan to search London's Jewish quarters. Every day during rush hours the family positioned themselves on street corners, stopping any likely candidate to inquire if he had ever lived in Russia and could his name be Horowitz. Six weeks later, this incredible venture paid off. Mrs. Chotzinoff stopped a man who replied affirmatively to inquiries about Russia and Vitebsk, but said his name was Harris. He had gone on when "suddenly he turned and came back to her. 'As a matter of fact,' he said slowly, 'it was Horowitz.' . . . Without a word my mother clutched him to her heart."[20]

Mr. Harris, it turned out, had been successful in London and he provided the family with a home and jobs until they were ready to go on.

Even with a valid ticket, even after reaching America, there were problems. Anna Oleson was put on the wrong train in Chicago and deposited at a small town in Iowa where she spent two nights and a day without sleep and very little to eat. In the words of her relatives, who filed a complaint against the railroad:

> The agent did nothing for her. When the trains came she went to the conductor with her ticket, but was not paid any attention to. At the station there were three young men who constantly kept an eye on her; one of them spoke broken Norwegian; they laid all kinds of plans to get her to go with them. The agent saw it but did not interfere. One of them took her handbag, and she had to follow them to a hotel, where she was taken into a room; she understood something was up, as one of them tried to persuade her to go back to Chicago with him. In the handbag she had between $26 and $30 which they stole from her. . .[21]

Despite the obstacles, young women could and did travel safely alone. In fact those people who worried over the protection of female travelers ended up making the sojourn more complex. In England, circa 1910, the Foreign Office took "special precautions in the case of women and young girls who desire to emigrate. Every application has to be personally supported by a responsible person, and all applications are the subject of very careful scrutiny. . . . It is necessary to provide a certificate of the relatives living abroad or . . . a certificate of the employers." The Greek government after 1920 stated flatly: "the emigration of women and minors of the female sex over 16 years of age is not allowed unless accompanied by a husband, father or mother, elder brother, uncle, son-in-law, brother-in-law or other near relation; or unless they are invited by such person or by their prospective husbands. . . ."[22]

It should be noted that while the horrors of steerage have been widely publicized, not everyone had a rough trip. The 1847 writings of Jannicke Saehle read like the travelogue of any happy tourist. Though she was somewhat seasick, she mentioned none of the horrible details other passengers dwell on; upon her arrival in New York, she rode around Central Park, visited a museum, and saw a play. The steamer to Buffalo was "very elegantly furnished;" the captain "treated us more as though we were relatives than passengers;" and after that leg of the journey "things went merrily on the railroads."[23] Nor was Jannicke a giddy girl; she also recorded sensible information about crops and prices.

Even on an Irish ship just after the potato famine, some passengers had no complaints. This woman's memories were not unpleasant:

> The ship was a sailin' vessel, the "Mary Jane." The passage was $12. You brought you own eating, your tea an' meal, an' most had flitch [cured meat]. There was two big stoves that we cooked on. The steerage was a dirty place and we were eight weeks on the voyage—over time three weeks. The food ran scarce, I tell you, but the captain give some to us, and them that had plenty was kind to others. I've heard bad stories of things that went on in the steerage in them old times— smallpox and fevers and starvation and worse. But I saw nothing of them in my ship. The folks were decent and the captain was kind.[24]

If one's expectations were low and attitude cheerful, bad conditions could be patiently endured. The attitude of the captain and crew seemed to matter more than the physical environment. If one could travel on a ship where the passengers and the crew were of the same nationality, where there was mutual understanding and respect, one's chances of a pleasant voyage were much greater.

There are many accounts of evening dances and entertainments amid these early, homogeneous travelers, and weddings also were not uncommon. "The bride wore a simple but pretty dress. . . . The groom wore a black coat and pantaloons. All the passengers and the whole crew were dressed in their best clothes. . . . In the evening there was dancing on board till midnight, and everybody had spent a very pleasant day."[25]

There were funerals as well as weddings, especially on the early ships with their longer, more harrowing voyages. Yet being in a smaller group in the company of one's compatriots could be a comfort. Gro Svendsen's ship even turned back after it had set sail so that a couple whose baby had died would have the consolation of laying their child to rest in the homeland.

Births of babies en route were also common events. Since most emigrants in this era departed only in the spring, to delay because of pregnancy would mean a whole year's wait, and by then one might be pregnant again. For women this meant danger and discomfort, and even if the delivery was safe, traveling with a small baby was difficult. Many did it, though, including Gro's mother-in-law. Being middle-aged, she risked her life traveling when pregnant. "She has been very ill," Gro wrote, "so for fourteen days we have had to take turns watching at her bedside. . . . She has been

ill largely because of the poor food. There is no fresh milk. . . .
There is not even good, nourishing beer." Her baby was born prematurely and died after their arrival.

Gro summarized in regard to her ship, "The officers on board
are friendly and eager to talk. I have often visited the captain and
mate in their cabins and browsed among their books. They were
astonished to know that I could write and that I like to read and
improve myself. . . . I have not had any of those unpleasant experiences that girls often have while traveling alone—but on this
subject there is much to be said."[26]

Her comments about her inland journey are very different.
American sailors on the Great Lakes looked differently upon a Norwegian girl than her compatriots did. Despite traveling with husband and in-laws, Gro had problems. "Adding to our discomfort,"
she wrote of the boat from Montreal to Minnesota, "were the sailors, most annoying and disgusting. I more than the others had to
suffer unwelcome attentions. I understood very little of what they
said, but their silly behavior was clear enough."[27]

Others complained of these Great Lakes vessels, too. One 1857
traveler recorded:

> The poor immigrants suffer horribly on the journey, especially
> from Quebec [to Wisconsin] because the Americans in charge
> of them treat them worse than animals. A few weeks ago a
> family arrived, one of whose children died immediately. The
> three children in the family all contracted measles on the jour-
> ney. To find a berth to put them in was too much to ask; so
> the parents had to carry them in their arms day and night,
> exposed to wind and weather. . . . When I comforted the
> mother at the funeral, she answered, "If only the child had
> not suffered so much on the voyage." She was grief-
> stricken. . . . Last Wednesday [they] buried their second
> child. . . . Their third child . . . will not live long.[28]

Much later, in 1911, a government report on inland steamers
read, "There seems to be no attention whatever paid to . . . care of
immigrants on these ships." They traveled with the freight, living
as best they could. Outrageously, "passengers other than aliens
who pay the same price as the aliens have regular berths with
mattresses and pillows, and a dining room is provided."[29]

Linka Preus, whose sea voyage had been pleasing, also found
travel in America less enjoyable. Her first train ride was distasteful:
"the speed worried me a bit; I was annoyed, too, when fiery cinders

came through the windows and burned holes in our clothes." But
an American inn was worse; the bed looked "decidedly alive" with
vermin.[30]

While these inland journeys were unpleasant, Caroline Hjort,
traveling to the Far West in the 1880s, felt her railroad trip to be
an agreeable adventure:

These sleepers are equipped in an unusually convenient and
comfortable manner, better than I had expected of an emigrant car. The seats are not stuffed—just plain wooden
benches—but even so, if one brings along a cover or two,
one can have quite a good seat. These seats are made to be
pulled out, so that two of them make up into a satisfactory
bed. One must bring along one's own bedding, except for mattresses, which can be purchased on the train. For every
two seats, too, there is a berth curtain, as on shipboard. At
one end of the car is a cooking stove, on which the passengers themselves can make their coffee and tea; the rest of the
necessary food is brought from home. Otherwise, one can go
into the adjoining car, where meals are served as in a first-
class hotel.[31]

American trains were likely to be the last leg of the journey, the
culmination of weeks and even months of travel. The preparation
for the journey is an aspect of emigration seldom considered, and
devolved mostly on women. Property had to be sold; sales might
be held to get rid of unuseable, but still treasured family posses-
sions. For those who emigrated on sailing ships, meat had to be
slaughtered and dried, vast quantities of bread baked, other food
bought and packed. Warm clothing and bedding had to be made
ready, the packing done, the legal necessities attended to, the
goodbyes said.

In some respects the weeks and months of preparation were
good emotionally; one had time to grow confident of her decision,
to begin to adjust. Rose Cohen recalled that when her father sent
her ticket, she suddenly became an important person in her village.
The attention a potential emigrant received was both gratifying and
pressuring. It made it difficult for her to change her mind and stay
home. Rose's feelings were typically ambivalent, "I remember that
when I convinced myself, by looking at the tickets often, that it
was not a dream like many others I had had, that I would really
start for America in a month or six weeks, I felt a great joy. Of

course I was a little ashamed of this joy. I saw that mother was unhappy. And grandmother's sorrow, very awful in its calmness, was double now."[32]

Older women had stronger roots in their native lands. Rose, under the care of an aunt, did not comprehend the mentally-taxing complexities of the voyage. For women who traveled with children and without husbands, as many did, the journey could be a real challenge. Men who were often essentially illiterate could not write letters sufficiently detailed for wives to benefit by their travel experience. Even when literate, some seemed indifferent. A Norwegian man spent more space in his letter describing a Fourth of July celebration than advising his wife on the move. He offered only the sketchiest information: "You should try to go either via Quebec or New York."[33] There is no word about disposing of their property in Norway, no advice on what goods to bring, no warnings of the difficulties she might expect, no estimation of the time it would take or how they would meet, no expression of hope for a safe journey. Apparently many women were similarly left very much alone with these problems.

For some, the most important part of preparation was planning how to leave the native land. Emigrants from many autocratic countries faced government opposition to their departure, but for Russian Jews particularly, well-laid plans could be a matter of life or death, as Rose Cohen wrote:

> I noticed that Aunt Masha did not want to go into a wagon with small children. Nor did other women who had none of their own. At last, after much talking and swearing on the part of the drivers, . . . we were all placed. I was put flat on my face with ill-smelling hay. We were covered up with more of it, heads and all, then drove off, it seemed to me, each wagon in a different direction.
>
> We might have been driving for an hour, though it seemed much longer for I could hardly breathe, when I heard the driver's hoarse whisper "Remember people, you are not to make a sound, nor move a limb for the next half hour."
>
> Soon after this I heard a rough voice in Russian, "Who is there?"
>
> "It is Mushka," our driver answered.
>
> "What have you in the wagon?" the Russian demanded.
>
> "Oh, just some bags of flour," Mushka answered.
>
> I felt a heavy hand laid on my back. . . . My heart began to thump so that I was sure he heard. And in my fear I began to pray. But I stopped at once, at a pinch from Aunt Masha

and a nudge from her friend. Then I heard the clink of money.
At last the rough voice called out loudly, "Flour? Go ahead."

As we started off again I heard the crying of children in the
distance, and shooting.[34]

Stealth had to be accompanied by bribery for government officials and fees for guides. Since so much hinged on their goodwill,
these men were in a position to extort whatever they wished.
Guides would sometimes insist upon more than the agreed-upon
price at the last minute, leaving women and children without sufficient money for the rest of their odyssey. Even when bribes were
unnecessary, unexpected expenditures depleted funds. A turn-of-
the-century study of single women debarking in Boston found that
83 of 500 arrived without a cent and were detained until a relative
or friend "called for them and guaranteed responsibility." The average amount these women had to begin life in America was $9.15,
varying from $22.02 for Scots to $6.85 for Russian Hebrews.[35]

The end of the journey did not end one's difficulties. Mrs.
Schneiderman, who slipped her children out of Russia at night by
bribery, had to cope with measles en route. On board ship this ill
fortune turned into good, as they were quarantined in a stateroom
and enjoyed unexpected luxury, but at New York it meant deten-
tion for the mother and two younger children. Her daughter Rose
was allowed to enter and join her father. But within a few days,
the baby became very ill, and mother and baby were rushed to a
hospital and quarantined there for ten days. Rose's four-year-old
brother was detained at the port and having no visitors must have
felt abandoned. "Father and I didn't know to what hospital they
had gone," Rose wrote, "and greenhorns that we were, we didn't
know how to find out. But we knew Mother would come home as
soon as she could." Little Rose stayed "alone all day in the apartment. I think it was the saddest, loneliest time of my life." When
mother and baby were at last released, "Mother had no idea where
she lived. . . . She took the baby and walked aimlessly for hours.
At last she remembered the name of the travel agency where our
passage tickets had been bought. Luckily she found someone who
could direct her to it, and even more luckily, the agency was able
to trace Father to the new address."[36]

The arrival of immigrants at their destination often seemed to
depend on luck. Many arrived with addresses no more specific
than "South Chicago." The Immigrants' Protective League of Chicago attempted to trace women who came alone to learn if they

had safely found their destination. In the first eighteen months of their investigation work, they received 734 addresses from ship manifests that were so inadequate they could not begin to locate them and another 1,203 addresses that seemed plausible, but no one at them knew the immigrant.[37]

Often the newcomer's knowledge of American geography was vague. When Elizabeth Hasanovitz left Russia, one of her neighbors delivered a sponge cake with the request that it be taken to her daughter in New York. When Elizabeth replied that she was bound for Canada, not New York, the woman replied, "Oh, it's all right, my child. America is one world. You'll find her, you'll surely recognize her."[38]

Sometimes friends or relatives moved after writing to Europe, leaving no forwarding address. Frequently the address used was that of a steamship line or a neighborhood saloon, those places being more permanent than most of the roving foreign ghetto. Sometimes an immigrant was detained at port or hadn't left Europe or joined another relative in America instead, all of which caused confusion for those trying to keep in touch.

The journey to America was a confused process, and more depended on luck than should have. It was almost impossible for the average immigrant woman, given her limited knowledge of the world, to plan the journey with confidence. All that she could do was simply to put one foot in front of the other and keep going, dealing with obstacles as best she could when they arose. Her most important intellectual baggage was her fatalism—her self-protective belief that what would be, would be.

AN OCEAN APART: SEPARATION AND ITS EFFECTS

R AFAELLA Peppo was fourteen when she was married to her twenty-four-year-old Italian husband Michael. In 1898, after they had been wed only a short while, her husband left for America. He stayed five years without sending a cent for Rafaella or their child. In 1903 he returned for a year and left again. This time he was gone ten years, while Rafaella had another child to support. At the end of that decade he sent word for her to join him in America; "however, he thoughtlessly failed to send money on which to come." Rafaella and her relatives managed to scrape together the fare: "After fifteen years of waiting, and by paying her own way across, Rafaella knew at last what it was to have at hand a husband and a father for her children."[1] But not for long. Michael found that having a family cramped his style and he soon moved to Chicago. Rafaella dutifully followed, but he fled again, leaving a message that he would never be a part of their family again.

Millions of women lived through such geographic separations. A wife could live in a state of uncertainty for years, not knowing if her husband was dead, or if he had deserted, or if she would soon hear from him or if, indeed, he no longer was her husband.

The memory of one's mate grew dim. While the woman usually had family, friends, and children whose presence prevented her from yielding to temptation, men footloose in America might well be attracted to others. "Americanization, in their cases meaning a taste for brighter lights, fancier clothing, more stirring amusements and less confined life, is not long in being acquired," said one sociologist. "Plain, hard-working Francisca or Gretchen in the Old Country cannot compare in style with their modernized counterparts in the cities of America."[2]

Bigamy was sometimes the result, for both his conscience and the legalities prevented an errant husband from getting a divorce. A woman in Europe continued to live in uncertainty while a woman here was deceived, and both usually had children, inadequately supported. A Jewish woman told of her separation:

> I was married six years ago in Russia. . . . [My husband] had no desire to serve Czar Nickolai and since I didn't want that either, I sold everything I could and sent him to . . . America. . . . He couldn't send me anything to live on . . . I couldn't go to work because I was pregnant. . . . Then his letters became fewer. Weeks and months passed without a word. In time I went to the rabbi of our town and begged him to have pity on a deserted wife. I asked him to write a New York rabbi to find out what had happened to my husband. . . . I imagined perhaps he was sick, maybe even dead.
>
> A month later an answer came to the rabbi. They had found out where my husband was but didn't want to talk with him

until I could come to America. My relatives from several towns collected enough money for my passage and I came to New York, to the rabbi. They tricked my husband into coming there, too. Till the day I die I'll never forget the expression on my husband's face when he unexpectedly saw me and the baby.[3]

The rabbi questioned the husband "sternly, like a judge," and the suspicions of bigamy proved true. The authorities saw that he was jailed, which, of course, made two families suffer instead of one.

Bigamy cases were sufficiently common that some immigrant parents took the trouble of checking out the backgrounds of their daughters' suitors, writing authorities back home to verify the man's unmarried state. Priests, too, gave thought to the matter. In one dramatic incident a foreigner was going to marry the daughter of a respected family. The banns had been published, an elaborate wedding prepared, and the guests were already assembled, when a priest rode up and informed the congregation that the intended groom had a wife in the Old World.[4]

While most men were conscious that what they were doing was illegal as well as immoral, bigamous practices were sufficiently common in some immigrant quarters that a simple man came to believe this was part of the Americanized life-style and did not try to hide his double marital status. One naive Slovak "brought his pregnant 'American wife' and two children to the . . . office of a charity . . . saying that the relatives in Europe of Anna, his first wife, had sent Anna to this country, and she was on the point of arriving. He added that, as manifestly it was not possible to support two families on his wages, he would like to provide for his second wife through 'the Charity.' "[5]

Second wives did suffer as much as the first, though theirs was likely to be a traumatic shock instead of years of doubt. A Bohemian woman lived with a man for six years and had three children, when he suddenly decided to send back to the Old Country for his first wife "and turned her out."[6]

Perhaps the saddest case of bigamy was that of Mary Adamski who suffered both rape and the loss of her children. She married in Poland in 1897 and was pregnant for the fourth time in 1903 when, "my husband decided to visit U.S.A., much against my wishes." She bore the baby alone and after a year her husband returned, only to leave again two years later. "My husband hardly ever sent me money and it was a pretty tough proposition for us to live. Many days I went hungry for I hated to beg." Mary soon found herself the victim of a rape that was indirectly caused by her husband. The rapist, a family friend, explained after his act: "You know I went to the U.S.A. before your husband and left my wife and children here. Your husband arrived in America sometime later and boasted of having intercourse with my wife. . . . It broke me up considerably for sometime, until once I told him I would do the same thing and let him taste the same medicine."[7]

The rape resulted in pregnancy. Having to bear this unwanted child, having to support her other children alone, she wrote her husband and begged for help, but he coldly replied that he no longer wanted to hear from her. Three years went by and then he sent for the children. Mary did not wish to part from them, but family and financial pressures prevailed and "against my consent they were brought." Mary followed to America and enlisted the support of a legal aid society to regain her children. Her husband was living with a woman who was extremely disreputable. Witnesses said of the couple, "They do things in front of the children so immoral that it is a pity that those children are kept . . . in such a house." Appallingly, despite this testimony, the judge awarded custody to the father, for he was earning $16.00 a week and "was able to look after the children better than their mother who could make only $7.50 a week." Mr. Adamski had no reason to doubt that his analysis of American justice was correct, for he had told a social worker that "he can have everything for money in this country."[8]

Cases of international bigamy became so frequent that some officials insisted a remedy must be had. A Scottish overseer of the poor, for instance, reported that during five years in his parish "340 families of emigrants involving 1,127 dependents, had applied to the parish for relief . . . Some of these emigrants have permanently separated themselves from their families and made new marriages abroad." His recommendation was to allow the emigration of married men without their families only under a system of probation whereby they would have to regularly report "to some constituted authority, with deportation on evidence of family desertion."[9]

Such detailed supervision, involving an international bureaucracy as it would, was far too much to expect *laissez-faire* Americans to consider. Yet there was concern in this country, too. One sociologist recommended that Congress legislate that "a foreign subject would be deported if . . . he . . . deserts his minor children and abandons his wife without supporting them according to their station of life and without due cause."[10] Uniform divorce laws in the states were also recommended to prevent women from unknowingly being divorced, but neither of these suggestions received any serious consideration from Congress.

Yet laws could not readily cope with such domestic problems. Very often, for instance, a woman could not say whether or not she had been deserted. Rose Schneiderman's mother probably did not think she had been deserted, for she had a sound marriage, but when her husband left Russia for America, he did not tell her of his intentions. He simply went, hurrying off, witnessed by one of his children. Rose explained, "I suppose Father didn't tell Mother about his plan to leave so that if the police questioned us about his disappearance, we would truly know nothing of it."[11] He wrote when he was safely out of the country and the family later followed in similar secrecy.

More frequently, though, desertion laws could not have been enforced because for both the women and men, their status and future were vague. The letters of Adam Strucinski reflect this uncertainty. He was loving and full of promises for reunion, but they did not materialize. His wife had asked him to end his sojourn in America, and in 1911, he replied, "When the work goes worse, then it may be that I will come, but I will work as long as we have not a thousand roubles." A month later the work was indeed "going worse" and now that became Adam's reason for not coming: "I cannot come because the work is going very weakly." Another year passed, and Adam continued to excuse himself: "I was already starting to go to the old country, but I detained myself in order to earn some 100 roubles more. . . ." Finally Adam came close to revealing the truth when he told his wife that he did not want her and the children to come to America, for now "if something bad happens, I take a train and go ahead . . . but it is not so with a woman."[12] As time edged dangerously near to World War I when he could not come back even if he so desired, Adam's letters continued to be filled with excuses and promises. Perhaps he had not deserted his family, but the attraction of America seemed stronger than the attraction of home.

A wife without children had even less claim. From 1893 to 1912 Teofila Borkowska humbled herself in letters to her husband, asking him first to come home or for her to go to him. She finally reached the point where she only hoped for occasional letters and money. Passages from her letters reveal Teofila's hardships and attitudes:

April, 1894: ... So, my dear, I beg you describe to me everything in detail, what I can take with me [to America] what clothes ... and other trifles. I will take the image and the cross. ...

January, 1896: ... You promised to send your photograph. I hoped always to see you at least on paper, but I was deceived. I sent you the books. .. .

December, 1896: ... Don't be angry that I send registered letters, but you see you write so seldom I should think that my letter did not reach you. ...

September, 1897: There are mostly days in my present situation when I have one small roll and a pot of tea for the whole day, and I must live so. And this has lasted almost 5 years since you left. If I were a plain country woman I would go to wash linen or floors, ... but you know I am unable to do it and I have no strength, while sewing by hand is terribly hard.

August, 1904: For God's sake answer, what is going on with you. Perhaps our Lord God will make you free soon. I wish it myself, for I am also tired with worrying myself so in this world. ...

August, 1910: I write you with great timidity, but despair obliges me. .... I tried to get from the Philanthropic Association at least a few tickets for a few pounds of bread and a few pints of gruel monthly, but they refused me, for they learned that I have a husband. They say that it is for them all the same whether this husband is in Warsaw or in America. ... I begin to lose my eyes with sewing and crying. ...

July, 1912: Have pity on me, for I am already barefooted and naked. They have taken everything for the rent. ... You won't let me die from hunger, for I know that you have a merciful and noble heart. ... Why, I have not much longer to live, for with such a hunger as I suffer now I shall not hold out long.[13]

Men did sometimes emigrate with the intention of shedding a bad marriage. Rosa Cavalleri said of one querulous woman in her village that it was gossiped that her husband "joined one of those gangs and went away to America just to get away from her scolding. And probably it was true, because he never sent back for her."[14] An Englishman wrote of his escape from his wife's family:

"that infernal crew... wished me a thousand miles off, but I got four thousand miles from them."[15]

There seems to have been little immorality on the part of women left behind in Europe. Certainly they were far more circumspect than the men in America. A Croatian schoolteacher made this assessment: "The women who are left alone here almost always remain faithful to their husbands. It is a rare case when now and then one forgets herself. But if it does occur the men show far more feeling and self-control than one might expect. A common peasant in such circumstances has often more strength and insight than an intelligent man from the better classes."[16]

Emigration also introduced new ideas on morality: "A curious story is quite widely rife in Croatia, and the returned emigrant seems to be responsible for it. It is reported, namely, that in America it is allowable to marry experimentally for a term of years. . . . Whether this is a *bona fide* impression made by American divorces . . . or possibly a convenient cover for American experiences of their own, I cannot say."[17]

Fear and suspicion on both sides of the Atlantic complicated these separations. Nor could anxieties find the relief of articulation, for people of that era, particularly illiterate peasants, could not verbalize sexual feelings. Even communication about much simpler problems was hard, for European women were often unlettered and had to dictate their messages, making the expression of their feelings difficult. In a series of messages from an illiterate Polish woman to her husband, for instance, we find great differences depending on who her secretary was; her daughter attempted to express her thoughts exactly, while the letters done by her son are perfunctory and short.[18] Misunderstandings were to be expected.

Such letters reveal the tension separation caused, and sometimes there were quarrelsome communications that must have left the recipient wondering whether he or she was indeed glad to get a letter. Scottish John Ronaldson, for instance, wrote angry letters to his wife:

You must [cease?] longwind stories. . . . It wont [do to?] speak of dieing yet. Then you say your patience has been great. It dont look like it when you speak of departing this life. . . . Dont speak that way again. . . . You want a few explanations of my seeming coldness. . . . You seem offended. I must say tis a pity. . . . You conclude by saying that you are to resume your complaints, abuse, and insinuations at another time. At any rate it means as much. . . .[19]

Later John was apologetic and pleasant, saying, "Eliza, you mention about coming out and about wearying to see me. I believe you. Tis high time. This wont do long. . . ."[20] Separation caused strain and the best of marriage partners could not help but question the activities of the other when they were parted so long. Nor were the complexities of human relationships the only source of dispute; women spent much of their letters informing their husbands on the details of family management, hoping their decisions were correct, attempting to mollify criticism of their actions. Maryanna Lazowska wrote typically: "Don't think I live here luxuriously with these children. I don't spend a single *grosz* in vain. It seems to you that you have sent me much money. But I have paid so many debts." When a daughter died and grief was added to the other frustrations, Maryanna wanted her husband so that she wrote, "If it were by land, I would go afoot to America."[21]

When one was responsible for a farm or business, the chances were even greater that her husband would disagree with her judgment on some matter. Therefore, letters are filled with interminable details justifying her actions before they were questioned:

Now you ask how much rye I have harvested. Well, I have harvested 5 *kopa* and 19 sheaves and of barley 2 *kopa* and 12 sheaves. I put it into the barn of Ignacy Pasek and I paid him 5 crowns, and the driving cost me 3 *gulden*. . . . The vegetables cost 3 *renski*. . . . I should like to by rye and wheat for sowing. I have spent 15 *renski* from this money. I have sold that pig. God keep us from such pigs! . . . Will you allow me to sell the cow? For she is so bold that I cannot manage her. She runs away . . . and does damage to other people, and I must pay. I would sell her and buy some older one; perhaps she would be gentler. . . . I have bad times now for I have no firewood. I have burned all, and it is far to the forest, difficult to drive, and I have little money left.[22]

Husbands who had been gone for years became detached and gave glib, unthinking replies which were of no help at all in dealing with the problems at hand. Another Polish woman wrote in exasperation to her husband that she would live apart no longer:

You have not even an idea how everything has stopped. . . . If there were anything to steal, I would steal, but even this is impossible. . . . You tell me to borrow, but I have already debts enough. . . . So I write you the last letter and tell you, let it be once, either take the children or come yourself and suffer together with us. I write you decidedly, let it be so or so, for here I am neither upon ice nor upon water.[23]

Her firmness, however, had no effect and six months later she was still alone, writing, "I have only wasted my young years in longing and grief, alone with these orphans, and I have no hope it will end soon."[24]

There was likely to be understanding and emotional support from women in the same condition. A Croatian wrote of the feminine—and abandoned—nature of her community:

Whoever has strength and youth is at work in America. At home are only the old men and women and the young wives with their children. Every wife has much to do for herself. . . . The women help one another and live from day to day, dragging along waiting for letters and money. The money generally comes in autumn. Everything is bought on credit through the year; the dealer waits, for he knows that in the autumn it will all be paid. If not then, danger threatens the little house or at least the cow in the stall. At Christmas and Easter, too, and at mid-summer presents of a few dollars come to the fortunate ones. Others who have a hard lot wait months and years and never receive anything . . . Oh, how bitterly those at home feel this! They not only suffer; they are ashamed that they have been forgotten.[25]

Aside from the shame of abandonment, a woman who did not hear from her husband naturally worried about his safety. Husbands did die in America and then both hope of reunion and financial improvement died. Nor did America concern itself with those aliens whose breadwinner may have laid down his life on the altars of our industry. Pennsylvania, home of the steel mills, had a law which barred workmen's compensation to families of aliens if they were not in the United States, even if the accident was due to gross negligence on the part of the employer.[26]

Despite the problems of those left behind and their geniune need of help, one can't help but feel that the reaction of a reader in America might well have been to rejoice that he (or she) was out of that situation. Letters from siblings and parents, full of family

quarrels and gossip, especially inspire this reaction. Swedish Kare
Jons Dotter, for instance, wrote in 1846 to her offspring in
America:

> . . . You can well imagine the sorrow with which you burdened
> my weak shoulders. . . . I wished to leave all this to you . . .
> [but] you did not regard it as a gift from God but rather as a
> poison that repelled you. This was the reward you gave me for
> all the unstinting efforts I made for your earthly future. . . .
> Consider, dear children, how first of all you were the means
> of the early death of your little son.[27]

But not all letters were somber; some were filled with humor
and affection, too. Women seemed especially likely to express loving feelings by talking about those of their children and quoting
their comments: "Mamma, where is papa? . . . When shall we go
to him? Perhaps tomorrow? Come, mamma, let us go!" and, from
another, "When I ask her 'What will father buy you?' she says,
'Shoes.' "[28] Children were the primary link that bound the separated
couple, and women probably thought that by talking of them they
would encourage the father to hasten the reunion. "The children
long awfully for you," reported a typical letter. "Joqus asks always
where is father. . . . Waldzio is already beginning to walk. Aniela
had a good school certificate. . . ."[29]

Aside from the routine problems of family and farm, occasionally
there were far more drastic problems when Europe erupted in one
of its periodic outbreaks of violence. Jewish women had special
reason to want the reassuring presence of a husband, for they
never knew when a pogrom might arise. One Russian Jew whose
husband and two teenagers had gone to America remained with
five young children: "It was to be a time of sharp, close saving and
poor living, until my husband could earn enough money . . . At
length . . . I received . . . the tickets . . . I hastened to secure my
passports. Everything was in readiness." She stayed on for Pass-
over, to spend the holidays in her old home, when suddenly the
rabbi warned people not to go out of their homes. "I . . . bolted the
heavy door behind us. . . . Even as I looked out . . . the flight of
stones at the houses near became a bombardment."

She had neither food nor water in the house, "but to seek either
was to tempt death. I set the ladder for the loft, bade my children

ascend, followed them, and drew the ladder up after me." Flames could be seen and screams heard and even the little children understood there was danger. For a day and a night they went without food or water, while her two year old cried pitifully but quietly. "The massacres went on. And yet . . . the low wailing of little Molka, who was fast losing her strength, forced me to reconnoiter." Taking the ladder so the children could not follow, she looked in vain for aid. That night "the strain became too great for the . . . boys. They began to moan and cry aloud." Deciding that quick death in the streets was as acceptable as slow death from thirst, she ventured successfully out of the house. The family continued in hiding for the rest of the week, when it finally was believed safe. She hired a carriage for concealment and rushed to the railroad station, but even on the train menacing Russians followed the fleeing Jews:

> From station to station the horror that had been within my mind grew worse, for the Cossacks and the loafers told us that they were going to follow us to America. I think I became somewhat insane. I told the ladies . . . that they would do me a great favor if they would take my children to their grandmother when the train reached Radziwill. I, for my part, would jump into the river. . . . Even after I . . . was safe on my way to America the fear of death and pursuit was on me. . . . It was only when I felt my husband's heart beating against mine, in Philadelphia, in the United States, that I felt we were truly safe.[30]

The years prior to World War I had seen millions of immigrants pass the Statue of Liberty and when the cannons boomed out across Europe in August of 1914, war left many stranded. If uncertainty had been their lot before, now with communications disrupted, it was doubly so. As Russian and German soldiers surrounded their town, a Polish family sent a desperate note to its breadwinner in America: "We send this letter through Japan, but whether it will reach you, we don't know. But a drowning man grasps even a razor. . . ."[31] Zofia Starkiewicz also felt the presence of war:

> . . . throngs of soldiers are passing by us afoot and on horses; we see no end of them . . . Now nothing else but everybody prays and prepares himself for death . . . Rich people go to far Russia; there is no war there, while here is the worst fire. . . . Perhaps we shall no longer be alive when your letter

comes. . . . Few people are left, only women, for men have
been taken, some to the war, others to digging trenches, others
to transports; horses and carts are all taken.[32]

When the war was over, Americans no longer extended their
welcome to Europeans and the flood of emigration narrowed to a
trickle. Within a few years, immigration quotas would be imposed
and separated families would suffer great hardship. The following
case is extreme, but illustrates how severe life could become for
women left behind.

In 1906, when Armenian Mrs. Demirjian was a three-month-old
baby, her father left for America, intending to send the money for
mother and child to follow. Like so many plans, his went astray;
the baby would not see her father until she was twenty-five years
old. She and her mother lived alone "with barely enough food to
keep us alive." The Turks massacred Armenians during this time
("I still have flashbacks from it—the dead bodies and the blood all
over the ground"), and then World War I prevented hope of emigration. The young woman married and when persecution broke
out again, she, her husband, and mother fled to Syria. Her mother,
at long last, went on to America as the wife of a citizen, but she
and her husband could go only as far as France. Misfortune struck
again; her husband died, leaving a penniless widow with two children. Her parents came to the rescue by arranging for marriage
to an Armenian who was an American citizen. He came to Marseilles and married her so that she could enter. Her daughter, who
had been born in France, was allowed to enter under that country's
quota. Her little seven-year-old son, however, had to be left behind
until his mother became a citizen and could bring him.[33] The complications of the law and the whimsicalities of international events
took no consideration of such human problems.

Separation from family members other than husbands of course
occurred, the saddest being the separation of a mother from her
young children. Kyra Goritzina was forced to leave a daughter behind in Russia and a son in Belgium, with little hope of sharing
their growing-up years. Yet she and other women apparently believed that their American dream was important enough to make
this sacrifice.

Older women usually had no realistic hope of ever seeing their
children again; except for letters, sending children to America was
as permanent as sending them to their graves. After Rose Cohen's
father had been arrested in Russia, but managed to escape and

Immigrants on a ship deck. (Courtesy of the National Park Service, The Statue of Liberty Monument.)

A vessel packed with newcomers. (Courtesy of the Library of Congress.)

A woman undergoing an eye examination at Ellis Island. (Courtesy of the Brown Brothers.)

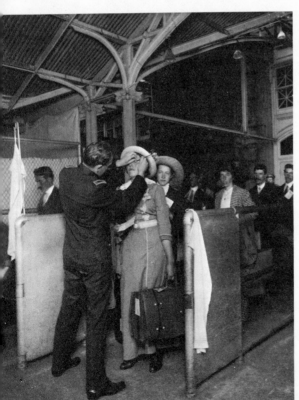

RIGHT: An Italian woman and her children arriving in America. (Photograph by Lewis Hine; courtesy of the George Eastman House Collection.)

A family on its way to the farms of the Great Plains. Note that the destination tag is pinned on the man. (Courtesy of the National Park Service, The Statue of Liberty Monument.)

LEFT: *Immigrants in "pens" at Ellis Island; Christmas season, 1906. (Courtesy of the Library of Congress.)*

BELOW: *An aerial view of Ellis Island, 1921. (Courtesy of the National Park Service, The Statue of Liberty Monument.)*

head for America, her grandmother commented philosophically, "If I had been told a year ago that my only son would go away to the other end of the world, and that I would continue to live knowing that I would never see him again, I would not have believed it possible. And yet it has come to pass and I am not only alive, but contented that he should be away. Ah, how strange is life and its ways!"[34]

Finally, it should be mentioned that it was not always the wife who was left behind while the husband emigrated. This was certainly the usual pattern, but there were exceptions. Considerable numbers of Bohemian female cigarmakers preceded their husbands to America. More surprising is that even some of the traditionally dependent Italian women came first to prepare a home for their husbands. A 1912 YWCA study in New York noted twenty-one women who had left their children in Italy; "in every case the mother was to send money back for the support of the child, even though it had been left in the care of its father."[35] In the case of betrothed couples, it was quite common for the woman to come first, particularly if her man had military obligations. Once in a while a woman, too, would fail to live up to her promises to one left behind: a young Polish man wrote with disappointment to his financeé, "I expected that you would say something about the ship-ticket or that you would send me money for the journey, while you write me in a totally different way."[36]

The majority of men and women worked hard to accommodate their aim of reunion and longed for that day. Many made great sacrifices to bring the time closer. When the peddler came into Rose Cohen's tailor shop selling breakfast, everyone ate except Rose's father; he went hungry and saved the two cents toward his wife's voyage. The strong, crude Slavs of Pennsylvania's steel mills may have seemed insensitive to the casual observer, but they too pathetically missed their families. An expert on them relates a simple but touching little tale that shows the lonely pathos of separation:

> As I waited one day in one of the little railroad stations of Homestead, a Slav came in and sat down by a woman with a two year old child. He made shy advances to the baby, coaxing her in a voice of heart-breaking loneliness. She would not come and finally her mother took her away. The Slav turned to the rest of the company, and taking us all into his confidence said very simply, "Me wife, me babe, Hungar."[37]

They did miss each other and love each other, and most clung steadfastly to their belief that marriage was forever and that the family was the most important aspect of life. Yet often the care of that family for long periods of time was left entirely to the one who was its traditional center—the woman. She alone ran the farm, transacted the business, made the decisions. It was she who closed the home and sold the property and led the children halfway around the world. It was she who dealt with the brusque steamship officials and the powerful immigration authorities. She had never done anything like this in her life, and it was an important growing experience. She had handled tremendous complexities, and it was a first taste of success, of individualism, of budding freedom.

PART VI

The Ties That Bind

F A M I L Y
R E L A T I O N S H I P S

HER independence in managing the household alone in Europe and her success in dealing with immigration obstacles were important factors in the emergence of the immigrant woman. Another factor that improved her status was her relative scarcity here. The scarcity of women is a point often made in discussions of the American West. Women were treated with greater respect where they were scarce; frontier states were quicker to grant women legal amenities. The same was true in immigrant cultures. Even as late as 1920, there remained a serious shortage of females in most immigrant groups:

NUMBER OF MEN PER 100 WOMEN, 1920[1]			
Irish	74	German	108
English Canadian	87	Norwegian	120
Bohemian	98	Slovak	122
French Canadian	104	Polish	126
English, Scotch, Welsh	106	Italian	128
Swedish	107	Russian	129
Yiddish	107	Danish	148

The three exceptions to the rule should be noted. From the 1840s, Irish women had emigrated alone, found jobs in America and remained, to a larger extent than most immigrants, unmarried. Like the Irish, English Canadian women were attracted to America because they encountered no language problem and because it offered work opportunities unavailable to them in their agricultural lands. Bohemian women established independent emigration patterns modeled after those of their compatriots who left in the 1870s to work in cigarmaking, leaving their husbands temporarily behind.

For all other immigrant groups, however, there was a scarcity of women. The situation gave women added status, for men were aware that if they did not treat a woman well, she could attract others who were willing to do so. One sociologist, working incognito as a hotel kitchen maid found that the foreign men there clamored for a date, saying how lonely they were. One was a shy Spanish man who wrote her notes and told her that though he had been in the United States two years, he had no friends and went nowhere on his time off because "it is no pleasure to go alone."[2]

The further west a woman went the more advantageous the ratio of the sexes became. While eastern cities sometimes had more immigrant women than men, in Detroit in 1920, there were 141 men for every 100 women, in San Francisco 145, and in Seattle 146.[3] Swiss Elise Isely, who lived in western Missouri in the 1850s and worked in her aunt's boarding house, wrote, "The frontier always has a preponderance of men, and St. Joseph was no exception. Most of the thirty men, perhaps all of them, who came to our table were bachelors. So great was the shortage of women in the West that many men of middle age were without wives. Girls of eighteen and twenty had their pick of suitors."[4]

Despite loneliness, however, foreign men generally waited until they had the opportunity to wed someone of their own nationality. The opinion was frequently expressed that American women were spoiled. One Scot declared, "I would not have a Yankee; they only eat candy all day long."[5]

Immigrant women also chose their partners from their own cultural group. Marriage data showed that even as late as 1920 most foreign-born women married men of the same nationality. In many ethnic groups 700 to over 800 of every 1,000 mothers listed the father of her child as having been born in the same country as herself. This was true for the Austrians, Hungarians, Italians, Poles, Russians and even—despite eighty years of heavy emigration and no language barrier—the Irish.[6]

When women did step out of their cultural group, they married an American or a man of a nationality close to their own. The Irish, for instance, married Scots, Welsh or English; Hungarians chose Austrians most commonly; Poles chose Russians, and so forth. The tendency of immigrant women to marry men of similar cultural and religious backgrounds leads one to strongly suspect that those Americans whom they wedded were in fact second-generation Americans of the same (or similar) nationality.*

*Where statistics bewilder, a personal example might clarify. My paternal grandmother Froslan would go down in the records as a foreign-born woman marrying

Endogamous marriages prevailed. A student of Lawrence, Massachusetts, an immigrant town, reported that marriages there fell into three categories: those between persons in the same ethnic group, which accounted for 77 percent of all marriages; those between immigrants and Americans, 19 percent; and those between immigrants from different areas, which were only 4 percent.[7] Those who believed that immigrant cities were vast melting pots did not look beyond the obvious surface.

Cities seem to have produced endogamous marriages longer than rural areas. To this day, many Italians in the Northeast incur the displeasure of their families when they marry non-Italians. On the prairies Scandinavians and Germans were marrying each other and Americans during the first generation.

For both city and rural immigrants, however, the societal rule of endogamous marriages would eventually lessen. Women in Europe who were limited to husbands from their own village and only those in occupations similar to their fathers' would in America have greater freedom of choice. Religion and ethnicity and finally even color became less important than personal merits in choosing a mate. Again, the group lost power while the individual gained.

———

Family structure saw other major changes because of immigration. People who had lived in large, extended families for as long as memory served left these units. Having once tasted greater freedom, few would return to the family fold that was dominated by the old and the male. Some security and economic advantages were lost with the disappearance of the extended family, but especially for its young female members, the change meant greater liberty. Even on American farms where large families were an asset, one couple tried to populate it with children, rather than include aunts and uncles and grandparents in the household.

The foundation of these nuclear families was the father–mother relationship, and here too there was important change. European males were regarded as the rulers of their families, but in America

———

an American, but her lifestyle continued to be Norwegian; she was not "marrying an American" in the sense of joining the mainstream of American life. Likewise my maternal grandfather Schultz would be listed in the records as a native marrying a native, yet he and Grandma were German in their background, religion, and language. Moreover, his brother August was statistically recorded as foreign-born, because he was born in Germany. He and Grandfather Schultz shared the same family background and culture—but the records would not show this.

women and children had more legal rights. Even more important was that economic reality here forced most immigrant fathers into sharing the breadwinner role. While in Europe wives and children had contributed to the family income, usually they were not directly paid; in American cities, however, pay envelopes came with an individual name on them.

It is indicative of the great attraction of America that at least some males were aware that their superior status would be lessened here, and yet they came. Italian men were forewarned in a 1911 advice book that, "It is a crime severely punished in all states for a man to strike his wife. . . . Treat women and children very kindly."[8] A sociologist traveling in remote Croatia found that "wives warn their husbands that in America things will be different, for women have more power there." One worried man inquired, "Is it true that when there is a lawsuit the woman goes to court and attends to it and the husband stays home?"[9] Though equality was not nearly so widespread as these women hoped, they saw the greater freedom of American females and wanted it for themselves. As a young Italian woman said to the Domestic Relations Court of her husband, "Now I am an American girl and I cannot stand for his treating me like a Dago."[10]

There were still many cases of arbitrary husbands and submissive wives, but while foreign marriages often gave the appearance of being far less than a real partnership, women may have had a greater voice than was easily seen from the outside. This was particularly likely to be true on a farm, where a farmwife was absolutely essential to its success. Speaking of Czechoslovakian farmers, one writer explained:

> The father's role as head of the family is frequently misunderstood by outsiders, who are shocked at the way he "works" his wife and children and the mean circumstances in which he "forces" them to live. . . . Upon closer examination, however, the relation of wife to husband does not prove to be one of submission on the one part and domination on the other. The wife is consulted in matters of general interest; she usually has a final voice in the buying and selling of land; she knows about the rotation of crops, and she knows which animals are to be sold and which retained. She is her husband's companion, intimately familiar with all details of managing the farm.[11]

While a common complaint was that husbands insisted on having the final word on everything, there were also those husbands who placed all the decision making on their wives. Of course this was the case with deserters and drunkards who abdicated their responsibilities without actually relinquishing their position as family head, but it was also sometimes true of sober men, especially scholars and rabbis who left financial worries to their wives and spent their days in the library or synagogue.

Anzia Yezierska's mother was so harried that she was woefully unhappy. Once when Anzia asked why she didn't have butter on her bread like a friend did, her mother shrieked, "Butter wills itself in you! Have you got a father a businessman, a butcher, or a grocer, a bread-giver? . . . You got a father a scholar. . . . He might as well hang the beggar's bag on his neck. . . ." When Anzia inquired what birthdays were and why she didn't have one, the reply was, "A birthday lays in your head? . . . You want to be glad that you were born into the world? A whole lot you got to be glad about. Wouldn't it be better if you was never born already?"[12] Perhaps life simply became too much for such sensitive men, and they fled to a spiritual realm where worldly pressures left them untouched. They were justified in their own eyes and in the eyes of the community as men whose lives had a higher purpose, but it caused suffering to their wives, who had to bear the practical burdens alone.

The marriage of Mary and Martin Grubinsky is one of the cases that seldom found their way into sociologists' records of a couple who cared deeply for each other. Even when they disagreed—as they did—they were careful of each other's feelings. They had gone from backwoods Hungary to Vienna and then Martin had continued to America. Mary soon followed, leaving their children in the Old World.

> Mrs. Grubinsky cooked in a restaurant until her first "American" baby came. . . . Three more "American" babies have been born. The children left in Hungary have begun to arrive. . . . The family expenses have mounted. . . .
>
> There has never been any question in Mary Grubinsky's mind as to whether she should work. . . . She is enterprising and adaptable and takes the lead in Americanizing the family. . . .
>
> Two months ago she moved her family from a two room into a three room apartment. . . . This was done in the face of Martin Grubinsky's flat command to the contrary. . . . How

should he know that an American family must have a sitting room besides a bedroom and kitchen, or that Tessie must have white shoes like the other girls?

... Mrs. Grubinsky... would like to go to a moving picture show occasionally with the children, but Grubinsky will not hear of that, and so she doesn't go. But on the day of the woman suffrage parade, she ran nearly all the way to Fifth Avenue to see the women pass by.... Sometimes Theresa brings home a story book in German ... and her mother sits up late at night ... and reads it ... in her slow, unpracticed way.... Martin Grubinsky cannot read and write. He once knew how, but has long since forgotten, which happens not uncommonly with working people.

The Grubinskys have ideals and hopes. These center around the possession of a little farm in New Jersey.... In the meantime, it is a sustaining hope equally for the husband and wife, and unites them through every other difference.[13]

In addition to the change from an extended to a nuclear family and the equalization of husband-wife roles, a third fundamental change in family structure was the relationship of parents and children. Women were particularly likely to be caught in the middle of this role-changing. While a woman was apt to side with children in the diminution of patriarchal power, she and her husband would, nevertheless, be united by challenges from their Americanized children. This change seemed the hardest of all, for parents had left everything they knew and endured suffering so that their progeny could live in a new land. Then they found those children ungrateful and disrespectful, and themselves the objects of their offspring's scorn.

"Shut up talking about Bohemia," was the cruel comment of a boy to his mother, a thought that was all too common in many other homes. His observation that "we are going to live in America, not in Bohemia,"[14] was true but not wise. His mother simply could not forget her homeland and moreover, the country beauty of her home compared to the ugliness of their Chicago stockyards district seemed an objective contrast worthy of comment.

A mother knew that her basic ideas on life had served her well and that one's system of morality should not be subject to change merely because one had crossed an ocean. Children, however, could not be convinced of this; everything their parents believed was questionable in their minds, especially if those ideas were different from the prevalent American creed.

Immigrant mothers probably made this antagonism worse because of their European notions on the infallible status of elders. "I never heard a mother tell a child honestly that she herself did know about a thing,"[15] said one social worker. Ultimately, a mother undermined her authority this way, for chances were that her child would soon know more about American life than she, and her pretension at knowing things she did not would damage her credibility in more important areas.

Nor was the change easy for the children. Rose Cohen, for example, was pained when she went against her parents' wishes, but she felt that she must leave them behind and adopt the ideas of the new country. She, like millions of others who had been born in Europe and had emigrated when young, did not really fit anywhere. They straddled two worlds and were different from both their parents and their American peers. Activities that natives viewed as wholly innocent, for example, were wild by the standards of Italian parents; some put daughters in homes for wayward girls because they came in at ten o'clock at night or went to a dance.[16]

Respect for the father was so strong in some southern Italian homes that children and even wives used the formal "you" when addressing him rather than the familiar "thou."[17] Indeed, in many immigrant homes the strongest emotion children had for fathers was not love, but fear. "The children fear Martin," reported a social worker of a tyrannical Irish father, "but mimic him in his absence. They do not ask God to bless him in their prayers."[18]

Elizabeth Stern suggests—and the conventional wisdom seems to agree—that there was a direct reversal in European and American views of fathers and mothers. She greatly respected and feared her father in the European tradition, while, she observed, her American boyfriend spoke of his mother with reverence and his father as more of a pal. Indeed, Americans have traditionally revered motherhood, whereas fathers are sometimes treated as a joke.

If the father ranked at the head of the family, the daughter ranked at the bottom. While this was true to some extent of all nationalities, Italians illustrated the point in its baldest form. A sociologist commented:

Here, as in Italy, the Italian girl is generally the least important member of the family. Her father and brothers, by the
very fact of their sex, hold complete authority . . . while the
mother has precedence. . . . In one family that I know the 19
year old daughter is the sole support of a hard-drinking, idle
parasite of a father, a sick mother and three shiftless younger
brothers, yet she is not allowed to eat at the table and sleeps
on a cot in the kitchen. . . . I have known an Italian to drag
his 13 year old daughter by the hair (its being unbobbed was
another proof of his authority) before the little statue of the
Virgin . . . and force her to remain on her knees before it for
3 hours, asking forgiveness for having helped herself before
him at the table to the Sunday chicken. . . . In fact, I have
known an Italian to take the strap to his married daughter
when he felt that her husband was handling her with too
American a leniency.[19]

Some Italian women grew to resent the way they had been exploited by their families. One fifty-nine-year-old woman remembered with venom that in the Old Country "girls never went to
school, but were made to work." "Nine years in the United States
had not yet softened the bitter memories of another woman who
had begun work on her father's land when only seven years old . . .
'I worked like a horse, not like a woman,' she said."[20]

While immigrant girls were subject to more severe family discipline than American girls, immigrant boys were less restrained
than natives. The primary reason for this was simply the superior
status of the European male. An additional factor may have been
the intervention of American law into family strife. The traditional
method of discipline in much of Europe was a severe beating, but
immigrants found that American society would not allow that. The
father was viewed as the offender, not the child. Their bewildered
response to this sometimes resulted in no discipline at all, since
they knew no method other than beating. The child, as he grew
old enough to grasp the situation, was apt to take unfair advantage
of the law.

The family strife caused by Lou Pagano, the Pagano's eldest son,
is an example of the problems families had with recalcitrant sons
and the divisions they could create between husband and wife.
Lou was in constant trouble with school authorities and dropped
out against his parents' wishes. He "moved in and out of the house
as he pleased" and went into professional boxing without his parents' knowledge. He gambled, chased women, got into fights and

even was stabbed in the chest. Finally his father learned of his
boxing activities, and was enraged that his son should follow such
a lowly profession, and worse, conceal it from his family. They had
a row and Lou ran away. Mrs. Pagano was full of recrimination for
her husband and worry for her son. Lou sent occasional postcards,
but was gone for a year. The following Christmas he turned up,
in answer to his mother's prayers.

His father ignored his presence, but the rest of the family welcomed him. To the younger children, he was a hero:

> It was almost as though he was boasting about his travels to
> irritate my father. And you could feel the breach widening
> between them. . . . But none of us cared. For the first time in
> our memory my father had been pushed into the back-
> ground. . . . And all of us shivered in secret delight. It was as
> though Lou were paying off the grievances which each of
> us . . . had accumulated against my father, and to which we
> had never, until now, had any recourse.[21]

Lou continued his dissolute habits and his father maintained an
icy silence as Lou drove the wedge deeper between him and his
wife. Mrs. Pagano was so grateful for his return that she defended
him blindly at first, but slowly she too grew disgusted with his
behavior. One day she burst out in agitated Italian: "Always it is
the same. First you do the bad thing to break your parents' hearts,
and then you tell us to keep quiet. Keep quiet yourself! You are
my son, and I am your mother."[22] Her admonition had no effect
and two weeks after this, Lou left again.

He turned up later in the Army, fighting in World War I. Now
the parental attitudes reversed. Mr. Pagano, carried away with the
patriotic hysteria that this war generated, was proud of his son,
while Mrs. Pagano disapproved. She was fearful for his safety, but
she also could see no logical difference between professional boxing and professional soldiering. Thus the gulf between them that
Lou caused grew deeper.

Mr. Pagano ". . . wanted to have the [Army] picture framed and
put on the mantel." Mrs. Pagano protested, "So that you can put
out your chest and act proud? You, who acted like a mad dog when
he was home!"[23] It developed into the first serious fight they had
in many years of marriage. She spat in his face and he left her.
He saw to the family's support, but he refused to go home. She
was equally stubborn and angrily refused relatives' appeals for

compromise. This went on for months—until the news came that Lou was dead. Mr. Pagano returned and the grieving parents, whose child had caused them such tragedy, mourned him to-gether. But the mistakes had been made when he was young and were typical of the mistakes immigrant parents made over and over again in giving their sons, especially the firstborn, more freedom than they could handle, while depriving their daughters of any.

———

Old age was a major impediment to emigration, both because the aged were more reluctant to leave home and because they were less capable of surviving the rigors of travel and admission. There-fore the first-generation home usually did not have grandparents as was the case in the Old World. For women this meant the loss of live-in help with family chores. For children it meant the loss of affection grandparents give. For the aged, it meant loneliness at the end of life. Rose Cohen's blind grandmother realized when her son fled to America that his family would soon follow and only her twenty-one-year-old unmarried daughter would be left. She understood that to burden this young woman with elderly parents and no dowry would ruin her chances in Russia, so she bravely determined that her daughter should go to America. She and her husband would remain in Russia to await their lonesome death. At last they were separated even from each other when no one was willing to board both of them. The sacrifices such mothers made for their families were every bit as great as the sacrifices of younger mothers in America.

While the aged did not generally emigrate, within a decade or two immigrant homes had their own elderly, for the hard work of America wore out bodies at an early age. The menial work at which most immigrants toiled required youthful vigor, and both men and women past age forty had a hard time finding jobs. Social workers commented that immigrants referred to themselves as old when they were still young by American standards. A forty-two-year-old Italian, for example, who earned only slightly more than his seven-teen-year-old daughter, excused himself from any greater share in supporting his nine-member family because "it is hard for an old man to find work."[24]

Older family members sometimes became a burden and resent-ment of the elderly began to appear. Old World traditions of ven-eration of the aged conflicted with the American necessity that everyone earn, and with American notions that vigor and youth were attributes more admirable than experience and wisdom. Yet Old World mores—and even those of America—would not yet permit exclusion of the elderly from the home, so they stayed, knowing perhaps that they were unwanted and unappreciated. An Italian woman succinctly explained, "My husband's mother lives with us. She makes me much work, but what can I do? We must keep her or lose face."[25]

The reluctance of the Americanized to assume responsibility for elderly parents is seen in this Jewish woman's missive:

> In Galicia, I was a respected housewife and my husband was a well-known businessman. God blessed us with three daughters and three sons and we raised them properly. When they grew up, one by one they left home, like birds leaving their nest. . . . I was left all alone. I longed for the children and wrote to them that I wanted to come to America to be with them and the grandchildren. But from the first they wrote to me that America was not for me, that they do not keep kosher and that I would be better off staying at home.[26]

The young were not entirely selfish, for it is true that the elderly did have difficulty in adjusting. Most knew this and did not attempt to uproot themselves in the autumn of their lives. Nonetheless it is plain that grandparents, who were an unquestioned feature of Old World households, came to be viewed as a liability in many American homes.

If the elderly became unwanted, there was a second category of person that was even less wanted: the stereotype of cruelty to stepchildren seems to have a great deal of basis in fact. Because of the greater likelihood of early parental deaths and because of the immigrants' distaste for the single state, stepchildren were common in immigrant homes. This was a frequent source of disruption as natural children and stepchildren battled each other and parents. A study of delinquent Chicago children in 1912 cites many examples of stepparents who were severe to the point of sadism, their cruelty leading to the delinquency of the child. One German-born woman was unabashed in her callousness towards her husband's children. "A person can barely care for her own children. How can she care for . . . strange ones?" The probation officer recorded that she said "she hated the children and that her only interest in them was due to the fact that they could earn when they were fourteen years old."[27]*

There were of course some loving stepmothers, too; Rebekah Kohut had one and became one. Yet, while her stepmother had reared her and five siblings without apparent resentment, when Rebekah wanted to marry a widower with eight children, her stepmother was adamantly opposed. After a year she saw them married, but "my marriage seemed to her more like a funeral ceremony. As she told me later, the thought of my being immured within the walls of a home that was already filled with children seemed too terrible."[28] Society did seem to feel that stepmothers were unfairly exploited by their foster children, and excused them when they were undeniably hardhearted.

There was another—and kindlier—surrogate mother in some immigrant homes. Older sisters were often forced into a motherhood role when still children because of the excessive burdens of their mothers. Rosa Cavalleri's oldest daughter, when she was still under ten, cared for the other children while her mother worked; Rose Cohen's maternal attitude toward her siblings is seen in her continual references to them as "our children." Sometimes, however, the sacrifices these girls made were unappreciated by the young, who instead resented the sister for trying to assume the authority of the mother. Even when they were older, the sister's efforts were often still not acknowledged. Theresa Malkiel wrote of her friend Clara, a big, clumsy girl whose work-roughened hands testified to her tender heart, for she had been in the factory since youth, working first to bring her siblings to America and then to educate them and provide them with luxuries she had never had. Their thanks was to scorn Clara's poor English and to be ashamed of her around their American friends.

Lotte Bauer was another sister who encountered all of the problems of mothers. A German girl, her father had been killed in one of Prussia's wars and her grandfather held strict control over the family. He had resisted appeals to emigrate, but as one after another of his young sons were killed in the military, he took his daughter-in-law and her family and went. At first things went well, but suddenly her mother sickened and died. Lotte had to redouble her efforts to replace this lost income. A younger child followed

---

*My own grandfather was sent out to earn his own living at age eleven by his German stepmother when his father died.

the mother to the grave, and Lotte was unable to keep her attractive and fun-loving fourteen-year-old sister out of trouble. The sister eventually ran away and entered a brothel. The final calamity came when her grandfather was hit by a falling barrel while he worked as a stevedore and left hopelessly paralyzed. For a year Lotte desperately tried to care for him and the younger children, while her long-time boyfriend abandoned her because she refused to institutionalize the children. She drove herself relentlessly, and it killed her. She suffered an apparent brain hemorrhage and died, quickly and young.[29]

The children of this family were then probably broken up and sent to foster homes and orphanages. It was something that happened with greater frequency to immigrant families, where death was more likely to claim parents before children were grown. The result was that children of many immigrant homes lived their adult lives without knowledge of their siblings. Oceanic separation and illiteracy of course increased the problem. An Irish woman said of her family: "There were seven children of us. John and Matthew they went to Australia. Mother was layin' by for five year to get their passage money. . . . We heard twice from thim and then no more. Not another word and this is forty year gone now—on account of them not reading and writing. . . . I suppose they're dead now—John would be 90 now—and in heaven."[30]

There was tremendous variation in the contact siblings kept with each other. Collections of immigrant letters show that some wrote home only every five or ten years, others wrote annually; still others much more often—and some never. What siblings had in common after many years of separation was a factor, too. Gro Svendsen, for example, kept in close contact with her family even after long years of separation; they were farmers as she was and they read the same Norwegian publications, for Gro often says, "You already know from the newspapers. . . ." On the other hand, women who adopted new factory occupations and a city life-style unlike their European siblings perhaps found they had few mutual interests and might give up communication with siblings who probably never would be seen again.

Many Europeans—especially the Irish—brought relatives here without thought of repayment, but paying interest to close relatives on loans was not at all uncommon. Occasionally exorbitant rates were demanded; one Jewish girl paid her brother-in-law 40 percent interest on a loan.[31] Likewise, some families welcomed a newly arrived relative and were glad to offer board without charge; others were grudging and charged more than the lodging was worth. Boarding with siblings also meant that they—or their spouses— then might adopt a dictatorial role. One Italian girl who lived with her sister found that her brother-in-law would not allow the women to drink the wine she had purchased for Christmas Eve. "He felt he could control my life the way he did hers. He resented the fact that I saved my money in a bank instead of handing it over to him to 'take care of it.' "[32]

Despite disapproving brothers-in-law, a sociologist who studied widowed and deserted mothers found that when they did go to a relative for help, women were far more likely to turn to sisters than brothers. "The brothers, no doubt," she added, "are making their contribution to the support of their wives' semi-dependent sisters."[33] It was an interestingly matriarchial arrangement whereby a man gave support to his wife's sister rather than to his own. On the whole, however, both this study and others showed that family members took their financial debts very seriously and there was little generosity based on blood—even to impoverished widows.

Irish families seem to exhibit particularly strong bonds between adult siblings. More than other immigrant groups, Irish women remained single, with over one-fourth of them in 1920 being unmarried.[34] Many Americans observed that Irish women were extremely devoted to their families, remaining single, staying in one job, and supporting parents and siblings with their wages. The autobiography of an Irish cook fits this pattern; she and her sister emigrated first and saved to bring their brothers and at last their parents. Her joy in accomplishing this goal is evident:

> We rented a little house in Kensington for them. There was a parlor in it and kitchen and two bedrooms and bathroom and marble door step, and a bell. That was in '66 and we paid $9 a month rent. . . . It took all our savings to furnish it, but Mrs. Bent and Mrs. Carr [employers] gave us lots of things to go in. To think of mother having a parlor and marble steps and a bell! They . . . got here at night, and we had supper for them and the house all lighted up. Well you ought to have seen mother's old face! I'll never forget that night if I live to be a hundred.[35]

All of the children in Mary Paul Hughes's Irish family remained single, one dying young and another being killed in the Civil War. When the mother died in 1865, the daughter and her remaining brother became a nun and a priest.[36] A Fall River weaver showed considerable resentment against the one member of her family who did marry, saying, "If our family had all stuck together and joined a buildin' club, and Tom he hadn't gotten married, we could have owned a cottage by now. . . ."[37] Her father and a younger brother were shiftless drinkers while she and her sister provided the steadying influence in the family, but she resented their alcoholism less than Tom's disloyalty in marrying.

Leaving the group was almost an essential part of Americanization. It was the way to grow, to become independent, and those were the qualities that Americans prized. Sometimes this gave one a perspective on her family that she would not have obtained at closer range. Elizabeth Hasanovitz, for example, had almost no contact with her siblings in America and she had not seen her European parents in years, but it was this distance that allowed her to develop an understanding of her mother that is unusual for a young person. Recalling her parents, she wrote:

> Of both of their lives, hers was the harder. From the time of her marriage she hardly had a carefree day—bearing children every two years, she fought with measles, scarlet fever, typhoid fever . . . she fed them; she clothed them. She gave her life to thirteen children, of whom she buried four. . . . She never saw a bright day until her children grew up. And then—Her oldest boy was in the hated Russian army, another was in prison for carrying the message of Freedom, three children scattered in far-away America—this was the reward of her long years of struggle.[38]

Perhaps it was these memories that made Elizabeth uninterested in marriage and suspicious of romance. Though she was over twenty, she had no thought of marriage and scorned those who saw it as a solution to problems. When World War I broke out, her family wrote of their suffering: "Your brother is being sent to the front. Nathan, who is such a youth, is being reserved. A fine was imposed on me for Sam. . . . I fear we shall face starvation before long."[39]

Of course she was distraught. Yet if Elizabeth had adopted the model of most immigrant women of putting family needs ahead of individual ones, she probably could have brought her loved ones out of Russia before the war. Being a skilled sample-maker, she earned high wages—but she lost job after job when she protested on behalf of workers less fortunate than she. Most women would have thought her devotion to this political ideal foolish; their ideal was the family and they gladly would have made the money and paid the passage. Elizabeth loved her family, but her career and her beliefs meant more to her.

America encouraged such individualism. Families changed from extended to nuclear; the male and the elderly lost their former power; the young had a right to assert themselves. The new nation emphasized the person, not the group, and ultimately this had an emancipating influence on women.

WOMEN'S PLACE IN THE NEW WORLD

IN 1920 only 14 percent of foreign-born women over age fifteen were single, but 37 percent of the second-generation remained unwed.[1] In all sections of the United States and for different time periods, the pattern holds: immigrant women married frequently and young; women of native parentage had the second highest marriage rate; and those who were most likely to be unwed were women who were born in America of foreign parents. There is a remarkable difference between 14 percent and 37 percent; immigrant mothers who married young reared daughters in America whose life pattern was very dissimilar.

Exactly why this was so is debatable. Certainly to some extent it was because young women saw the miserable lives their mothers had and saw that America offered alternatives. The dependency of their mothers made young women wary of taking on a husband and children early in life. The case of Rachael Solomon and her sister-in-law is illustrative. The Solomons came from Syria and did well financially in America. "Mr. Solomon," a sociologist wrote, "has an unmarried daughter who lives at home, but being an American-born girl she is not satisfied to stay at home to look after her father and three brothers but wishes to earn her own living. Bringing a Syrian girl from the Old Country to marry David and keep house was Mr. Solomon's solution of the difficulty."[2] Rachael, the immigrant, would marry young while her sister-in-law, the daughter of immigrants, would remain single.

Daughters of immigrants did not view marriage as necessarily desirable and they rejected arranged marriages as "Old World." On the other hand, their decision to marry later was not always a result of choosing independence, but because of family responsibilities. Many immigrant girls found that instead of the traditional pressure to marry, they were pressured to remain single because their income was essential.

When they did marry, the daughters of immigrants rejected the large families their mothers had.

PERCENTAGE OF WOMEN UNDER 45 AND MARRIED 10 TO 19 YEARS, BEARING MORE THAN 5 CHILDREN, 1900[3]		
	FIRST GENERATION	SECOND GENERATION
Austrian	38.9	19.1
Bohemian	43.9	29.1
Danish	40.8	22.5
English	22.4	10.7
German	39.2	23.4
Irish	40.8	30.2
Norwegian	39.7	34.3
Polish	61.9	38.5
Scotch	23.2	11.6
Swedish	28.7	18.9

Because they stayed single longer and had fewer children, it is to be expected that daughters of immigrants would be more frequently employed, and indeed, that is the case, with more second-generation women working than either immigrants or natives.[4] Whether they worked from choice or because they were scrambling to support their parents' too-numerous offspring is debatable. There was at least some upward mobility in their jobs; one study of working mothers found that while 70 percent of them worked as domestics, over 90 percent of their daughters were in trade and manufacturing.[5] The daughters went to offices and factories that their mothers saw only as cleaning women.

While daughters of immigrants worked more frequently than foreign-born women, the sons of immigrants were less often employed than foreign-born men.[6] Upward mobility for the women meant a factory job instead of domestic work, but for their brothers

it apparently meant higher education or increased leisure while a
larger share of family support fell to the women.

The improvement in female status was admittedly slow, but compared with the treatment of women in much of Europe, there were
tremendous strides. Such a major attitudinal change had to begin
with discontent and self-examination on the part of the women
themselves. Finding the courage and independence to question the
accepted ways was a painful process, but while Europeans were
concerned with "place," Americans encouraged the ambitious, and
this atmosphere made it easier for women to raise themselves. A
Jewish woman who felt her husband's idea of her status was wrong
wrote to a newspaper advice column in 1910 to find support for
her goals:

> Since I do not want my conscience to bother me, I ask you
> to decide whether a married woman has the right to go to
> school two evenings a week. My husband thinks I have no
> right to do this.
> I admit that I cannot be satisfied to be just a wife and
> mother... My children and my house are not neglected...
> My husband is not pleased and when I come home at night
> and ring the bell, he lets me stand outside a long time inten-
> tionally, and doesn't hurry to open the door.... When I am
> alone with my thoughts, I feel I may not be right.[7]

Linka Preus began questioning her sex role much earlier, in the
1840s, while she was still unmarried. She prefaces her comments
with self-denigrating remarks, but goes ahead with her discon-
tented musings:

> Frequently I think of the many advantages a man has over
> a woman.... Since I am convinced that Nature has equally
> endowed us, why then should we not without reproach de-
> velop our abilities? Certainly Nature has not given them to us
> just in order that we should season food and darn stockings.
> The Lord's purpose without a doubt is that we should cultivate
> our minds, not forgetting that first and foremost we should
> become capable housemothers.[8]

Linka apparently put her independent ideas to the back of her
mind as she grew older. Weighed down by the responsibilities of
managing a parsonage and farm and in poor health, she made little
effort to see that her daughters got a better opportunity. Her sons
were educated at Lutheran institutions, but since no such insti-

tutions existed for girls, their formal learning was much more sketchy.

Some women grew more determined with age. This was especially likely if one came from continental Europe where girls were literally beaten into subordination. Rosa Cavalleri was entirely submissive to her mother and husband when she was young, but after she freed herself of them in America, she grew very independent. Many times she speaks with contempt of the way she and other Italian girls were easily frightened and with admiration of American females who were, in Rosa's view, beautifully self-reliant.

Likewise, Mrs. Pagano began life in America as a half-starved waif, but as a married woman she grew more and more assertive, taking the lead in pushing her family's upward mobility. It was she who insisted they move away from the Colorado coal camps, while her husband complacently replied that they had enough to eat. Slowly, though, it dawned on him that she was right: the children would have better opportunities in a larger town. But he could not admit that she was right—he simply went out and bought a partnership in a saloon in a nearby town. Then he ran excitedly home to inform her:

> If he had expected her to give him any satisfaction, however, he was to be sorely disappointed. Secretly nettled, no doubt, that he had not taken her into his confidence beforehand, [she] merely nodded her head, straightened her apron, and looking at him pointedly, gave vent for the first time to the phrase which he was to hear more than once during the ensuing years. "So! You finally realized I was right after all!"[9]

Nor was Mrs. Pagano content to stay in Rockton. If business was good there, she reasoned, it would be even better in Denver. This time they were not so lucky, but when her husband suggested going back to the smaller town, she was determined to tough it out. Ultimately the family moved on to Salt Lake City and Los Angeles with Mrs. Pagano always insisting that her children—especially the boys—have the best educational opportunities. The outwardly passive Italian wife who appeared to be dominated by her husband might in fact be very independent within her home.

Dominant women were exceptional. More commonly men and women joined forces to keep sex roles well-defined and to put defiers in their place. For example, although it was generally a source of family and community pride when a woman became a nun (and certainly when a man became a priest), the Italians among Sister Blandina Segale's family and friends did not want her to be too independent. When she was assigned to travel alone to a mission in frontier Colorado, they (especially her father) tried to dissuade her.[10]

While she was strong enough to insist upon her right to choose, many others were not, and families were sometimes so fearful of independence in women that they discouraged even a convent career. "I got married like everyone else. I did what was expected of me," said one Italian woman. "The only other possibility I had considered as a young girl was to become a nun, but my parents were against this. Even my grandparents, who were very kind and loving, told me to pray for a husband."[11]

Girls were taught from birth not to have high expectations, to accept inferior treatment without regret or question. Many even understood that they should expect less love, especially from fathers whose pride in their sons caused them to overlook daughters. The baldest cases of this came from eastern cultures. An Armenian woman who already had two sons wrote that when a daughter was born, "My husband was so disappointed because she was a girl that he refused to see her or name her."[12] A young Polish girl, writing to her father in America, likewise complained of disparate treatment of her and her brother, "I received one rouble from you, for which I thank you heartily. I am somewhat pained that you always make a difference between us two. We are never equally treated, but he always gets more than I do, as if I were not your daughter. But nothing can be done. Dear father, if you love Romek more than me, what can I do?"[13]

In this case the very fact that she dared to complain and question is probably based on her knowledge that she was loved as much or more, for her father himself wrote of his son, "he is very sentimental . . . while Hela has my iron nature."[14] But while he takes pride in his daughter and is somewhat contemptuous of his son, discrimination against her is automatic. Mothers joined with fathers in discouraging daughters. One, who had "read in the paper what is going on in the world," would not allow her daughter to go out unaccompanied. When the girl argued that her brothers could do so, the stock reply came, "It is permitted to the boys, for they are boys. . . . So, my dear husband," she continued, "admonish her always. . . ."[15]

A girl's goal was marriage, not independence, and all her training was aimed at this end. If by some fluke she failed to marry, she could expect to be considered almost unnatural. "Many a time," wrote a sociologist, "has one of our investigators met with kindly and courteous, but pitying, comments of Italian men and women who have marveled at her cheerfulness though still unmarried after the ripe age of twenty-five."[16]

Social workers commented that sometimes women were so rigid in their wifely roles that they seemed incapable of anything else. Though many met hardships with resourcefulness, others seemed totally dependent upon "the charity." Even when such women worked, they found it hard to concede that they were stepping out of traditional roles. An enterprising Italian who had learned book-keeping and typing could not wholly acknowledge this break with tradition, for her typing was "not fast like you have to do it here, but like a lady would know how to do it."[17]

Work roles and family training taught females subservience, but perhaps the most serious of all pressures came from religious teachings. Linka Preus's rebellion quoted earlier was tempered largely because she believed that submission of women was divinely ordained, as taught to her by her church. Indeed, both Christians and Jews taught that women were lesser beings, whose inferior place was the intention of God. While almost all held this doctrinal belief, it was more easily ignored in some religions than in others. Probably those who agonized most over sex roles were Mormon women. Fanny Stenhouse, an English Mormon who also lived in France and Switzerland, said in part:

> I now began to feel perfectly reckless, and even willing to throw aside my religion and take "my chance of salvation," rather than submit to Polygamy; for I felt that the new doctrine was a degradation to womankind. I asked myself "Why did the Lord wish to humiliate my sex in this manner?"
> ... I would not have my readers think that I bore all my troubles meekly, like a saint. Indeed I did not . . . I was a sore trial to my husband. I was wicked and rebellious at times, and said very bitter things of the "Prophet of the Lord," and all his sex, my husband included; for I began to hate the very name "Man." . . . I felt that womankind was insulted whenever the subject [polygamy] was mentioned, and I never got over the feeling. . . .

I was told by my husband, and the other elders . . . that it
devolved on me to teach the hateful doctrine to the women of
Switzerland. That was to be my mission, and I, poor, deluded
thing that I was, believed it to be so. I concealed my feelings
as best I could.[18]

After her emigration to Salt Lake City Mrs. Stenhouse wrote that
young women were beginning to question the doctrine of polygamy, for it had "made such bad men of their fathers and such
victims of their mothers. It is not our city girls who maintain so
much the plural marriages, but it is chiefly the newly arrived English and country girls who supply the Patriarchs."[19] One such
immigrant woman had promised while still in Europe to marry a
missionary, but changed her mind en route to Utah. He insisted
that her oath to marry him had the full effect of marriage and
breaking it would put her salvation in jeopardy. She finally agreed,
but said, "I have fulfilled my covenant, but I have wrecked my
happiness, for I cannot bear the man I have married. I have told
him so . . . but he does not care."[20]

Polygamous marriages often had the ironic effect of making
women more independent. Men with a dozen or more families
could not support them all, and women were enjoined to "eat their
own bread." Sometimes a husband traveled a circuit between his
various "homes" and wives saw him only a few weeks of the year.
Women farmed alone and supported themselves and their children; the only thing a polygamous husband gave to the family was
his name and his "glory."

Though women supported the doctrines of the church into
which they had been catechized, doubtless there was much quiet
rejoicing when Congress made Utah's statehood contingent upon
the outlawing of polygamy. In this, at least, American society aimed
at uplifting the status of women. Most of the changes in the New
World did mean a gain for women, but there would also be an
occasional loss. One was the customary insistence in America that
a woman take her husband's name, whereas in some European
cultures a woman individualized her surname.

Polish women used their husband's names, but personalized
them by adding an "a" where he used an "i." Wiktorya Osinska,
for example, was the wife of Antoni Osinski. Children in Latin
cultures sometimes were given part of the mother's name as well
as the father's; Czech women individualized their husband's

names by adding "ova" as a suffix, and similar variations appear in other groups. Scandinavian women, including Danes, used "datter"—a woman would be Pattersdatter while her brother would be Patterson.

In most of Gro Svendsen's letters, for instance, she signed her name either "Gro" or "Gro Nilsdotter." When she signed both her and her husband's names, she wrote either "Ole Svendsen and Gro Nilsdot" or "Gro and Ole Svendsen." The last form of signature is used only four times in the entire collection of her letters, and those are at the end when perhaps she was beginning to accept the American way, although even then she did not use it consistently. (Once she indicated her awareness of American names by writing "Svendsen" as "Swenson.") In the vast majority of letters, Gro called herself by her maiden name and obviously thought of that as her name.

Slavic women had their own name forms, but one writer who was sympathetic to Slavs could find no charitable words to say about the status of women in that part of Europe:

> . . . abhorrent even to the strongest "Slavophile" is the position occupied by women. . . . To escape the charge of prejudice, I shall quote a few proverbs current among the Southern Slavs—a few out of many hundreds:
> "The man is the head, the woman is grass."
> "One man is worth more than ten women."
> "A man of straw is worth more than a woman of gold."
> "Let the dog bark, but let the woman keep silent."
> . . . She is valued only for the work she can do . . . and for the children she can bear. . . . In Montenegro the proverb says, "My wife is my mule," and she is treated accordingly. . . . It would, of course, be unjust to charge every Slav with beating his wife, but unfortunately, it is the rule rather than the exception. . . . That the Slavic woman possesses the qualities to make of herself a "new woman" can be plainly seen among the women of the higher class in Russia, where there is a second paradise for women; America, by common consent, being the first.[21]

Kyra Goritzina was one of those Russian women who enjoyed the "second paradise;" she, too, consistently spelled her name thus even after long residence in America while calling her husband "Goritzin." Even more interesting is that she apparently believed in "a room of one's own." In most jobs she and her husband took as cook and butler, they were given two rooms. Although they were

very close and she had great admiration and love for him, instead
of using one room as a sitting room and the other as bedroom,
they maintained separate rooms. This seemed to be important to
her, for among her most happy writing is commentary on furnishing and improving "my" room.

But it was "women of the higher class" who gained advantages
in Europe. Class was probably a more important factor than nationality, for women of the upper class had more in common with
women halfway across Europe than they did with the manor slaves
who served them—and lower-class women felt likewise. Though
America likes to think of herself as classless, the era from the Civil
War to World War I, when most immigrants arrived, saw the most
well-defined classes of our history. Emigration almost always
meant at least a temporary reduction in class status.

This happened to Jewish Mrs. Frowne, who was nothing in the
new land, but an important person in the old. Her daughter Sadie
wrote that she had run a grocery store in her village. "That was
in Poland, somewhere on the frontier, and mother had charge of
a gate between the countries, so that everybody who came through
had to show her a pass. She was much looked up to by the people,
who used to come and ask her for advice. Her word was like law
among them."[22]

That the poorly dressed woman who could scarcely make herself
understood had once been an authority figure would seldom occur
to Americans. They would instead presume her inferiority, and she,
being treated this way so entirely, would accept it. The inferiority
that Americans imposed because of class and origin would be rein-
forced by her family because of sex.

Situations of course varied depending on the power of individual
personalities, and there were variations among the cultures as well,
but throughout immigrant society, the fundamental inequality of
the sexes was undebatable. Most women as well as men accepted
that this was the way life was and therefore ought to be. The fa-
talists were many, and the rebels few. Linka Preus would not have
found many receptive listeners had her musings been aloud, and
knowing that, she tried to repress them. Sometimes, though, the
truth would out when she thought "of the many advantages a man
has over a woman:"

It is not my opinion that he is more gifted than a woman, but
that his mind has been better developed by many kinds of
knowledge than has woman's. Her intellectual growth is re-

garded as of secondary importance, as something useless, bringing no benefit to the world. When these thoughts occupy my mind, I frequently become embittered, as it all seems so unjust.[23]

PART VII

Content
and
Discontent

VIEWS OF THE
NEW WORLD

THOUGH the life-styles of daughters of immigrants varied from those of their mothers, they were still inextricably bound to the home and family. This was even more true for first-generation women. It would be economic need that would bring change. The need to survive forced a woman out of the lethargy of fatalistic acceptance, and into the competitiveness of American life. She began to develop a sense of self-worth and independent capabilities. She made a tremendous and still largely unrecognized contribution to the growth of her adopted land. It was her labor—on farm, in factory and store, streets and homes—which built a nation.

Change was accompanied by ambivalence. Changes in areas so seriously fundamental as sex roles and morality and the basic beliefs by which we guide our lives take place at a rate that is imperceptible. Though there were those occasional people—usually young and adventurous—who flung themselves with abandon into everything American, for most there were years of holding back, years of acceptance.

Even those who are credited with easy assimilation had mixed feelings about this acculturation, holding on to parts of the old life. The Scandinavians in the Midwest certainly rank high on a historian's list of easily assimilated groups, yet the diaries of the women who lived there show another point of view. Except for rare references to a Yankee storekeeper or postmaster, their writings focus almost entirely on each other. While their emigration was permanent and they did not hope to return to their native land, many of these women considered Scandinavian culture to be superior. They had no intention of changing their fundamental beliefs and made as few changes as possible in their life-style.

Nor did surface indications of assimilation necessarily mean that one was in fact becoming Americanized. Usually an immigrant began work within a few days of her arrival, an apparent indication of rapid acculturation, but whether or not that was the case depended on where one worked. Rose Cohen went to work immediately, but her tailor shops were filled with other aliens. Her first trip out of the East Side took place several years later when she was hospitalized; only then did she meet Americans and see another way of life:

> Although almost five years had passed since I had started for America it was only now that I caught a glimpse of it. For though I was in America I had lived in practically the same environment which we brought from home. Of course there was a difference in our joys, in our hardships . . . but on the whole we were still in our village in Russia. A child that came to this country and began to go to school had taken the first step into the New World. But the child that was put into the shop remained in the old traditions, held back by illiteracy. Often it was years before he could stir away from it, sometimes it would take a lifetime.[1]

Though Rose felt those five years had been wasted, actually she and her family made significant adjustments long before. This description of an incident that took place four years earlier shows how momentous changes could occur, and yet the process of assimilation had only begun:

> Mother had been here only a short time when I noticed that she looked older and more old-fashioned than father . . . It was so with most of our women, especially those who wore wigs or kerchiefs on their heads. So I thought that if I could persuade her to leave off her kerchief she would look younger and more up to date. But remembering my own first shock, I decided to go slowly . . . So, one day, when . . . we two were alone in the house, I asked her playfully to take off her kerchief and let me do her hair, just to see how it would look.
>
> She consented reluctantly. She had never before in her married life had her hair uncovered before anyone. . . . I was surprised how different she looked. . . . I handed her our little mirror. . . . She glanced at herself, admitted frankly that it looked well and began hastily to put on her kerchief. . . .
>
> "Mamma," I coaxed, "please don't put the kerchief on again—ever!"
>
> At first she would not even listen to me. . . . I began to coax and beg and reason. I . . . pointed out that wives often looked so much older because they were more old-fashioned, that the husbands were often ashamed to go out with them. . . .
>
> Mother put her finger on my lips.

"But father trims his beard," I still argued. Her face looked sad. "Is that why," she said, "I too must sin?"

But I finally succeeded.

When father came home that evening and caught sight of her while still at the door, he stopped and looked at her with astonishment. "What!" he cried, half earnestly, half jestingly, "Already you are becoming an American lady!" Mother looked abashed for a moment; in the next, to my surprise and delight, I heard her brazen it out in her quiet way.

"As you see," she said, "I am not staying far behind."[2]

Another way in which Rose had begun to Americanize even before the arrival of her mother was in changing her name. She had gone from Rahel to Ruth to Rose, encouraged by her co-workers to have a New World name. This was standard procedure for many; Rose Schneiderman was originally named Rachel; her brothers Ezekial and Aaron became Charles and Harry. Their parents thought the new names "sounded nicer."[3] A Norwegian writer commented that "Aase, Birthe, Siri, became changed at an incredible speed to Aline, Betsy and Sarah."[4] Still there certainly were those—such as Linka Preus and Gro Svendsen—who found such imitation distasteful and proudly clung to their native names.

Adults were sufficiently rooted in their traditional ways that they could ignore the winds of change. Children had no such roots, and nothing is worse to a child than the mockery of his peers. Rose Cohen's brother was embarrassed by his sturdy Russian shoes that the neighborhood children scorned. In desperation to be rid of this proof of his greenhorn status, he went to a strange neighborhood, climbed to the roof of a tenement and flung the hated shoes in opposite directions into the dark. He knew he would incur the wrath of parents too poor to buy new shoes, but he felt it was worth it.

Swiss Elise Isely had more understanding adults around her, but the teasing of children was the same: "As I walked to school, I was taunted by 'Know-Nothing' children for being Dutch," she wrote of her childhood in the 1850s. "To them all foreigners were Dutch or Irish; and while they did not know my nationality, they knew I was not Irish."[5] The failure of Americans to draw distinctions between the various Europeans was sometimes more serious. A victim of the Russian revolution, Kyra Goritzina wrote that many American women refused even to interview her for a job when they found she was Russian, their knowledge of world affairs being too meager for them to understand that not all Russians were Bolsheviks.

———————

Historians generally have accepted the notion that women suffered more from homesickness than men, and that it was more difficult for women, often homebound, to become assimilated. The comment of a sociologist speaking of Slavs was typical:

> I get the impression that women are more apt to be homesick than the men, and that in consequence wives often make their husbands return against their wishes. . . . They miss, I think, the variety of work, the employment within doors alternating with field work . . . and most of all the familiar, sociable village life where everyone knows everyone else, and there are no uncomfortable superior Yankees to abash one, and where the children do not grow up to be alien and contemptuous. The men live more out in the world. They get more from America.[6]

Estrangement from one's husband and children was indeed a serious problem. Some women did suffer seriously from homesickness; Gro Svendsen's letters can be almost neurotic on this point. Years after she had emigrated she tormented herself with attacks of conscience over the grief she had caused her parents in leaving them. As the sociologist quoted above believed Slavic women in the steel towns missed farm life, so a German writer at mid-century averred that his female compatriots in the Midwest, particularly the educated ones, missed German town life. "In the country she is obliged . . . to stoop to do work which at home would fall to the most ordinary servant. She has also renounced all the charming enjoyments of a more elegant household . . . and finds herself banished in a solitude which is only enlightened by pictures of the past which seem all the more dazzling from a distance."[7]

On one point there was almost no ambivalence—at least among women—and that was the attitude of men towards women. America encouraged both greater respect and freedom. Young women had more opportunity to live without supervision and more choice in deciding on a husband. The dowry, a symbol of inequality, soon disappeared. Yet while these are changes of real significance and while they occurred very quickly from a historian's point of view, to the individual woman, a longing for her brick oven might indeed be more real than the fact that her daughter wouldn't have to have a dowry, and so the larger ambivalence about America remained.

An important factor in assimilation was whether or not returning home was feasible. To early immigrants from northern Europe, that option was remote; one emigrated with the knowledge that the decision was permanent. The Jews who came later also made a permanent decision; they knew they would never go back to a land of pogroms. These groups were considered good candidates for assimilation.

When transatlantic crossing became easier, the slow assimilation of immigrants from southern and eastern Europe was a subject of frequent comment and criticism. Often illiterate and superstitious, the women trained to timidity, it is natural that adjustment would take some time. Yet the younger women, especially those who were able to go to school here, became Americanized. Rosa Cavalleri's time of triumph came when she returned to Italy for a visit. Though she had been gone only a few years (to Americans she still would be unassimilated, for she knew very little English), Rosa was already proud to be an American. Her new-found confidence in contrast to the timidity of the Italian women became apparent when Rosa went to the bank on business:

All the time more men kept coming and the women had to wait and let the men go first. I stood there waiting and waiting and I got tired. There were some nice chairs there on the other side of a little railing—chairs for the high people. But why should the high people have chairs and not the poor? . . . So finally I did it; I pushed open the little gate and went in and sat down.

"Oh, Rosa,!" gasped the other poor women in the line. "Come back! Come back! You'll get arrested. They'll put you in jail!"

"The chairs are here and nobody is sitting in them," I said.

Soon the janitor came. *"Che impertinenza!"* he said. "Who gave you the permission to sit down?"

"Myself," I said and I smiled at him because I was no longer afraid. "The chairs belong to the bank, isn't that so? And the people who have money in the bank have the right to use them, no?"

"You think you're smart because you come from America!"

"Yes," I said, "In America the poor do get smart. We are not so stupid anymore."

. . . At last all the men had finished their business . . . When it was my turn the officer smiled and bowed and didn't say anything at all about my sitting in the chair.

"If you please," I said in English. "How do you do. Thank you. Goodbye." That Italian officer wouldn't know that the words didn't fit and I wanted to show him that I was learning to speak English. And there he was bowing and smiling so polite and the women were all looking and looking, with their mouths hanging open.[8]

Those who returned home were little noticed by Americans. It is but natural that natives would choose to ignore the fact that some returned, and that those who rejected America would be forgotten. Yet the truth is that from 1908, when the immigration authorities began keeping records on departures, until the end of the era, there were large numbers of aliens who left. The numbers varied with business cycles and war, but the surprising fact is that three of eight arrivals from 1908–20 returned to their native lands.[9]

Moreover, the Immigration Commission concluded that most of these departures were permanent, and not caused by seasonal migratory labor: "a very large proportion of those who return to Europe do not come again to this country."[10] Exactly what role women played in this return rate is not clear. Those who believe that women were likely to be homesick and urged their mates to return will find that the statistics do not necessarily validate this opinion. The Immigration Commission noted after study of its data "a striking predominance of males in the movement from the United States to Europe, 82.7 percent of all departing aliens . . . being of that sex."[11] In 1908–10 those with the lowest rates of return—6 and 8 per 100 admissions—were Scottish, Irish and Jewish, groups with large numbers of female immigrants. On the other hand, those with the highest return rates—69, 64, and 62 per 100—were the Turks, Magyars, and Italians, groups that contained many more male immigrants than females.[12] It seems likely that women viewed the decision to emigrate as a permanent change, whereas males, both single and married, were more likely to view it as a fortune-seeking fling.

Even when the original aim had been to earn money and return, often residence in America changed women's minds. They enjoyed the superior status of women here, and while they still missed their homes, ambivalence grew and time dimmed the memories. A sociologist writing in the 1930s said of her Italian clients:

> Generally speaking few Italians wish to return to Italy to live. Although this may not have been their original intention, immigrants usually stay. Despite early plans to save enough money to return to live in comfort in their old homes, children and the World War and other complications eventually made the prospects seem less alluring. "To visit Italy for a month or two, yes," commented a woman, "but not to stay. They always fight there; every ten years there is a war. The man he goes to fight and the woman she work like the jackass."[13]

Another Italian agreed, commenting perceptively, "I have never been back to the old country. When I had enough money, the war was on; when the war was over I couldn't afford it. Finally, when everything was right I just couldn't go back. Sometimes memories are better than reality."[14] English Kate Bond had similar intentions of returning that did not materialize. She lived in Connecticut in the 1870s and had definite plans to go back. In 1898 the long-postponed return was recognized as only a whim; "I would like to see you," she wrote, "but I shall never leave Kansas. This is my home as long as I am on this earth."[15]

Elise Waerenskjold had written in 1857, "If all goes well . . . it could happen that we might be able to visit."[16] Elise lived thirty-eight more years, but she never returned. Elisabeth Koren, on the other hand, was one of the few Midwesterners of the early era to return for a visit. In the 1870s the Korens and their seven children made a six-month trip to Norway, fulfilling her 1854 promise to herself. "To stay here forever—I cannot think of such a thing, nor can Vilhelm either. . . . No matter if we were ever so comfortable here, and even ever so contented, I would still return. Never to gaze again on what I have left behind—that would be too heavy a burden."[17]

Yet though she went back, it was only for a visit. Her home was in America. As steamers replaced sailing vessels and fares dropped, more and more immigrants would be able to cross the Atlantic merely to visit. Women as well as men went home to settle an estate, do a bit of legal work, tend sick relatives, or simply see old friends. A scholar traveling in Europe circa 1910 mentioned, for example, meeting "a simple peasant woman who had gone home on business" and who was so familiar with her route that she "knew every detail. . . , down to the right street car in Vienna."[18]

A 1911 report on women in the cotton-goods industry showed that many enjoyed visits home:

PERCENTAGE OF WOMEN REPORTING ONE OR MORE VISITS ABROAD AFTER 10 YEARS IN THE U.S.[19]			
Scotch	37	German	23
English	32	Polish	23
Portuguese	32	Irish	21
Swedish	25	Italian	13

Sometimes the motivation to return was not homesickness or even nostalgia; going back could be the immigrant's way of proving to herself and to her peers that she had "made good." Perhaps because she had visited Italy once and enjoyed the respect given her, Rosa Cavalleri wished to go again in her old age. The first time, although her Americanization was sufficient to impress the villagers, Rosa knew that she was still green; if she could go back again, her triumph would be complete.

> Only one wish more I have; I'd love to go to Italia again before I die. Now I speak English good like an American. I could go anywhere—where millionaires and high people go. I would look the high people in the face and ask them what questions I'd like to know. . . . I'd be proud I come from America and speak English. . . . They wouldn't dare hurt me now I come from America. Me, that's why I love America. That's what I learned in America: not to be afraid.[20]

As the debarkation figures indicate, there certainly were those who did return permanently. Some had come with high hopes, were disappointed and went back; others came with the expectation of returning after they had made enough money in America to live comfortably in the Old World. There was the German candymaker who was saving for a farm back home;[21] the Portuguese family whose aim was to return to the sunny Azores with a fortune;[22] the French dressmaker who candidly said she came "on account of the money, as there is no country like France."[23] They were not dissatisfied with the American economic system. They recognized that it helped them to achieve their aims, but they apparently were unimpressed with other aspects of American life.

Some, like the French dressmaker and her roommate, did not try to accommodate themselves to this country. Their world was their work, and there they did very well. They had risen from beginning salaries of six dollars a week—which they viewed as a huge improvement over their salaries in Paris—to the truly munificent sum of forty dollars weekly in early-century dollars. But money was their object only in that it could be used to return: "To one born in England, Germany, Austria, Holland or Scandinavia this [America] may appear fine, but not so to the French. There is but one France and only one Paris in all the world, and soon, very soon, Annette and I will be aboard some great ship that will bear us back there."[24]

Returning often was not necessarily related to dissatisfaction with America, but rather some factor of one's personal life. The Scandinavian woman whose husband, parents, and son died soon after their arrival surely would have returned if she could have. "How hard and miserable it will be for me," she wrote, "left behind with six small children, to settle on land that has not even been cleared. . . . If I could talk to any of you, my . . . most fervent plea would be that you never think of America."[25] The Irish nursemaid whose little charge died at the same time her boyfriend took her savings and disappeared, probably returned not because of any fault of the country but because her personal loss was more than she could bear. Danish milliner Anna Walther also was unhappy for her first several years here, again, not because she was particularly disillusioned with America, but because of a frustrated love affair.

Sometimes women returned because someone in Europe needed their aid. An Austrian girl whose father was blind knew that he would never be admitted to the United States and that the day might come when duty would call her home to care for her aging parents.[26] Some returned for their health; Italians particularly when afflicted with tuberculosis went back to the sunshine of home.[27] A number of Italian girls told interviewers that they came to earn a dowry and their intention was to return to improved marital prospects.[28]

Even those who returned because they wanted to often found that home was not as they remembered it. Their experiences abroad had affected them and they no longer "fit in" at home.

American attitudes made returnees less willing to show deference to officials and social superiors, more assertive and impatient. A story is told of a traveler in Croatia who asked the villagers why they did not fix the tremendous hole in their road where vehicles broke down. The answer was, "No one told us to, sir."[29] One who had lived in America could no longer accept such attitudes.

A returnee could become a person without a country; no longer happy in the Old World, yet unwilling to accept the New. As Europe had appeared doubly attractive from afar, so the memories of America might improve as time dimmed reality. The woman who had lived abroad generally was accorded a special respect in her community, and self-importance could change her mind about the experience. "In a little village in Hungary," noted one writer, "I know a woman who in her youth had tasted . . . the freedom of life in Chicago. Now, although she has been married fifteen years and has lived away from America longer than that, she speaks with glowing eyes of the time when she lived on South Halstad Street, ate thin bread with thick jam on it, and the land was flowing with sausages, lager beer, and chewing gum."[30]

Whether or not they were ultimately pleased with their decision, the fact remains that many more immigrants left our land than we generally acknowledge. Others probably would have left if the body could move as easily as the mind. Only poverty kept some from making the return voyage. A Jewish woman who wanted "to mention that she came from a respectable family" and that her dowry had been six hundred rubles, described the trauma of her first years in the Promised Land:

> When we came to America . . . we . . . went through a lot. . . . Our two little children stretched out their bony little hands to us, begging for food. . . . Because we owed the landlord six dollars for rent, he put us out on the street. I huddled with the two children near our few belongings. . . . The neighbors and passers-by threw a few cents into a plate. . . . But the clung of the coins falling into the plate tore at my heart and I wept bitter tears.[31]

Ida Lindgren never got over her initial disappointment and returned to Sweden in 1881. Her diary written in 1870 reads:

> What shall I say? Why has the Lord brought us here? Oh, I feel so oppressed, so unhappy! . . . We drove across endless,

endless prairies.... The rooms Albinson had written he
wished to rent us were not available but we were quartered
here in Albinson's attic.... When I asked ... to go up with
the children and put them to bed, there was no table, no chair,
no bed, *nothing,* and there we were to stay! I set the candle
on the floor, sat down beside it, took the children in my lap
and burst into tears. . . .[32]

The contrast between expectation and reality made it all so
much harder to bear. Almost everyone in Europe believed that if
American streets were not actually paved with gold, then some
lesser version of that tale was indisputably true. They expected
their virtue to be rewarded; they thought that in a growing nation
there should be work for willing hands. Yet they found that when
work was available, the pittance often paid barely kept starvation
from the door. An elderly German woman cried bitterly, "It is early
that we begin ... and all day we shall sew and sew. We eat no
warm *essen.* . . . We sit not down. . . . No, we stand and eat as we
must and sew more and more. . . . It is fourteen hours efery day—
yes, many times sixteen. . . . My back have such pain that I fall
on the bed to say, *Ach Gott!* is it living to work so in this rich, free
America?"[33]

Maja Johnsson also saw no hope in the remainder of her days.
She was displaced from their farm when her husband died, and
wrote to her niece in Sweden: "Now I am alone in a foreign land,
but I take comfort for His help. He is the same God here as at
home. . . . If you could send me a little money it would be good,
for I am too old to do any work. . . . Forget not one who is alone
in a strange land."[34]

The disillusionment for youth could also be stunning. The
higher one's goals, the greater seemed the likelihood of disappointment. If a woman came merely to get a job or get married, that
end could be fulfilled. If her expectations were more lofty, she was
apt to become bitter.

Elizabeth Hasanovitz was one whose expectations were too high
for the reality. Her hopes were bright when she came, and she
attempted suicide a short time later. Sick from cold and hunger
and seriously depressed, she wrote:

Two years in America! Two years in the golden country! What
had I accomplished?—a weak stomach, headaches every other
day, a pale face, inflamed eyes ... I wanted a doctor and I
could not afford one. . . .

I always got headaches travelling in the subways. In Russia
no more passengers than seats are allowed. Here in free America the people are free to choke themselves with the suffo-
cating subway air. They are thrown together like cattle and
carried down to the industrial market. . . .

If I could forget all the humiliations and return to my old
days, which, though very unhappy because of the Government's brutality to us, though unendurable at the time, still
after . . . American life, seemed the happiest.[35]

It is important to note that Elizabeth never did get out of her
bad situation through the traditionally proclaimed methods of hard
work or good marriage. It was only the merest chance; an American man whom she knew through union activity decided that she
would be an ideal person to write a book encapsulating the strug-
gles of workers. Her life changed overnight, and not because of
anything she did differently. Doubtless there were other Elizabeth
Hasanovitzes who were not so lucky, whose suicide attempts did
not fail.

But it was only because her mind was clouded by illness that
Elizabeth wrote that she would be happier in czarist Russia. No
rational Jew—certainly not an opinionated, freedom-loving one like
herself—could say that in sane moments. For her, and for most
women, the decision to emigrate had been long-considered and
their commitment was a permanent one. It was men, as we have
seen, who were more likely to be fortune-seeking adventurers who
gave up and returned when reality hit them squarely.

While they may have resented an economic system they could
neither understand nor manage, these women seldom resented
those who did control it. The Elizabeth Hasanovitzes were an
anomaly. Most envied the rich only in the sense that they would
ape them if they could. Rose Cohen, working in a nineteenth-
century dress shop, heard a customer refer to a sixty-four dollar
hat as "a bargain" and was amazed, but she was not resentful. Her
attitude seems typical of the mass of workers, especially the young,
who pored over the society pages and followed the activities of the
Morgans and Belmonts with vicarious pleasure. But it was only in
youthful fantasies that a woman compared her life to that of society
ladies. Her European background had instilled strong beliefs about
the propriety of "keeping one's place." She might hope to rise in

America, but it was only a modest improvement that she expected, and that mostly for the sake of her family and not herself.

Because she did not expect to be wealthy, it was easier to find contentment with her lot. Because she thought of the family first, it was easy to believe that even if life in America had not measured up to her hopes, her children would one day bless her for her decision to emigrate. "Children," said a group of Swedes interviewed in the 1850s, "have a better prospect here for their future than at home. They are admitted into schools for nothing; receive good education and easily have an opportunity of maintaining themselves."[36]

For almost everyone the evaluation of America was mixed; there seldom was the quick acceptance of the new land and the complete renunciation of the old that Americans liked to believe of the "wretched, huddled masses." For many immigrants, the move actually involved a reduction in social status and a loss of economic security which was not regained for a decade or a generation.

Rosalie Roos, a woman of some wealth who spent four years in the antebellum South before deciding to return to Sweden, was at first impressed by America but quickly grew disenchanted. She wrote upon arrival, "I felt as though I were in a dream . . . like a princess. . . . Wherever my eyes turned they came upon new, unusual, remarkable objects. . . . It is a little paradise here." Yet soon after she recorded, "I would not wish to advise anyone to come over who believes he is in a position to earn his bread in his homeland. . . . May none of my brothers hit upon the idea of seeking their fortune in America!"[37]

Elise Waerenskjold, whose long life in Texas was filled with praise for her adopted land, nevertheless held to the overwhelming practicality of immigrant women and was candid enough to acknowledge that emigration was not for everyone:

> Anyone who is well situated in Norway ought, in my opinion, to remain. Provided he can lead an independent life there and has the means to hire others to work for him, he will not be better off here but probably worse, since he might not be able to hire help. . . . For the poor and destitute, on the other hand, who have never enjoyed things . . . but from early childhood have been inured to drudgery and toil, there is little to lose and much to gain.[38]

It was a land for the poor, a land where those "inured to hardship and toil" could work and save and eventually build their fortune.

Letters going back to Europe gave realistic encouragement to those who were willing to live by the sweat of their brow; they bore witness to the contentment of the writers. "Please to tell my Father," wrote English textile worker Jane Morris, "that . . . I am often uneasy when I think about him having so large a family to maintain in that country while there is a free and plentiful country so near. . . . If sister Betty was here she could do very well . . . this would be the very place for brother William. . . ."[39] Some Norwegian sisters in 1850 implored their brother: "We all fear that after working so long on the farm in Norway you may eventually end up poor. . . . While here you can work ahead to success and get to own a good deal of property, even though you did not have a penny to begin with. . . ."[40] Likewise, Emily Tongate writing from rural New York in 1874, was perplexed at why others did not follow her example: "John and I have talked quite a good deal about you all and wondered you did not try and come to America. . . . You could have done well out here. This is a good country for working people."[41]

Lisa Jonsdotter Hertman wrote in 1850, "We arrived here . . . in 1846 . . . without any means. Now we owe nobody, own a nice farm, have fenced our property. . . . This is a wonderful country, richly blessed by God. . . . Those who move here can count on coming to the land of Canaan."[42] Maria Steffansson wrote that while her husband "speaks a great deal of moving to Sweden, I don't favor it. . . . I do not believe that I can leave this place until death takes me away. . . . You will not regret coming here if you do not encounter misfortunes—and misfortunes are met with in every country."[43]

The Swedish government in 1907, concerned by emigration, sought anonymous reports from immigrants and many responded, including a North Dakota woman who offered this information and creative advice:

> I am a woman, born in Varmland and belonged to the poor class. I had to go out and earn my bread already at the age of eight. . . . I got rotten herring and potatoes, served out in small amounts. . . . But I was not allowed to neglect Sunday school, for they wanted to drill into us poor people certain Biblical passages, such as "Be godly and let us be contented." . . . Would be best to get the Chinese to emigrate to Sweden. I remember when I was at missionary meetings in Sweden, how they cried and complained over the poor Chinese and his poor soul, and gave substantial contributions to im-

prove his condition. Best to chase out your poor countrymen and take in the dear Chinese.[44]

"I had to work like a dog," said another anonymous respondent. "Go out and spread manure and dirt from the ditches during the summer, and on the snowiest days of winter I had to carry water. . . . Here . . . I was ashamed to get paid for what little I did. . . . Whoever wants to work can get ahead in America. It is a good country and has been a support to many poor people."[45]

Millions joined the chorus, and millions responded by packing their bags to come. It was "a good country for working people;" it was a place for the practical, the ambitious, the optimistic. Naturally there were those—especially the young—who were charmed by the tinsel, the shining newness of this most modern of lands. There was the German girl who thought Coney Island to be "just like what I see when I dream of heaven,"[46] and the young Hungarian who thought "America is the best country" because there she had "white bread and butter and candy, and I can chew gum to beat the band."[47]

Most were more sober and serious. Yet all of these little things did go into building the attraction of the new land. The reasons for liking or disliking America were varied and complex, and they ranged from the profound to the trivial. They differed from woman to woman and within the same woman at different stages of acculturation, in different circumstances and moods.

Though there are very few scientific studies of contentment, in one interview of 500 Boston women at the turn of the century, only 10 percent "felt that their object in coming to this country had not been realized, or expressed a definite discontent or want."[48]

Ultimately the best proof of their satisfaction is that they kept coming. They wrote back for their loved ones who streamed across the sea in ever-increasing waves until finally America closed her gates. Even when a woman felt that she would never totally adjust, even when she judged her emigration to have been too costly in emotional terms, still she believed that the objective reality showed she had done what was best for her children. Her offspring—if they ever stopped to think on it at all—would be plagued by no such questions. The individual born in this country who chose to emigrate to another would be a rare one; future generations would validate their foremothers' decision by assuming that America, whatever its faults, was the best place to live. They would seldom stop to think of the sacrifice that had been made to give them this opportunity, and they could never completely understand the heartache and internal conflict that had been endured. An anonymous emigrant from Arendal, Norway, explains to us through the mists of time her ambivalence and her loneliness and her hope that the decision which was so painful for her in the present would prove right in the future:

> My dear sisters, it was a bitter cup for me to drink, to leave a dear mother and sisters and to part forever in this life, though living. Only the thought of the coming world was my consolation; there I shall see you all. . . . Thanks be to the Lord who gave me the strength to carry out this step, which I hope will be for my own and my children's best in the future. So I hope that time will heal the wound, but up to the present I cannot deny that homesickness gnaws at me hard. When I think, however, that there will be a better livelihood for us here than in poor Norway, I reconcile myself to it and thank God, who protected me and mine over the ocean's waves and led us to a fruitful land.[49]

NOTES

I. THE BODY AND THE SOUL
FATALISTIC CONCEPTIONS

1. Niles Carpenter, *Immigrants and Their Children, 1920: A Study Based on Census Statistics Relative to the Foreign Born and the Native White of Foreign or Mixed Parentage* (Washington, D.C.: U.S. Government Printing Office, 1927; re-issued by Arno Press and the *New York Times*, American Immigration Collection, 1969), p. 183.

2. Donald B. Cole, *Immigrant City: Lawrence, Massachusetts, 1845–1921* (Chapel Hill: University of North Carolina Press, 1963), p. 107.

3. Elsa G. Herzfeld, *Family Monographs: The History of Twenty-Four Families Living in the Middle West Side of New York City* (New York: James Kempster Printing Co., 1905), p. 19.

4. Mary Van Kleeck, *Artificial Flower Makers* (New York: The Russell Sage Foundation, 1913), p. 95.

5. Gro Svendsen, *Frontier Mother: The Letters of Gro Svendsen,* trans. and ed. by Pauline Farseth and Theodore C. Blegen, (Northfield, Minnesota: The Norwegian-American Historical Association, 1950), p. 134. (Letters written between 1862 and 1878.)

6. Elizabeth G. Stern, *I Am a Woman—and a Jew* (New York: J. H. Sears & Co., Inc., 1926; re-issued by Arno Press and the *New York Times*, American Immigration Collection, 1969), p. 76.

7. Herzfeld, *Family Monographs*, p. 130.

8. Priscilla Long, Collection of Oral Histories (Cambridge, Mass.: Schlesinger Library of Radcliffe College), Folders 2–7. Lola Marot, "Oral Interview: Lola Anguini," p. 12.

9. The Vice Commission of Chicago, *The Social Evil in Chicago* (Chicago: Gunthorp-Warren Printing Co., 1911; re-issued by Arno Press and the *New York Times*, 1970), p. 224.

10. Phyllis H. Williams, *South Italian Folkways in Europe and America* (New York: Russell & Russell, 1938; re-issued 1969), pp. 105–06.

11. Ibid.

12. Herzfeld, *Family Monographs*, p. 140.

13. Katherine Anthony, *Mothers Who Must Earn* (New York: Survey Associates and the Russell Sage Foundation, 1914), p. 154.

14. Long, Oral Histories. Sarah Demirfian, "An Interview with My Mother," p. 5.

15. Edward Shorter, "Female Emancipation, Birth Control, and Fertility in European History," *American Historical Review,* Vol. 78, No. 3, June 1973.

16. Vice Commission, *Social Evil*, p. 225. For an extensive study see James C. Mohr, *Abortion in America* (New York: Oxford University Press, 1978). Pages 91–93, 207, and 243 refer specifically to immigrants. In general, Mohr asserts that immigrant women were far less likely than natives to seek abortions during most

of the nineteenth century. However, by the early twentieth century, when state legislatures had passed strongly restrictive anti-abortion laws (largely because of the lobbying efforts of organized medicine), a shifting of patterns seems to have occurred. Then, he states, "there is some evidence to indicate that a substantial proportion of the married women still having recourse to abortion by 1900 were lower-class and immigrant wives."

17. Elsa Herzfeld, "The Tenement House Family," *The Independent* 59, 12-28-05, p. 1521.

18. Caroline Dorothea Margrethe Keyser Preus, *Linka's Diary on Land and Sea, 1845–64*, trans. and ed. by Johan C. K. Preus and Diderikke Brandt Preus (Minneapolis: Augsberg Publishing House, 1952), p. 256.

THOSE UNCONTROLLED BIRTHS

1. Williams, *South Italian Folkways*, pp. 87 and 103.

2. Herzfeld, *Family Monographs*, pp. 19–20.

3. Williams, *South Italian Folkways*, p. 35.

4. 12th Census of the United States, 1900, Vol. 3, *Vital Statistics*, p. ccxlviii.

5. Emily Balch, *Our Slavic Fellow Citizens* (Philadelphia: William F. Fell Co., 1910; re-issued by Arno Press and the *New York Times,* American Immigration Collection, 1969), p. 376.

6. Charlotte Erickson, *Invisible Immigrants* (Coral Gables, Florida: University of Miami Press, 1972), pp. 175–78.

7. Jo Pagano, *Golden Wedding* (New York: Random House, 1943), p. 60.

8. Ibid., pp. 138–39.

9. Marie Hall Ets, *Rosa: The Life of an Italian Immigrant* (Minneapolis: University of Minnesota Press, 1970), p. 178.

10. Ibid., pp. 157–58.

11. Ibid., p. 181.

12. Ibid., pp. 229–31.

13. Michael M. Davis, Jr., *Immigrant Health and the Community* (New York: Harper & Brothers, 1921), p. 201.

14. Upton Sinclair, "Is *The Jungle* True?" *The Independent,* Vol. 60, 5-17-06, p. 1130.

15. Davis, *Immigrant Health,* p. 211.

16. Ibid., pp. 212–13.

17. Ibid., p. 214.

18. Ibid., p. 214, citing Dr. Abraham Jacobi, "The Best Means of Combating Infant Mortality," *Journal of the American Medical Association,* 6-8-12, pp. 1740–44.

19. Davis, *Immigrant Health,* p. 220.

IN SICKNESS AND IN HEALTH

1. Davis, p. *Immigrant Health,* p. 193.

2. Rose Cohen, *Out of the Shadow* (New York: George H. Doran Co., 1918), p. 233.

3. Williams, *South Italian Folkways,* p. 172.

4. 61st Congress, 2nd Session, Senate Document 645, *Report on Condition of Woman and Child Wage-earners in the United States,* (Washington, D.C.: U.S. Government Printing Office, 1911–13), Vol. 2, *Men's Ready-Made Clothing,* p. 312.

5. Ets, *Rosa,* p. 251.

6. Bessie Olga Pehotsky, *The Slavic Immigrant Woman* (Cincinnati: Powell & White, 1925), pp. 49–50.

7. Louise C. Odencrantz, *Italian Women in Industry* (New York: Russell Sage Foundation, 1919), p. 234. (Although published in 1919, the data was collected in 1912–13.)

8. Anthony, *Mothers Who Must Earn,* p. 159.

9. Davis, *Immigrant Health,* p. 351, citing Peter Roberts, *The New Immigration,* 1914, p. 134.

10. Williams, *South Italian Folkways,* p. 5.

11. Ets, *Rosa,* p. 12.

12. Marjorie Roberts, "Italian Girls on American Soil," *Mental Hygiene,* Vol. 13, October 1929, p. 766.

13. Stern, *I Am a Woman,* p. 72.

14. Knut Gjerset and Ludvig Hektoen, "Health Conditions and the Practice of Medicine Among the Early Norwegian Settlers, 1825–1865," Norwegian-American Historical Association *Studies and Records* Vol. 1, 1926, p. 33.

15. Williams, *South Italian Folkways,* p. 168.

16. Constance McLaughlin Greene, *Holyoke, Massachusetts: A Case History of the Industrial Revolution in America* (New Haven: Yale University Press, 1939), p. 119.

17. 12th Census, Vol. 3, p. lxxxviii.

18. Theodore C. Blegen, *Land of Their Choice: The Immigrants Write Home* (St. Paul: University of Minnesota Press, 1955), p. 77.

19. Anthony, *Mothers Who Must Earn,* p. 25. For another view of immigrant health care see Lillian D. Wald, *The House on Henry Street* (New York: Henry Holt & Co., 1915).

THE IMMIGRANT WAY OF DEATH

1. Cole, *Immigrant City,* pp. 64 and 76.

2. Ibid., p. 76.

3. Jacob Riis, *How the Other Half Lives* (New York: C. Scribner's Sons, 1890; re-issued by Sagamore Press, New York, 1957), p. 27.

4. Anthony, *Mothers Who Must Earn,* p. 154.

5. Gjerset and Hektoen, "Health Conditions," p. 32.

6. Senate Document 645, Vol. 13, *Infant Mortality and Its Relation to the Employment of Mothers,* 1912, p. 143.

7. Ibid., pp. 138–61.

8. Herzfeld, "Tenement House Family," p. 1522.

9. Anthony, *Mothers Who Must Earn,* p. 155.

10. Stern, *I Am a Woman,* pp. 57–58.

11. Elisabeth Koren, *The Diary of Elisabeth Koren, 1853–1855,* trans. and ed. by David T. Nelson, (Northfield, Minnesota: Norwegian-American Historical Association, 1955), p. 159.

12. Preus, *Linka's Diary,* p. 239.

13. Elise Waerenskjold, *The Lady with the Pen: Elise Waerenskjold in Texas,* trans. and ed. by C. A. Clausen, (Northfield, Minnesota: Norwegian-American Historical Association, 1961), pp. 64–65.

14. Herzfeld, *Family Monographs,* pp. 107–08.

15. Ibid., p. 64.

16. Ibid., p. 69.

17. Erickson, *Invisible Immigrants,* p. 221.

18. Ibid., p. 222.

19. Ibid., p. 223.

20. Svendsen, *Frontier Mother,* pp. 145–47.

21. Erickson, *Invisible Immigrants,* p. 366.

22. Waerenskjold, *Lady with the Pen,* p. 48.

23. Riis, *How the Other Half Lives,* p. 196.

24. Louise B. More, *Wage-Earners' Budgets: A Study of Standards and Cost of Living in New York City* (New York: Henry Holt and Co., 1907), p. 145.

25. Mary E. Richmond, and Fred S. Hall: *A Study of Nine Hundred and Eighty-five Widows* (New York: The Russell Sage Foundation, 1913), p.15.

26. Theodore C. Blegen, *Grass Roots History* (Port Washington, New York/London: Kennikat Press, 1947; re-issued in 1969 by Kennikat Press), pp. 93–94.

RELIGION HERE AND HEREAFTER

1. Cohen, *Out of the Shadow,* pp. 78–79.

2. Koren, *Diary of Elisabeth Koren,* p. 281.

3. Svendsen, *Frontier Mother,* p. 33.

4. Elise Dubach Isely, as told to her son, Bliss Isely, *Sunbonnet Days* (Caldwell, Idaho: The Caxton Printers, 1935), pp. 185–86.

5. Erickson, *Invisible Immigrants,* pp. 182–83.

6. Waerenskjold, *Lady with the Pen,* p. 40.

7. Blegen, *Land of Their Choice,* p. 324.

8. Ruth Fritz Meyer, *Women on a Mission* (St. Louis: Concordia Publishing House, 1967). See also Ludwig Ernest Fuerbringer, *Persons and Events* (St. Louis: Concordia Publishing House, 1947) and same author and publisher, *Eighty Eventful Years* (1944).

9. Kenneth O. Bjork, *West of the Great Divide: Norwegian Migration to the Pacific Coast, 1847–1893* (Northfield, Minnesota: Norwegian-American Historical Association, 1958), pp. 182 and 191.

10. Ibid., p. 200.

11. Ibid., p. 204.

12. Cohen, *Out of the Shadow,* p. 86.

13. Ibid., p. 104.

14. Ibid., p. 105.

15. Herzfeld, *Family Monographs,* p. 140.

16. Ibid., p. 24.

17. Ibid., p. 23.

18. Herzfeld, "The Tenement House Family," p. 1521.

19. Odencrantz, *Italian Women in Industry,* p. 206.

20. Hamilton Holt, *The Life Stories of Undistinguished Americans As Told by Themselves* (New York: James Pott & Co., 1906), p. 88.

21. Williams, *South Italian Folkways,* p. 152.

22. Helen Campbell, *Prisoners of Poverty: Women Wage-Workers, Their Trades and Their Lives* (Boston: Roberts Brothers, 1895), pp. 137–38.

23. Thomas Capek, *The Čechs (Bohemians) in America* (Boston: Houghton Mifflin, 1920), p. 119.

24. Williams, *South Italian Folkways,* p. 102.

25. Cohen, *Out of the Shadow,* p. 162.

II. AMBIVALENCE IN MORALITY
COURTING CUSTOMS

1. Long, Oral Histories. Lola Marot, "Oral Interview," p. 6.

2. Ibid., p. 7.

3. Roberts, "Italian Girls," p. 764.

4. Long, Oral Histories. Lola Marot, "Oral Interview," p. 7.

5. Cohen, *Out of the Shadow,* p. 201.

6. Ibid., p. 204.

7. Ets, *Rosa,* p. 157.

8. Ibid., p. 160.

9. Arnold H. Barton, *Letters from the Promised Land: Swedes in America, 1840–1914* (Minneapolis: University of Minnesota Press, 1975), p. 266.

10. Mari Sandoz, *Old Jules* (Boston: Little, Brown & Co., 1935), pp. 164–65.

11. Edith Abbott, *Immigration: Select Documents and Case Records* (Chicago: University of Chicago, 1924; re-issued by Arno Press and the *New York Times,* American Immigration Collection, 1969), pp. 783–84.

12. William I. Thomas, and Florian Znaniecki: *The Polish Peasant in Europe and America.* Five Volumes. (Chicago: University of Chicago Press, 1918; re-issued by Dover Publications, 1958; Vol. 1, p. 592.

13. Balch, *Our Slavic Fellow Citizens*, p. 185, from the notebook of one Miss Gazvoda.

14. Holt, *Life Stories*, pp. 141–42.

15. Abbott, *Immigration*, p. 745.

16. Isaac Metzker, ed. *A Bintel Brief: Sixty Years of Letters From the Lower East Side to the Jewish Daily Forward* (Garden City, New York: Doubleday & Co., 1971), pp. 103–04.

17. Cohen, *Out of the Shadow*, pp. 302–03.

18. Williams, *South Italian Folkways*, p. 194.

19. Thomas and Znaniecki, *The Polish Peasant*, Vol. 1, pp. 582–84.

MARRIAGE, DIVORCE, AND DESERTION

1. Kate Claghorn, *The Immigrant's Day in Court* (New York: Harper & Bros., 1923; re-issued by Arno Press and the *New York Times*, American Immigration Collection, 1969), p. 82.

2. Herzfeld, *Family Monographs*, p. 138.

3. Anthony, *Mothers Who Must Earn*, p. 20.

4. Ibid., p. 22.

5. Erickson, *Invisible Immigrants*, pp. 480–81.

6. Anthony, *Mothers Who Must Earn*, pp. 23–24.

7. Herzfeld, "Tenement House Family," p. 1522.

8. Cornelia Stratton Parker, *Working With the Working Woman* (New York: Harper & Brothers, 1922), p. 53.

9. Preus, *Linka's Diary*, pp. 127–28.

10. Herzfeld, *Family Monographs*, p. 104.

11. Thomas and Znaniecki, *The Polish Peasant*, Vol. 2, pp. 1708–09, from the records of the Chicago Legal Aid Society.

12. Ibid., pp. 1722–23.

13. Ibid., p. 1709.

14. Abbott, *Immigration*, p. 799.

15. Metzker, *A Bintel Brief*, p. 121.

16. Joanna C. Colcord, *Broken Homes: A Study of Family Desertion* (New York: Russell Sage Foundation, 1919), pp. 101–02.

17. Ets, *Rosa*, pp. 204–05.

18. Ibid., p. 205.

19. Ibid., pp. 205–06.

20. Colcord, *Broken Homes*, p. 8.

21. Earle Edward Eubank, *A Study of Family Desertion.* (Chicago: University of Chicago Libraries and City of Chicago Department of Public Welfare, 1916), p. 16.

22. Lillian Brandt, *Five Hundred and Seventy-four Deserters and Their Families* (New York: The Charity Organization Society, 1905), pp. 15–16.

23. Colcord, *Broken Homes*, p. 21 and Eubank, *Study of Family Desertion*, p. 20.

24. L. Brandt, *Deserters*, p. 39.

25. Eubank, *Study of Family Desertion*, p. 45.

26. L. Brandt, *Deserters*, pp. 26–27. See also William H. Baldwin, *Family Desertion and Non-Support Laws* (Washington, D.C.: The Associated Charities, 1904).

27. Gwendolyn Salisbury Hughes, *Mothers in Industry: Wage-Earning by Mothers in Philadelphia* (New York: New Republic, Inc., 1925), p. 80.

28. Colcord, *Broken Homes*, p. 50.

29. Metzker, *A Bintel Brief*, pp. 108–09.

30. Claghorn, *Immigrant's Day in Court*, p. 209.

31. Eubank, *Study of Family Desertion*, p. 49, citing *Report of the National Desertion Bureau*, 1912–15, p. 7.

32. Hughes, G., *Mothers in Industry*, pp. 69–70.

33. Metzker, *A Bintel Brief*, pp. 83–84.

34. Thomas and Znaniecki, *The Polish Peasant*, Vol. 2, p. 1709.

35. Eubank, *Study of Family Desertion*, p. 47.

36. Metzker, *A Bintel Brief*, pp. 111–12.

37. Eubank, *Study of Family Desertion*, p. 45.

38. L. Brandt, *Deserters*, p. 35.

39. Colcord, *Broken Homes*, pp. 34–35.

40. Anthony, *Mothers Who Must Earn*, p. 181.

41. L. Brandt, *Deserters*, p. 53. See also, Eubank, *Study of Family Desertion*, p. 42, citing Zilpha D. Smith, *Deserted Wives and Deserting Husbands*.

42. Ibid., p. 46.

43. Anthony, *Mothers Who Must Earn*, p. 183.

44. Claghorn, *Immigrant's Day in Court*, p. 88.

ILLICIT SEX

1. Abbott, *Immigration*, pp. 377–82.

2. Ibid., p. 382–83. See also Balch, *Our Slavic Fellow Citizens*, p. 51.

3. Carpenter, *Immigrants and Their Children*, p. 245.

4. Senate Document 645, Vol. 15, *Relation Between Occupation and Criminality of Women*, pp. 84–87.

5. Williams, *South Italian Folkways*, p. 99.

6. Riis, *How the Other Half Lives*, p. 143.

7. Thomas and Znaniecki, *The Polish Peasant*, Vol. 2, pp. 1721–22.

8. Claghorn, *Immigrant's Day in Court*, p. 78.

9. Svendsen, *Frontier Mother*, pp. 9–10.

10. Charles Booth, *Life and Labour of the People in London*, (New York: AMS

Press, 1970, originally published in London and New York, 1902–4.) 3rd Series, Vol 1, p. 55.

11. Claghorn, *Immigrant's Day in Court*, p. 84.

12. Elizabeth Beardsley Butler, *Women and the Trades* (New York: Charities Publication Committee and the Russell Sage Foundation, 1909; part of *The Pittsburgh Survey: Findings in Six Volumes*, ed. by Paul H. Kellogg), p. 348.

13. Women's Educational and Industrial Union: *Report of an Investigation of 500 Immigrant Women in Boston*, June, 1907 (Schlesinger Library, Radcliffe College), p. 15.

14. Vice Commission of Chicago, *Social Evil*, pp. 43 and 97. See also Walter C. Reckless, *Vice in Chicago* (University of Chicago, 1933, re-issued by Patterson Smith Publishing, 1969).

15. Edward A. Steiner, *On the Trail of the Immigrant* (New York and London: Fleming H. Revell Co., 1906), pp.316–17.

16. 61st Congress, 3rd Session, Senate Document 753. *Reports of the Immigration Commission: Importation and Harboring of Women for Immoral Purposes* (Washington, D.C.: Government Printing Office, 1911), p. 62.

17. Ibid., pp. 62–64. See also 61st Congress, 3rd Session, Senate Document 750, *Immigration and Crime*, pp. 100–01 and p. 157.

18. Vice Commission of Chicago, *Social Evil*, p. 227.

19. See Senate Document 753, *Importation and Harboring of Women*, for examples of such letters.

20. Ibid., p. 82.

21. Ibid., pp. 104–06.

22. Metzker, *A Bintel Brief*, p. 104.

23. Ibid.

24. Blandina Segale, S.C., *At the End of the Santa Fe Trail* (Milwaukee: The Bruce Publishing Company, 1948), p. 5, in an introduction by Sister Therese Martin.

25. Senate Document 753, *Importation and Harboring of Women*, p. 79.

26. Senate Document 645, Vol. 15, *Relation*, p. 99. See also Thomas and Znaniecki, *The Polish Peasant*, Vol. 2, pp. 1800–27 on "Sexual Immorality of Girls," and George J. Kneeland, *Commercialized Prostitution in New York City* (New York: The Century Co., 1913).

III. DOMESTICITY: THE OLD AND THE NEW
THE FRUIT OF THE LAND

1. Blegen, *Land of Their Choice*, pp. 262–63.

2. Ets, *Rosa*, p. 172 and 175.

3. Blegen, *Land of Their Choice*, p. 268.

4. Williams, *South Italian Folkways*, p. 63.

5. Davis, *Immigrant Health*, p. 246.

6. Ibid., pp. 249–50.

7. Ibid., p. 268.

8. Svendsen, *Frontier Mother,* p. 39.

9. Robert Coit Chapin, *The Standard of Living Among Workingmen's Families in New York City* (New York: The Russell Sage Foundation, 1909), p. 132.

10. Waerenskjold, *Lady with the Pen,* p. 135.

11. Koren, *Diary of Elisabeth Koren,* p. 156.

12. Ibid., p. 231.

13. Ets, *Rosa,* p. 215.

14. Senate Document 645, Volume 5, *Wage-Earning Women In Stores And Factories,* p. 149.

15. Cole, *Immigrant City,* p. 163.

16. Odencrantz, *Italian Women in Industry,* p. 227.

17. Anzia Yezierska, *Children of Loneliness: Stories of Immigrant Life in America* (New York & London: Funk and Wagnalls, 1923), p. 18. Some of Yezierska's work is autobiographical fiction.

18. Green, *Holyoke,* p.125, citing the *Holyoke Transcript,* August 1, 1868.

19. Williams, *South Italian Folkways,* pp. 65–66.

20. Balch, *Our Slavic Fellow Citizens,* pp. 363–64.

21. John Curtis Kennedy, *Wages and Family Budgets in the Chicago Stockyards District* (Chicago: University of Chicago Press, 1914), pp. 68 and 72–73.

22. Odencrantz, *Italian Women in Industry,* pp. 198–99.

23. See More, *Wage-Earners' Budgets.*

24. Senate Document 645, Vol. 16, *Family Budgets of Typical Cotton-Mill Workers,* pp. 223 and 220.

25. Erickson, *Invisible Immigrants,* p. 182.

26. Waerenskjold, *Lady with the Pen,* pp. 29, 93, and 37.

27. Svendsen, *Frontier Mother,* p. 71.

28. Blegen, *Land of Their Choice,* p. 29.

29. Pagano, *Golden Wedding,* p. 276.

OF HOVELS, HOMES, AND HOPES

1. Cohen, *Out of the Shadow,* p. 304.

2. Cole, *Immigrant City,* pp. 70–71.

3. Steiner, *Trail of the Immigrant,* p. 265.

4. G. Hughes, *Mothers in Industry,* p. 306.

5. Cole, *Immigrant City,* p. 66.

6. Riis, *How the Other Half Lives,* p. 51.

7. Mary Buell Sayles, "Housing and Social Conditions in a Slavic Neighborhood," *The Survey,* Vol. 13, December 3, 1904, p. 261.

8. Edith Abbott, *The Tenements of Chicago, 1908–1935* (Chicago: University of Chicago, 1936), p. 23, citing Colbert and Chamberlin: *Chicago and the Great Conflagration* (1871), pp. 273–75.

9. Riis, *How the Other Half Lives,* p. 8.

10. Julius Wilcox, "The Greatest Problem of Great Cities," *The Independent*, Vol. 59, October 19, 1905, p. 906.

11. Senate Document 645, Vol. 2, *Men's Ready-Made Clothing*, p. 263.

12. Abbott, *Chicago*, p. 263.

13. Ibid., p. 346.

14. Ets, *Rosa*, p. 225.

15. Helen I. Wilson, and Eunice W. Smith, "Chicago Housing Conditions Among the Slovaks in the Twentieth Ward," *American Journal of Sociology*, Vol. 20, September, 1914, p. 154. See also Annie Marion MacLean, "Life in the Pennsylvania Coal Fields, with Particular Reference to Women," *American Journal of Sociology*, Vol. 14, November, 1908, p. 334, for other commentary on sanitation.

16. Barton, *Letters from the Promised Land*, p. 236.

17. Gjerset and Hektoen, "Health Conditions," p. 19.

18. Waerenskjold, *Lady with the Pen*, p. 83.

19. Koren, *Diary of Elisabeth Koren*, p. 330.

20. Preus, *Linka's Diary*, p. 194.

21. Ibid., p. 213.

22. Koren, *Diary of Elisabeth Koren*, pp. 382–83.

23. Mrs. Realf Ottesen Brandt, "Social Aspects of Prairie Pioneering: The Reminiscences of a Pioneer Pastor's Wife," Norwegian-American Historical Association *Studies and Records*, Vol. 7, p. 5.

24. Koren, *Diary of Elisabeth Koren*, p. 222.

25. Brandt, Mrs. R. O., "Social Aspects," p. 15.

26. Preus, *Linka's Diary*, p. 281.

27. Riis, *How the Other Half Lives*, p. 4.

28. Cohen, *Out of the Shadow*, p. 186.

29. Senate Document 645, Vol. 4, *The Silk Industry*, pp. 310–11.

30. Abbott, *Chicago*, p. 378.

31. Ibid.

32. Sayles, "Housing and Social Conditions," p. 258.

33. Herzfeld, *Family Monographs*, pp. 14–16.

HOUSEWORK AND CHILD CARE

1. G. Hughes, *Mothers in Industry*, p. 176.

2. Svendsen, *Frontier Mother*, p. 28.

3. Blegen, *Land of Their Choice*, p. 422.

4. Emilie Lohmann Koenig, "Letters From America to a Family in Germany," *Concordia Historical Institute Quarterly*, Vol. 28, No. 4, Winter 1956, pp. 6, 8, 19.

5. Cole, *Immigrant City*, p. 73.

6. Samuel Chotzinoff, *A Lost Paradise* (New York: Knopf, 1958), pp. 307–09.

7. Williams, *South Italian Folkways*, p. 49.

8. Mrs. R. O. Brandt, "Social Aspects," p. 37.

9. Anthony, *Mothers Who Must Earn*, p. 91.

10. Abbott, *Chicago*, p. 223.

11. Balch, *Our Slavic Fellow Citizens*, p. 372.

12. Sayles, "Housing and Social Conditions," p. 258.

13. Jane E. Robbins, "The Bohemian Women in New York," *Charities and the Commons*, Vol. 13, December 12, 1904, pp. 195–96.

14. Long, Oral Histories. Anonymous, "An Italian Immigrant Woman—1920," p. 6.

15. Senate Document 645, Vol. 1, *Cotton Textile Industry*, pp. 540–41.

16. G. Hughes, *Mothers in Industry*, pp. 178–79.

17. Chapin, *Standard of Living*, pp. 170–181.

18. Riis, *How the Other Half Lives*, p. 45.

19. Long, Oral Histories. Lola Marot, "Oral Interview," pp. 3–4.

20. Ets, *Rosa*, p. 233.

21. G. Hughes, *Mothers in Industry*, p. 194.

22. Ibid., p. 7.

23. Anthony, *Mothers Who Must Earn*, p. 140.

24. Green, *Holyoke*, pp. 345, 362.

25. Frances E. Lane, *American Charities and the Child of the Immigrant: A Study of Typical Child Caring Institutions in New York and Massachusetts Between the Years 1845 and 1880*, (Washington, D.C.: The Catholic University of America, 1932), pp. 82–83.

26. Ibid., p. 112.

27. Ibid., p. 128.

28. See Colcord, *Broken Homes*, and Richmond, *Study*, for examples.

29. Lane, *American Charities*, p. 71.

30. Rose Schneiderman, with Lucy Goldwaite: *All For One* (New York: Paul S. Eriksson, Inc., 1967), pp. 30–33.

CUSTOM IN COSTUME

1. Balch, *Our Slavic Fellow Citizens*, pp. 370–72.

2. Ibid.

3. Butler, *Women and the Trades*, p. 347.

4. Odencrantz, *Italian Women in Industry*, p. 64.

5. Balch, *Our Slavic Fellow Citizens*, p. 370.

6. Williams, *South Italian Folkways*, p. 71.

7. Balch, *Our Slavic Fellow Citizens*, p. 372.

8. Ibid., pp. 106–07.

9. Holt, *Life Stories*, p. 46.

10. Odencrantz, *Italian Women in Industry*, p. 232.

11. Ibid. p. 233.

12. Sue Ainslie Clark, and Edith Wyatt: *Making Both Ends Meet: The Income and Outlay of New York Working Girls* (New York: The Macmillan Company, 1911).

13. Odencrantz, *Italian Women in Industry*, p. 201.

14. Cohen, *Out of the Shadow*, p. 115.

15. Chapin, *Standard of Living*, p. 164.

16. Ibid., p. 234.

17. Herzfeld, *Family Monographs*, pp. 146–47.

18. Ets, *Rosa*, p. 5.

19. Anthony, *Mothers Who Must Earn*, p. 147.

20. Balch, *Our Slavic Fellow Citizens*, p. 92.

21. Williams, *South Italian Folkways*, p. 27.

22. Balch, *Our Slavic Fellow Citizens*, pp. 106–07.

23. Svendsen, *Frontier Mother*, p. 29.

24. Preus, *Linka's Diary*, p. 203.

25. Ibid., pp. 187–88.

26. Robert Ernst, *Immigrant Life in New York City: 1825–1863* (Port Washington, New York: Ira J. Friedman, Inc., 1949; re-issued by same publisher 1965), pp. 67–68 citing the *Irish American*, November 29, 1856.

27. Blegen, *Grass Roots History*, p. 107.

IV. THE CONTRIBUTIONS OF THESE WOMEN
SUPPORTING FAMILIES

1. Margaret Byington, *Homestead: The Households of a Mill Town* (New York: The Russell Sage Foundation, 1910), p. 108.

2. Anne Webster Noel, "On Twelve a Week," *The Independent*, Vol. 59, October, 26, 1905, p. 959.

3. G. Hughes, *Mothers in Industry*, p. 13.

4. Van Kleeck, *Artificial Flower Makers*, p. 74.

5. More, *Wage-Earners' Budgets*, p. 88.

6. Odencrantz, *Italian Women in Industry*, p. 172.

7. Ibid., p. 187.

8. Kennedy, *Wages and Family Budgets*, p. 66.

9. Chapin, *Standard of Living*, p. 64. See also U.S. Department of Labor, Women's Bureau Bulletin No. 49, *Women Workers & Family Support*, a study made by students in the economics course at the Bryn Mawr summer school under the direction of Prof. Amy Hewes; (Washington, D.C.,: Government Printing Office, 1925).

10. Holt, *Life Stories*, pp. 38–39.

11. Ibid., pp. 39–40.

12. Clark, *Making Both Ends Meet*, p. 50.

13. Emilie Josephine Hutchinson, *Women's Wages* (New York: Columbia University Press, 1919, re-issued by AMS Press, New York, 1968), pp. 43–44.

14. Odencrantz, *Italian Women in Industry*, p. 100.

15. Senate Document 645, Vol. 12, *Women in Laundries*, p. 81.

16. Riis, *How the Other Half Lives*, p. 128.

17. Odencrantz, *Italian Women in Industry*, p. 212.

18. Ibid., pp. 214–15.

19. Herzfeld, *Family Monographs*, p. 38.

20. Aagot Raaen, *Grass of the Earth*, (Northfield, Minnesota: Norwegian-American Historical Association, 1950; reprinted by Arno Press & the *New York Times*, 1979), p. 119.

21. Odencrantz, *Italian Women in Industry*, p. 176.

22. Van Kleeck, *Artificial Flower Makers*, pp. 229–35.

23. Anthony, *Mothers Who Must Earn*, p. 53.

24. Van Kleeck, *Artificial Flower Makers*, pp. 84–85.

25. Odencrantz, *Italian Women in Industry*, pp. 307 and 315, in a supplement by Henriette R. Walter.

26. Clark, *Making Both Ends Meet*, p. 104.

27. Ibid., p. 58.

28. Ibid., p. 100.

29. Senate Document 645, Vol. 12, *Women in Laundries*, p. 99.

30. Ibid., p. 118.

31. Cohen, *Out of the Shadow*, p. 115.

THEIR WORK AND THEIR WAGES

1. Ernst, *Immigrant Life*, p. 68.

2. Frances A. Kellor, "The Immigrant Woman," *The Atlantic*, Vol. 100, September, 1907, p. 401.

3. Senate Document 645, Vol. 4, *The Silk Industry*, p. 15.

4. Butler, *Women and the Trades*, p. 62.

5. Senate Document 645, Vol. 4, *The Silk Industry*, p. 194.

6. Van Kleeck, *Artificial Flower Makers*, p. 17.

7. Ibid., p. 29.

8. Parker, *Working Woman*, p. 28.

9. Senate Document 645, Vol. 18, *Employment of Women and Children in Selected Industries*, p. 362.

10. Butler, *Women and the Trades*, p. 46.

11. Parker, *Working Woman*, p. 16.

12. Edith Abbott, *Women in Industry*, (New York: Appleton & Co., 1909), p. 199. See also Senate Document 645, Vol. 9, *History of Women in Industry in the U.S.*, p. 198.

13. Balch, *Our Slavic Fellow Citizens*, pp. 357–58.

14. Odencrantz, *Italian Women in Industry*, pp. 48–49.

15. Gary R. Mormino, and Anthony P. Pizzo: *Tampa: The Treasure City*, (Tulsa, Okla.: Continental Heritage Press, Inc., 1983), p. 108.

16. Robbins, "Bohemian Women," p. 195.

17. Campbell, *Prisoners of Poverty*, p. 205.

18. Caroline Manning, *The Immigrant Woman and Her Job*, United States Department of Labor, Bulletin of the Women's Bureau, No. 74, (Washington, D.C.: U.S. Government Printing Office, 1930; reprinted New York: Arno Press and the *New York Times*, 1970), p. 129.

19. Gertrude Barnum, "The Story of a Fall River Mill Girl," *The Independent*, Vol. 58, April 27, 1905, p. 242.

20. Green, *Holyoke*, p. 105.

21. Senate Document 645, Vol. 1, *Cotton Textile Industry*, p. 590.

22. Cole, *Immigrant City*, p. 76.

23. Barnum, "Fall River Mill Girl," p. 242.

24. Ernst, *Immigrant Life*, p. 68.

25. Senate Document 645, Vol. 2, *Men's Ready-Made Clothing*, p. 491.

26. Ibid., p. 495.

27. Senate Document 645, Vol. 12, *Women in Laundries*, p. 13.

28. Butler, *Women and the Trades*, p. 182.

29. Parker, *Working Woman*, p. 87.

30. Senate Document 645, Vol. 12, *Women in Laundries*, p. 60.

31. Anonymous, "A Collar Starcher's Story," *The Independent*, Vol. 59, August 10, 1905, p. 307.

32. Ibid.

33. Manning, *Immigrant Woman*, pp. 151–52.

34. Balch, *Our Slavic Fellow Citizens*, p. 375.

35. Pehotsky, *Slavic Immigrant Woman*, p. 47.

36. Abbott, *Chicago*, p. 346.

37. Balch, *Our Slavic Fellow Citizens*, p. 352.

38. Ibid.

39. Ibid., p. 252.

40. Pehotsky, *Slavic Immigrant Woman*, p. 35.

41. G. Hughes, *Mothers in Industry*, p. 96.

42. Claghorn, *Immigrant's Day in Court*, p. 78.

43. *New York Times*, Grossinger obituary, November 21, 1972. I am indebted to Jean Christensen of Marshfield, Mass., for bringing this item to my attention.

44. Margaret Byington, "The Mill Town Courts and Their Lodgers," *Charities and the Commons*, Vol. 21, Feb. 6, 1909, p. 921.

45. Riis, *How the Other Half Lives*, p. 144.

46. Senate Document 645, Vol. 18, *Employment of Women and Children*, p. 138.

47. Ibid., pp. 180–194.

48. Ibid., p. 234.

49. Butler, *Women and the Trades*, pp. 210, 228.

50. Ibid., p. 210.

51. Ibid., p. 227.

52. Theresa Wolfson, *The Woman Worker and the Trade Unions* (New York: International Publishers, 1926), p. 36.

53. G. Hughes, *Mothers in Industry*, p. 131.

54. Balch, *Our Slavic Fellow Citizens*, p. 355.

55. Capek, *The Čechs*, p. 85.

56. Long, Oral Histories. Anonymous, "An Italian Immigrant Woman," p. 9.

57. Hutchinson, *Women's Wages*, p. 26, citing *Census of Manufacturers, 1905:* Bulletin No. 93, p. 11.

58. Abbott, *Immigration*, p. 269.

59. Butler, *Women and the Trades*, p. 340.

60. Anthony, *Mothers Who Must Earn*, p. 116.

61. Van Kleeck, *Artificial Flower Makers*, p. 66.

62. Elizabeth Hasanovitz, *One of Them: Chapters from a Passionate Autobiography* (Boston and New York: Houghton Mifflin Company, 1918), pp. 115–16.

63. Ibid., p. 115.

64. Odencrantz, *Italian Women in Industry*, in a supplement by Henriette R. Walter p. 317.

65. Manning, *Immigrant Woman*, p. 117.

66. Butler, *Women and the Trades*, p. 261.

67. Odencrantz, *Italian Women in Industry*, p. 132.

68. Butler, *Women and the Trades*, p. 4, statement made by Paul U. Kellogg, in the editor's foreword.

69. Abbott, *Immigration*, p. 585, quoting from Massachusetts Bureau of Immigration, *Second Annual Report*, 1920, pp. 38–39.

70. Claghorn, *Immigrant's Day in Court*, pp. 17–18.

71. Anna Walther, *A Pilgrimage With a Milliner's Needle* (New York: Fredrick A. Stokes Company, 1917), p. 229.

THE WAYS OF WORK

1. Clark, *Making Both Ends Meet*, p. 48.

2. Odencrantz, *Italian Women in Industry*, p. 157.

3. Rose Schneiderman, "A Cap Maker's Story," *The Independent*, Vol. 58, April 27, 1905, p. 936.

4. Odencrantz, *Italian Women in Industry*, p. 159.

5. Campbell, *Prisoners of Poverty*, p. 177.

6. Ibid, p. 178.

7. Cohen, *Out of the Shadow*, pp. 87–88.

8. Hasanovitz, *One of Them*, p. 109.

9. Riis, *How the Other Half Lives*, p. 176.

10. Ibid., p. 183.

11. Parker, *Working Woman*, pp. 153–54.

12. Dorothy Richardson, *The Long Day: The Story of a New York Working Girl as Told by Herself* (New York: The Century Co., 1905), p. 188.

13. Butler, *Women and the Trades*, p. 224.

14. Clark, *Making Both Ends Meet*, p. 194.

15. Senate Document 645, Vol. 2, *Men's Ready-Made Clothing*, p. 421.

16. Parker, *Working Woman*, pp. 111–12.

17. Ibid., p. 110.

18. Cohen, *Out of the Shadow*, p. 287.

19. Women's Educational and Industrial Union, *Report*, p. 16.

20. Odencrantz, *Italian Women in Industry*, p. 315, in a supplement by Henriette R. Walter.

21. Abbott, *Historical*, p. 597.

22. Frances A. Kellor, *Out of Work* (New York: G. P. Putnam's Sons, 1904). See also Grace Abbott, "The Chicago Employment Agency and the Immigrant Worker," *American Journal of Sociology*, Vol. 14, November, 1908.

23. Odencrantz, *Italian Women in Industry*, pp. 272–73.

24. Ibid., p. 275.

25. Manning, *Immigrant Woman*, pp. 103–05.

26. Odencrantz, *Italian Women in Industry*, pp. 115, 121, and 283.

27. Ibid., p. 124.

28. Ets, *Rosa*, p. 211.

29. Clark, *Making Both Ends Meet*, pp. 141–46.

30. Parker, *Working Woman*, p. 50.

31. G. Hughes, *Mothers in Industry*, p. 226.

32. Cole, *Immigrant City*, p. 75.

33. Butler, *Women and the Trades*, p. 108.

34. Odencrantz, *Italian Women in Industry*, p. 67.

35. Cole, *Immigrant City*, p. 32.

36. "Disastrous Fire in the Woonasquatucket Valley," *Providence Daily Journal*, February 3, 1866.

37. Hasanovitz, *One of Them*, p. 216.

38. *New York Times*, March 26, 1911.

39. Ibid.

40. Ibid., March 27, 1911.

41. Ibid., December 28, 1911.

42. Ibid., March 26, 1911.

43. Schneiderman, *All For One*, p. 47.

44. Green, *Holyoke*, p. 48.

45. Senate Document 645, Vol. 10, *History of Women in Trade Unions*, pp. 60 and 93.

46. Holt, *Life Stories*, pp. 45–46.

47. Parker, *Working Woman*, pp. 113–14.

48. Hasanovitz, *One of Them*, pp. 252–53.

49. Clark, *Making Both Ends Meet*, p. 81.

50. Green, *Holyoke*, p. 57.

51. Senate Document 645, Vol. 10, *History of Women in Trade Unions*, p. 164.

52. Cohen, *Out of the Shadow*, pp. 124–127.

53. Abbott, *Women in Industry*, p. 145.

54. Clark, *Making Both Ends Meet*, p. 62.

55. *New York Times*, December 9, 1909.

56. Clark, *Making Both Ends Meet*, p. 63. See also Theresa Serber Malkiel, *The Diary of a Shirtwaist Striker* (New York: The Cooperative Press, 1910); and Andria Taylor Hourwich & Gladys L. Palmer, eds., *I Am a Woman Worker* (New York: Affiliated Schools for Workers, Inc., 1936; reprinted by Arno Press, 1974). Pages 109–152 deal especially with strikes.

57. *New York Times*, January 16, 1912, p. 1.

58. *Evening Tribune*, Lawrence, Mass., January 30, 1912.

59. Richard Child, "The Industrial Revolt at Lawrence," *Colliers*, Vol. 48, March 9, 1912, p. 15.

60. Priscilla Long, *Mother Jones, Woman Organizer*, p. 18, citing letters from F. L. Abbey to Governor Ferris, September 3, October 4, and August 29, 1913; Michigan Historical Commission, Ann Arbor.

61. From unidentified, undated clippings in the scrapbook of Eva W. White (Schlesinger Library, Radcliffe College, Cambridge, Mass.).

62. Van Kleeck, *Artificial Flower Makers*, p. 36.

63. Anthony, *Mothers Who Must Earn*, p. 81.

64. Parker, *Working Woman*, p. 134.

65. Richmond, *Study*, p. 70.

66. Graham Wallas, *The Great Society: A Psychological Analysis* (New York: The Macmillan Co., 1929), pp. 341–43.

67. Ibid.

68. Manning, *Immigrant Woman*, pp. 112 and 114.

69. Wallas, *Great Society*, p. 341. For additional information on general working conditions, see also Carroll D. Wright, *The Working Girls of Boston* (Boston: Wright & Potter Printing Co., 1889; reprinted by Arno Press and the *New York Times*, 1969); and *Working Girls of Cincinnati*, an Arno Press 1974 reprint of three Cincinnati studies done in 1918, 1927, and 1930.

FOREIGN DOMESTICS

1. Blegen, *Land of Their Choice*, p. 436.

2. Ibid., p. 76.

3. Bjork, *Great Divide*, p. 160; citing a letter from Rev. Christian Hvistendahl in *Foedrelandet og emigranten*, May 18, 1871.

4. Women's Educational Industrial Union, *Immigration as a Source of Supply*

for Domestic Workers, 1905 (Schlesinger Library, Radcliffe College, Cambridge, Mass.,) p. 1. See also Robert Ernst, *Immigrant Life in New York City, 1825–1863* (Port Washington, New York: Ira J. Freidman, 1949; reissued by same publisher, 1965); and Carroll D. Wright, *The Working Girls of Boston* (Boston: Wright & Potter Printing Co., 1889; reissued by Arno Press, 1969). Both contain similar statistics showing the overwhelming number of foreign-born women among domestics.

5. Kellor, "The Immigrant Woman," p. 402. On employment agencies for domestics, see also Frances Kellor: *Out of Work,* as well as Kellor's "Immigration and Household Labor," *Charities,* Vol. 12, February 6, 1904.

6. Ibid.

7. Carpenter, *Immigrants and their Children,* pp. 288–89.

8. John Francis Maguire, *The Irish in America* (London, 1868), pp. 313–32. Cited in Edith Abbott, *Historical Aspects of the Immigration Problem* (Chicago: University of Chicago Press; re-issued by Arno Press and the *New York Times* as part of the American Immigration Collection, 1969), pp. 522–24.

9. Ernst, *Immigrant Life,* p. 67.

10. Abbott, *Historical,* p. 385.

11. Harriet Prescott Spofford, *The Servant Girl Question* (Boston: Houghton Mifflin Co., 1881; reprinted by Arno Press and the *New York Times,* 1977), p. 44.

12. Ernst, *Immigrant Life,* p. 245.

13. Women's Educational and Industrial Union: *Immigrant Women and Girls in Boston, 1905–06,* (Cambridge, Mass.: Schlesinger Library, Radcliffe College).

14. Kyra Goritzina, *Service Entrance: Memoirs of a Park Avenue Cook* (New York: Carrick and Evans, Inc, 1939), p. 77.

15. Raaen, *Grass of the Earth,* p.131.

16. Ets, *Rosa,* p. 221.

17. Anthony, *Mothers Who Must Earn,* pp. 115–16.

18. Koenig, *Letters from America,* Vol. 29, No. 1, Spring 1956, p. 13.

19. Steiner, *Trail of the Immigrant,* p. 337.

20. Lucy Maynard Salmon, *Domestic Service,* second edition, (New York: The Macmillan Co., 1901), p. 132.

21. Ibid., pp. 133 and 135–36.

22. Holt, *Life Stories,* pp. 133–34.

23. Joan Morrison and Charlotte Fox Zabusky, *American Mosaic,* (New York: E. P. Dutton, 1980), pp. 42–43.

24. Salmon, *Domestic Service,* pp. 107–08.

25. Byington, *Homestead,* p. 79.

26. More, *Wage-Earners' Budgets,* p. 137.

27. Salmon, *Domestic Service,* pp. 98–101.

28. Ibid., pp. 91–92.

29. Claghorn, *Immigrant's Day in Court,* pp. 14–15.

30. Yezierska, *Children of Loneliness,* pp. 41–42.

31. Parker, *Working Woman,* p. 203.

32. Cohen, *Out of the Shadow,* p. 176.

33. Parker, *Working Woman,* p. 203.

34. Goritzina, *Service Entrance,* p. 76.

35. Salmon, *Domestic Service,* p. 158.

36. Ibid., p. 154.

37. Hutchinson, *Women's Wages,* pp. 168–69.

38. Cohen, *Out of the Shadow,* pp. 180–81.

39. Erickson, *Invisible Immigrants,* pp. 312–13.

HOMES ON THE RANGE

1. Svendsen, *Frontier Mother,* p. 40.

2. Brandt, Mrs. R. O., "Social Aspects," p. 35.

3. Sandoz, *Old Jules,* p. 300.

4. Isely, *Sunbonnet Days,* pp. 196–98.

5. Waerenskjold, *Lady with the Pen,* p. 51.

6. Paul Knapland, *Moorings Old and New,* (State Historical Society of Wisconsin, 1964), p. 215.

7. Brandt, Mrs. R. O., "Social Aspects," pp. 26–28.

8. Koren, *Diary of Elisabeth Koren,* p. 258.

9. Ibid.

10. Isely, *Sunbonnet Days,* p. 174.

11. Waerenskjold, *Lady with the Pen,* pp. 29–30.

12. Svendsen, *Frontier Mother,* p. 32. See also Theodore C. Blegen, "Immigrant Women and the American Frontier," Norwegian-American Historical Association *Studies and Records,* Vol. 5, 1930, p. 27.

13. Blegen, *Land of Their Choice,* p. 427.

14. Richard O'Connor, *The German-Americans* (Boston: Little, Brown & Company, 1968), p. 192, citing Evan Jones, *The Minnesota: Forgotten River.*

15. Blegen, *Land of Their Choice,* pp. 429–30. See also Blegen, *Grass Roots,* pp. 67 and 78, citing Lawson, Tew & Nelson, *History of Kandiyohi County* (St. Paul, 1905), pp. 106–10.

16. Gjerset and Hektoen, p. 11.

17. Henry S. Lucas, *Dutch Immigrant Memoirs and Related Writings* (Assen, Netherlands: Van Gorcum & Co., 1955), pp. 407–09.

18. Isely, *Sunbonnet Days,* p. 180.

19. Erickson, *Invisible Immigrants,* pp. 184–85.

20. Ibid., pp. 219 and 221.

21. Fredrika Bremer, *America of the Fifties: Letters of Fredrika Bremer,* Selected and edited by Adolph B. Benson (New York: The American-Scandinavian Foundation, 1924), pp. 208–09.

22. Ibid., p. 209.

23. Waerenskjold, *Lady with the Pen,* p. 60.

24. Ibid., p. 30.

25. Koren, *Diary of Elisabeth Koren*, p. 321.

26. Svendsen, *Frontier Mother*, p. 35.

27. Koren, *Diary of Elisabeth Koren*, p. 201.

28. Ibid., p. 280.

29. Preus, *Linka's Diary*, p. 262.

30. Isely, *Sunbonnet Days*, pp. 171–72.

31. Nels Anderson, "Czecho-Slovaks in Virginia," published in Edmund Brunner, *Immigrant Farmers and Their Children*, (Garden City, New York: Doubleday, Doran, and Company, 1929), p. 194.

32. Ibid., pp. 189–90.

33. Balch, *Our Slavic Fellow Citizens*, p. 329.

V. THE COMPLEXITIES OF IT ALL
STANDARDS AND DOUBLE STANDARDS

1. Abbott, *Immigration*, p. 420.

2. Ibid., p. 426.

3. Ibid., p. 300.

4. Ibid., pp. 268–69.

5. Ibid., pp. 303–07.

6. Ibid., p. 312.

7. Long, Oral Histories. Anonymous, "An Italian Immigrant Woman," p. 2.

8. Metzker, *A Bintel Brief*, p. 97.

9. Abbott, *Immigration*, pp. 392–95.

10. Ibid., pp. 350–51.

11. Ibid.

12. Ibid., p. 345.

13. Martha Reid Robinson, "Immigrants at the Port of New York," *World Events*, March, 1905, p. 195.

14. Metzker, *A Bintel Brief*, pp. 62–63.

15. Claghorn, *Immigrant's Day in Court*, p. 317.

16. Ibid.

17. Ibid.

18. Ibid., pp. 437–48, citing *The Survey*, January 10, 1920.

19. Ibid., p. 436.

20. Ibid., p. 462.

TRAVAILS OF TRAVEL

1. Isley, *Sunbonnet Days*, p. 40.

2. Cohen, *Out of the Shadow*, pp. 62–64.

3. 61st Congress, 3rd session, Senate Document 753, *Reports of the Immigration Commission: Steerage Conditions* (Washington, D.C.: Government Printing Office, 1911), p. 8.

4. Kellogg Durland, "Steerage Impositions," *The Independent,* 61, Vol. 61, August 30, 1906, pp. 499–504.

5. Elizabeth Hampsten, *To All Inquiring Friends: Letters, Diaries & Essays in North Dakota* (Grand Forks: University of North Dakota, 1979), p. 217.

6. Isley, *Sunbonnet Days,* p. 31.

7. Senate Document 753, *Steerage Conditions,* p. 19.

8. Cohen, *Out of the Shadow,* p. 60.

9. Durland, "Steerage Impositions," pp. 499–504.

10. Senate Document 753, *Steerage Conditions,* p. 37.

11. Abbott, *Immigration,* pp. 82–86.

12. Isely, *Sunbonnet Days,* p. 28.

13. Morrison and Zabusky, *American Mosaic,* p. 85.

14. Hasanovitz, *One of Them,* p. 13.

15. Senate Document 753, *Steerage Conditions,* p. 30.

16. Ets, *Rosa,* p. 163.

17. Ibid., p. 168.

18. Francis A. Kellor, "The Protection of Immigrant Women," *Atlantic,* Vol. 101, February, 1908, p. 248.

19. Chotzinoff, *Lost Paradise,* pp. 46–51.

20. Ibid., p. 51.

21. Abbott, *Immigration,* p. 598, from the files of the Chicago Immigrants' Protective League.

22. Ibid., pp. 62–63, from International Labor Office, *Emigration and Immigration: Legislation and Treaties* (Geneva, 1922), pp. 13–24.

23. Blegen, *Land of Their Choice,* p. 260.

24. Holt, *Life Stories,* p. 145.

25. Blegen, *Land of Their Choice,* pp. 97–98.

26. Svendsen, *Frontier Mother,* pp. 6–7.

27. Ibid., p. 23.

28. Blegen, *Land of Their Choice,* p. 383.

29. Senate Document 753, *Steerage Conditions,* p. 40.

30. Preus, *Linka's Diary,* p. 178.

31. Bjork, *Great Divide,* 412; quoting a letter from Caroline C. Hjort in the *Decorah-posten,* 12-1-1886.

32. Cohen, *Out of the Shadow,* p. 34.

33. Blegen, *Land of Their Choice,* p. 298.

34. Cohen, *Out of the Shadow,* pp. 55–56.

35. Women's Educational & Industrial Union: *Report,* p. 8.

36. Schneiderman, *All For One,* p. 25.

37. Abbott, *Immigration,* p. 472.

38. Hasanovitz, *One of Them,* p. 214.

AN OCEAN APART: SEPARATION AND ITS EFFECTS

1. Eubank, *Study of Family Desertion*, p. 40.

2. Ibid., p. 39.

3. Metzker, *A Bintel Brief*, pp. 56–57.

4. Segale, *Santa Fe Trail*, pp. 193–94.

5. Colcord, *Broken Homes*, p. 100.

6. Senate Document 645, Vol. 12, *Women in Laundries*, p. 107.

7. Thomas & Znaniecki, The Polish Peasant, Vol. 2, p. 1712.

8. Ibid., pp. 1713–14.

9. "Probation for All Emigrant Husbands," *The Survey*, Vol. 30, no. 12, June 21, 1913, p. 385.

10. Hugo Eugene Varga, "Desertion of Wives and Children by Emigrants to America," *Proceedings of the National Conference of Charities and Correction,* (Fort Wayne, Indiana: Fort Wayne Printing Co., 1912), p. 260.

11. Schneiderman, *All For One* pp. 18–19.

12. Thomas & Znaniecki, *The Polish Peasant*, Vol. 1., pp. 863–68.

13. Ibid., pp. 874–93.

14. Ets, *Rosa*, p. 140.

15. Erickson, *Invisible Immigrants*, p. 241.

16. Balch, *Our Slavic Fellow Citizens*, p. 188.

17. Ibid., pp.170–71.

18. Thomas & Znaniecki, *The Polish Peasant*, Vol. 1, pp. 394–450, the Osinski series.

19. Erickson, *Invisible Immigrants*, pp. 372–77.

20. Ibid.

21. Thomas & Znaniecki, *The Polish Peasant*, Vol. 1, pp. 837–38.

22. Ibid., pp. 825–26.

23. Ibid., p. 909.

24. Ibid., p. 913.

25. Balch, *Our Slavic Fellow Citizens*, p. 186, from the notebook of Miss Gazvoda.

26. Byington, *Homestead*, p. 161.

27. Barton, *Letters from the Promised Land*, p. 44.

28. Thomas & Znaniecki, *The Polish Peasant*, Vol. 1, pp. 851, 592.

29. Ibid., p. 825.

30. Tauba Leah Meyer Cohen Forman, "The Blood Thirst in *Kishineff*," *The Independent*, Vol. 55, June 18, 1903, pp.1430–33.

31. Thomas & Znaniecki, *The Polish Peasant*, Vol. 1, p. 900.

32. Ibid., pp. 850–52.

33. Long, Oral Histories. Sarah Demirfian, "Interview with My Mother," unpaged.

34. Cohen, *Out of the Shadow*, p. 22.

35. Odencrantz, *Italian Women in Industry*, p.309, in a supplement by Henriette R. Walter.

36. Thomas & Znaniecki, *The Polish Peasant*, Vol. 1, p. 973.

37. Byington, *Homestead*, p. 181.

VI. THE TIES THAT BIND
FAMILY RELATIONSHIPS

1. Carpenter, *Immigrants and their Children*, p. 169.

2. Parker, *Working Woman*, p. 205.

3. Carpenter, *Immigrants and their Children*, p. 408.

4. Isely, *Sunbonnet Days*, p. 107.

5. Koren, *Diary of Elizabeth Koren*, p. 94.

6. Carpenter, *Immigrants and their Children*, p. 235.

7. Cole, *Immigrant City*, p. 104.

8. John Foster Carr, *Guide for the Immigrant Italian*. Published under the auspices of the Connecticut Daughters of the American Revolution, (New York: Doubleday, 1911; re-published as part of *Assimilation of the Italian Immigrant*, Arno Press, 1975), pp. 36–37.

9. Balch, *Our Slavic Fellow Citizens*, p. 377.

10. Claghorn, *Immigrant's Day in Court*, p. 98.

11. Brunner, *Immigrant Farmers*, p. 200.

12. Yezierska, *Children of Loneliness*, p. 20.

13. Anthony, *Mothers Who Must Earn*, pp. 186–190.

14. Mary E. McDowell, "The Struggle in Family Life," *Charities*, Vol. 13, Dec. 3, 1904, p. 197.

15. Herzfeld, *Family Monographs*, p. 57.

16. Williams, *South Italian Folkways*, p. 96.

17. Ibid., p. 77.

18. Herzfeld, p. 94.

19. Roberts, "Italian Girls," pp. 760–61.

20. Odencrantz, *Italian Women in Industry*, p. 28.

21. Pagano, *Golden Wedding*, pp. 67, 107.

22. Ibid., p. 128.

23. Ibid., p. 179.

24. Van Kleeck, *Artificial Flower Makers*, p. 235.

25. Williams, *South Italian Folkways*, p. 190.

26. Metzker, *A Bintel Brief*, p. 128.

27. Sophonisba Breckenridge and Edith Abbott: *The Delinquent Child and the Home: A Study of the Delinquent Wards of the Juvenile Court of Chicago* (New York: The Russell Sage Foundation, 1917), p. 285.

28. Rebekah Kohut, *My Portion* (New York: Thomas Seltzer, 1925), p. 118.

29. Campbell, *Prisoners of Poverty*, pp. 88–99.

30. Holt, *Life Stories*, pp. 143–44.

31. Viola Paradise, "The Jewish Immigrant Girl in Chicago," *The Survey*, Vol. 30, September 6, 1913, p. 703.

32. Long, Oral Histories. Anonymous, "An Italian Immigrant Woman," pp. 3–4.

33. G. Hughes, *Mothers in Industry*, p. 99.

34. Carpenter, *Immigrants and their Children*, p. 424.

35. Holt, *Life Stories*, p. 147.

36. Leona Murphy, S.C., *The Life Story of the Sisters of Charity of Cincinnati, Ohio*, unpublished monograph, 1941, Sisters of Charity Archives, College of Mount St. Joseph, Mount St. Joseph, Ohio, p. 246.

37. Barnum, "Fall River Mill Girl," p. 242.

38. Hasanovitz, *One of Them*, p. 236.

39. Ibid, p. 249.

WOMEN'S PLACE IN THE NEW WORLD

1. Carpenter, *Immigrants and their Children*, p. 220.

2. Abbott, *Immigration*, pp. 353–54.

3. 61st Congress, 2nd session, Senate Document 282, *Reports of the Immigration Commission: Fecundity of Immigrant Women*, pp. 811–12.

4. Carpenter, *Immigrants and their Children*, p. 270.

5. Anthony, *Mothers Who Must Earn*, p. 61.

6. Carpenter, *Immigrants and their Children*, p. 281.

7. Metzker, *A Bintel Brief*, pp. 109–110.

8. Preus, *Linka's Diary*, pp. 198–99.

9. Pagano, *Golden Wedding*, pp. 38–9.

10. Segale, *Santa Fe Trail*, p. 15.

11. Long, Oral Histories. Marot, "Oral Interview," p. 11.

12. Ibid., Demirfian, "Interivew with My Mother," p. 2.

13. Thomas and Znaniecki, *The Polish Peasant*, Vol. 1, p. 923.

14. Ibid., p. 930.

15. Ibid., p. 952.

16. Mary Van Kleeck, *Working Girls in Evening Schools*, (New York: Survey Associates for The Russell Sage Foundation, 1914), p. 25.

17. Odencrantz, *Italian Women in Industry*, p. 28.

18. Fanny Stenhouse, *Exposé of Polygamy in Utah: A Lady's Life Among the Mormons. A Record of Personal Experience as One of the Wives of a Mormon Elder During a Period of More than Twenty Years*, (New York: American News Company, 1872), pp. 34–36.

19. Ibid., p. 78.

20. Ibid., p. 81.

21. Steiner, *Trail of the Immigrant*, p. 187.

22. Sadie Frowne, "The Story of a Sweatshop Girl," *The Independent,* Vol. 54, September 25, 1902, p. 2279.

23. Preus, *Linka's Diary,* p. 198.

VII. CONTENT AND DISCONTENT
VIEWS OF THE NEW WORLD

1. Cohen, *Out of the Shadow,* p. 246.

2. Ibid., p. 153.

3. Schneiderman, *All For One,* p. 27.

4. Blegen, *Land of Their Choice,* p. 307.

5. Isley, *Sunbonnet Days,* p. 62.

6. Balch, *Our Slavic Fellow Citizens,* pp. 59–60.

7. Abbott, *Historical,* p. 309.

8. Ets, *Rosa,* pp. 190–91.

9. 67th Congress, 1st Session, Committee on Immigration, Report No. 17, April 28, 1921, p. 6.

10. 61st Congress, 3rd session, Senate Document 748, *Reports of the Immigration Commission: Emigration Conditions in Europe,* 1911, p. 41.

11. Ibid., p. 45.

12. Ibid., p. 41.

13. Williams, *South Italian Folkways,* p. 17.

14. Long, Oral Histories. Anonymous, "An Italian Immigrant Woman," p. 10.

15. Erickson, *Invisible Immigrants,* p. 225.

16. Waerenskjold, *Lady with the Pen,* p. 45.

17. Koren, *Diary of Elisabeth Koren,* p. 244.

18. Balch, *Our Slavic Fellow Citizens,* p. 119.

19. 61st Congress, 2d Session, Senate Document 633, Reports of the Immigration Commission: *Immigrants in Industries,* "Cotton Goods Manufacturing in the North Atlantic States," 1911, Vol. 72, p. 166.

20. Ets, *Rosa,* p. 254.

21. Parker, *Working Woman,* p. 25.

22. Senate Document 645, Vol. 16, *Family Budgets,* pp. 212–14.

23. Holt, *Life Stories,* pp. 108–09.

24. Ibid., p. 124.

25. Blegen, *Land of Their Choice,* p. 187.

26. Clark, *Making Both Ends Meet,* pp. 91–92.

27. Davis, *Immigrant Health,* p. 55.

28. Odencrantz, *Italian Women in Industry,* p. 26.

29. Balch, *Our Slavic Fellow Citizens,* p. 61.

30. Steiner, *Trail of the Immigrant,* p. 337.

31. Metzker, *A Bintel Brief,* p. 106.

32. Barton, *Letters from the Promised Land,* p. 143.

33. Campbell, *Prisoners of Poverty,* p. 106.

34. Barton, *Letters from the Promised Land,* p. 224.

35. Hasanovitz, *One of Them,* pp. 193–94, 199, 308–09.

36. Bremer, *America of the Fifties,* pp. 218–9.

37. Rosalie Roos, *Travels in America, 1851–55* (Carbondale: Southern Illinois University Press, 1982), pp. 24, 43.

38. Waerenskjold, *Lady with the Pen,* p. 36.

39. Erickson, *Invisible Immigrants,* p. 153.

40. Blegen, *Land of Their Choice,* pp. 268–69.

41. Erickson, *Invisible Immigrants,* p. 207.

42. Erik Wiken, "Olof Bäck & the Hertman Family," *Swedish American Genealogist,* Vol. 4, March, 1984, No. 1, pp. 16–17. My thanks to my brother, Norman Barge, for bringing this item to my attention.

43. Barton, *Letters from the Promised Land,* pp. 100, 120, 136.

44. Ibid., pp. 290–92.

45. Ibid., pp. 285–86.

46. Holt, *Life Stories,* p. 140.

47. Steiner, *Trail of the Immigrant,* p. 336.

48. Women's Educational and Industrial Union, *Immigrant Women and Girls in Boston.*

49. Blegen, *Land of Their Choice,* p. 265.

SELECTED BIBLIOGRAPHY

(SEE NOTES FOR FURTHER DETAIL)

ABBOTT, EDITH. *Historical Aspects of the Immigration Problem.* Chicago: University of Chicago Press, 1926; re-issued by Arno Press and the *New York Times* as part of The American Immigration Collection, 1969.

————. *Immigration: Select Documents and Case Records.* Chicago: University of Chicago Press, 1924; re-issued by Arno Press and the *New York Times* as part of The American Immigration Collection, 1969.

————. *The Tenements of Chicago, 1908–35.* Chicago: University of Chicago Press, 1936.

————. *Women in Industry.* New York: Appleton & Co., 1909.

ANTHONY, KATHERINE. *Mothers Who Must Earn.* New York: Survey Associates and The Russell Sage Foundation, 1914.

BALCH, EMILY. *Our Slavic Fellow Citizens.* Philadelphia: Wm. F. Fell Co., 1910; re-issued by Arno Press and the *New York Times* as part of The American Immigration Collection, 1969.

BARNUM, GERTRUDE. "The Story of a Fall River Mill Girl." *The Independent* 58 (April 27, 1905).

BARTON, H. ARNOLD. *Letters From the Promised Land: Swedes in America, 1840–1914.* Minneapolis: University of Minnesota Press, 1975.

BJORK, KENNETH O. *West of the Great Divide: Norwegian Migration to the Pacific Coast, 1847–1893.* Northfield, Minnesota: Norwegian-American Historical Association, 1958.

BLEGEN, THEODORE C. *Grass Roots History.* Port Washington, New York/London: Kennikat Press, 1947; re-issued in 1969 by Kennikat Press.

————. "Immigrant Women and the American Frontier." Norwegian-American Historical Association *Studies and Records* 5 (1930).

————. *Land of Their Choice: The Immigrants Write Home.* St. Paul: University of Minnesota Press, 1955.

BRANDT, LILIAN. *Five Hundred and Seventy-four Deserters and Their Families.* New York: The Charity Organization Society, 1905.

BRANDT, MRS. REALF OTTESEN. "Social Aspects of Prairie Pioneering: The Reminiscences of a Pioneer Pastor's Wife." Norwegian-American Historical Association *Studies and Records* 7 (1956).

BRECKINRIDGE, SOPHONISBA, and EDITH ABBOTT: *The Delinquent Child*

and the Home: A Study of the Delinquent Wards of the Juvenile Court of Chicago.
New York: The Russell Sage Foundation, 1917.

BREMER, FREDRIKA. *America of the Fifties: Letters of Fredrika Bremer.* Selected and edited by Adolph B. Benson. New York: The American-Scandinavian Foundation, 1924.

BRUNNER, EDMUND. *Immigrant Farmers and Their Children.* Garden City, New York: Doubleday, Doran, and Company, 1929.

BUTLER, ELIZABETH BEARDSLEY. *Women and the Trades.* New York: Charities Publication Committee and The Russell Sage Foundation, 1909. (Part of *The Pittsburg Survey: Findings in Six Volumes,* edited by Paul U. Kellogg.)

BYINGTON, MARGARET. *Homestead: The Households of a Mill Town.* New York: The Russell Sage Foundation, 1910.

––––––. "The Mill Town Courts and Their Lodgers." *Charities and the Commons* 21 (February 6, 1909).

CAMPBELL, HELEN. *Prisoners of Poverty: Women Wage-Workers, Their Trades and Their Lives.* Boston: Roberts Brothers, 1895.

CAPEK, THOMAS. *The Čechs (Bohemians) in America.* Boston: Houghton Mifflin, 1920.

CARPENTER, NILES. *Immigrants and Their Children, 1920: A Study Based on Census Statistics Relative to the Foreign Born and the Native White of Foreign or Mixed Parentage.* Washington, D.C.: U.S. Government Printing Office, 1927; reissued by Arno Press and the *New York Times* as part of The American Immigration Collection, 1969.

CHAPIN, ROBERT COIT. *The Standard of Living Among Workingmen's Families in New York City.* New York: The Russell Sage Foundation, 1909.

CHOTZINOFF, SAMUEL. *A Lost Paradise.* New York: Knopf, 1958.

CLAGHORN, KATE. *The Immigrant's Day in Court.* New York: Harper & Bros., 1923; re-issued by Arno Press and the *New York Times* as part of The American Immigration Collection, 1969.

CLARK, SUE AINSLIE and EDITH WYATT. *Making Both Ends Meet: The Income and Outlay of New York Working Girls.* New York: The Macmillan Company, 1911.

COHEN, ROSE. *Out of the Shadow.* New York: George H. Doran Company, 1918.

COLCORD, JOANNA C. *Broken Homes: A Study of Family Desertion.* New York: The Russell Sage Foundation, 1919.

COLE, DONALD B. *Immigrant City: Lawrence, Massachusetts, 1845–1921.* Chapel Hill: University of North Carolina Press, 1963.

"A Collar Starcher's Story." *The Independent* 59 (August 10, 1905).

Commonwealth of Massachusetts: State Department of Health. *The Food of Working Women in Boston.* Boston: Wright & Potter Printing Co., 1917.

DAVIS, MICHAEL M., JR. *Immigrant Health and the Community*. New York: Harper & Bros., 1921.

DURLAND, KELLOGG. "Steerage Impositions," *The Independent* 61 (August 30, 1906).

ERICKSON, CHARLOTTE. *Invisible Immigrants*. Coral Gables, Florida: University of Miami Press, 1972.

ERNST, ROBERT. *Immigrant Life in New York City: 1825–1863*. Port Washington, New York: Ira J. Friedman, Inc., 1949; re-issued in 1965 by Ira. J. Friedman.

ETS, MARIE HALL. *Rosa: The Life of an Italian Immigrant*. Minneapolis: University of Minnesota Press, 1970.

EUBANK, EARLE EDWARD. *A Study of Family Desertion*. Chicago: University of Chicago Libraries and City of Chicago Department of Public Welfare, 1916.

FORMAN, TAUBA LEAH MEYER COHEN. "The Blood Thirst in Kishineff." *The Independent* 55 (June 18, 1903).

FROWNE, SADIE. "The Story of a Sweatshop Girl." *The Independent* 54 (September 25, 1902).

GJERSET, KNUT and LUDVIG HEKTOEN. "Health Conditions and the Practice of Medicine Among the Early Norwegian Settlers, 1825–1865." Norwegian-American Historical Association *Studies and Records* 1 (1926).

GORITZINA, KYRA. *Service Entrance: Memoirs of a Park Avenue Cook*. New York: Carrick and Evans, Inc., 1939.

GREEN, CONSTANCE MCLAUGHLIN. *Holyoke, Massachusetts: A Case History of the Industrial Revolution in America*. New Haven: Yale University Press, 1939.

HASANOVITZ, ELIZABETH. *One of Them: Chapters from a Passionate Autobiography*. Boston and New York: Houghton Mifflin Company, 1918.

HERZFELD, ELSA G. *Family Monographs: The History of Twenty-four Families Living in the Middle West Side of New York City*. New York: The James Kempster Printing Company, 1905.

———. "The Tenement House Family," *The Independent* 59 (December 28, 1905).

HOLT, HAMILTON, ed. *The Life Stories of Undistinguished Americans As Told by Themselves*. New York: James Pott & Co., 1906.

HOURWICH, ANDRIA TAYLOR. *I Am a Woman Worker: A Scrapbook of Autobiographies*. New York: The Affiliated School for Workers, Inc., 1936.

HUGHES, ELIZABETH. "Chicago Housing Conditions: The Lithuanians in the Fourth Ward," *American Journal of Sociology* 20 (November, 1914).

HUGHES, GWENDOLYN SALISBURY. *Mothers in Industry: Wage-Earning by Mothers in Philadelphia*. New York: New Republic, Inc., 1925. (Data was collected in 1918–1919.)

HUTCHINSON, EMILIE JOSEPHINE. *Women's Wages*. New York: Columbia University Press, 1919; re-issued by AMS Press, New York, 1968.

ISELY, ELISE DUBACH, as told to her son, Bliss Isely. *Sunbonnet Days*. Caldwell, Idaho: The Caxton Printers, 1935.

KELLOR, FRANCES A. "The Immigrant Woman." *The Atlantic* 100 (September, 1907).

————. "Immigration and Household Labor." *Charities* 12 (February 6, 1904).

————. *Out of Work*. New York: G. P. Putnam's Sons, 1904.

————. "The Protection of Immigrant Women." *Atlantic* 101 (February, 1908).

KENNEDY, JOHN CURTIS. *Wages and Family Budgets in the Chicago Stockyards District*. Chicago: University of Chicago Press, 1914.

KITCHELT, FLORENCE. Florence Kitchelt Papers. Cambridge, Mass.: Schlesinger Library, Radcliffe College. "Little Italy Neighborhood Association," Brooklyn, 1906. "Bureau of Information for Foreigners," Rochester, 1910.

KOENIG, EMILIE LOHMANN. "Letters from America to a Family in Germany." *Concordia Historical Institute Quarterly* 28, no. 4 (Winter 1956).

KOHUT, REBEKAH. *My Portion*. New York: Thomas Seltzer, 1925.

KOREN, ELISABETH. *The Diary of Elisabeth Koren, 1853-1855*. Translated and edited by David T. Nelson. Northfield, Minnesota: Norwegian-American Historical Association, 1955.

LANE, FRANCIS E. *American Charities and the Child of the Immigrant: A Study of Typical Child Caring Institutions in New York and Massachusetts between the Years 1845 and 1880*. Washington, D.C.: The Catholic University of America, 1932.

LONG, PRISCILLA. Collection of Oral Histories. Cambridge, Mass.: Schlesinger Library, Radcliffe College.
    Demirfian, Sarah: "An Interview with My Mother."
    Marot, Lola: "Oral Interview: Lola Anguini."
    Anonymous: "An Italian Immigrant Woman—1920."

LUCAS, HENRY S. *Dutch Immigrant Memoirs and Related Writings*. Assen, Netherlands: Van Gorcum and Co., 1955.

MACLEAN, ANNIE MARION. "Life in the Pennsylvania Coal Fields, with Particular Reference to Women." *American Journal of Sociology* 14 (November, 1908).

MALKIEL, THERESA SERBER. *The Diary of a Shirtwaist Striker*. New York: The Co-operative Press, 1910.

MANNING, CAROLINE. *The Immigrant Woman and Her Job*. U.S. Department of Labor, Bulletin of the Women's Bureau, No. 74. Washington, D.C.: U.S. Government Printing Office, 1930.

MASARYK, ALICE G. "The Bohemians in Chicago." *Charities* 13 (December 3, 1904).

MCDOWELL, MARY E. "The Struggle in Family Life." *Charities* 13 December 3, 1904.

METZKER, ISAAC, ed. *A Bintel Brief: Sixty Years of Letters from the Lower East Side to the Jewish Daily Forward*. Garden City, New York: Doubleday & Co., 1971.

MORE, LOUISE B. *Wage-Earners' Budgets: A Study of Standards and Cost of Living in New York City*. New York: Henry Holt and Company, 1907.

MORRISON, JOAN and CHARLOTTE FOX ZABUSKY. *American Mosaic*. New York: E. P. Dutton, 1980.

MURPHY, LEONA, S. C. "The Life Story of the Sisters of Charity in Cincinnati, Ohio." Unpublished Monograph, 1941, Sisters of Charity Archives, College of Mount St. Joseph, Mount St. Joseph, Ohio.

NORTON, GRACE P. "Chicago Housing Conditions: Two Italian Districts." *American Journal of Sociology* 18 (January 1913).

ODENCRANTZ, LOUISE C. *Italian Women in Industry*. New York: The Russell Sage Foundation, 1919.

PAGANO, JO. *Golden Wedding*. New York: Random House, 1943.

PARADISE, VIOLA. "The Jewish Immigrant Girl in Chicago." *The Survey* 30 (September 6, 1913).

PARKER, CORNELIA STRATTON. *Working With the Working Woman*. New York: Harper & Bros., 1922.

PEHOTSKY, BESSIE OLGA. *The Slavic Immigrant Woman*. Cincinnati: Powell & White, 1925.

PREUS, CAROLINE DOROTHEA MARGRETHE KEYSER. *Linka's Diary on Land and Sea, 1845–1864*. Translated and edited by Johan C. K. Preus and Diderikke Brandt Preus. Minneapolis: Augsburg Publishing House, 1952.

"Probation for All Emigrant Husbands." *The Survey* 30 (June 21, 1913).

RAAEN, AAGOT. *Grass of the Earth*. Northfield, Minnesota: Norwegian-American Historical Association, 1950.

RICHARDSON, DOROTHY. *The Long Day: The Story of a New York Working Girl as Told by Herself*. New York: The Century Co., 1905.

RICHMOND, MARY E. and FRED S. HALL. *A Study of Nine Hundred and Eighty-five Widows*. New York: The Russell Sage Foundation, 1913.

RIIS, JACOB. *How the Other Half Lives*. New York: C. Scribner's Sons, 1890; reissued by Sagamore Press, 1957.

ROBERTS, MARJORIE. "Italian Girls on American Soil." *Mental Hygiene* 13 (October, 1929).

ROBBINS, JANE E. "The Bohemian Women in New York." *Charities* 13 (December 12, 1904).

ROBINSON, MARTHA REID. "Immigrants at the Port of New York." *World Events* (March, 1905).

ROOS, ROSALIE. *Travels in America, 1851–55*. Carbondale: Southern Illinois University Press, 1982.

SALMON, LUCY MAYNARD. *Domestic Service.* Second edition. New York: The Macmillan Co., 1901.

SANDOZ, MARI. *Old Jules.* Boston: Little, Brown, & Company, 1935.

SAYLES, MARY BUELL. "Housing and Social Conditions in a Slavic Neighborhood." *The Survey* 13 (December 3, 1904).

SCHNEIDERMAN, ROSE with LUCY GOLDWAITE. *All For One.* New York: Paul S. Eriksson, Inc., 1967.

———. "A Cap Maker's Story." *The Independent* 58 (April 27, 1905).

SEGALE, BLANDINA, S. C. *At the End of the Santa Fe Trail.* Milwaukee: The Bruce Publishing Company, 1948.

SPOFFORD, HARRIET PRESCOTT. *The Servant Girl Question.* Boston: Houghton Mifflin Co., 1881; re-issued by Arno Press and the *New York Times,* 1977.

STEINER, EDWARD A. *On the Trail of the Immigrant.* New York and London: Fleming H. Revell Co., 1906.

STENHOUSE, FANNY. *Exposé of Polygamy in Utah: A Lady's Life Among the Mormons.* New York: American News Company, 1872.

STERN, ELIZABETH G. *I Am a Woman—and a Jew.* New York: J. H. Sears & Co., Inc., 1926; re-issued by Arno Press and the *New York Times* as part of The American Immigration Collection, 1969.

SVENDSEN, GRO. *Frontier Mother: The Letters of Gro Svendsen.* Translated and edited by Pauline Farseth and Theodore C. Blegen. Northfield, Minnesota: The Norwegian-American Historical Association, 1950.

THOMAS, WILLIAM I. and FLORIAN ZNANIECKI. *The Polish Peasant in Europe and America.* 5 Vols. Chicago: University of Chicago Press, 1918; re-issued in 1958 by Dover Publications, Inc.

U.S. Government Publications (Selected).

61st Congress, 2nd Session, Senate Document 645. *Report on Condition of Woman and Child Wage-Earners in the United States.* Washington, D.C.: U.S. Government Printing Office, 1911–13.
    Volume 1: *Cotton Textile Industry.*
    Volume 2: *Men's Ready-Made Clothing.*
    Volume 4 *The Silk Industry.*
    Volume 5: *Wage-Earning Women in Stores and Factories.*
    Volume 9: *History of Women in Industry in the U.S.*
    Volume 10: *History of Women in Trade Unions.*
    Volume 12: *Employment of Women in Laundries.*
    Volume 13: *Infant Mortality and Its Relation to the Employment of Mothers.*
    Volume 14: *Causes of Death Among Women and Child Cotton-Mill Operatives.*
    Volume 15: *Relation between Occupation and Criminality of Women.*
    Volume 16: *Family Budgets of Typical Cotton-Mill Workers.*
    Volume 18: *Employment of Women and Children in Selected Industries.*

61st Congress, 3rd Session, *Reports of the Immigration Commission.* Washington, D.C.: Government Printing Office, 1911.

    Senate Document 282: *Fecundity of Immigrant Women.*

    Senate Document 748: *Emigration Conditions in Europe.*

    Senate Document 750: *Immigration and Crime.*

    Senate Document 753: *Importation and Harboring of Women for Immoral Purposes.*

    Senate Document 753: *Steerage Conditions.*

    Senate Document 756: *Statistical Review of Immigration, 1820–1910.*

VAN KLEECK, MARY. *Artificial Flower Makers.* New York: The Russell Sage Foundation, 1913.

————. *Working Girls in Evening Schools.* New York: Survey Associates for The Russell Sage Foundation, 1914.

VARGA, HUGO EUGENE. "Desertion of Wives and Children by Emigrants to America." *Proceedings of the National Conference of Charities and Correction,* Fort Wayne, Indiana: Fort Wayne Printing Co., 1912.

The Vice Commission of Chicago. *The Social Evil in Chicago.* Chicago: Gunthorp-Warren Printing Company, 1911; re-issued by Arno Press and the *New York Times,* 1970.

WAERENSKJOLD, ELISE. *The Lady with the Pen: Elise Waerenskjold in Texas.* Edited by C. A. Clausen. Northfield, Minnesota: Norwegian-American Historical Association, 1961.

WALLAS, GRAHAM. *The Great Society: A Psychological Analysis.* New York: The Macmillan Company, 1929.

WALTHER, ANNA. *A Pilgrimage with a Milliner's Needle.* New York: Fredrick A. Stokes Company, 1917.

WILLIAMS, PHYLLIS H. *South Italian Folkways in Europe and America.* New York: Russell & Russell, 1938; re-issued in 1969.

WILSON, HELEN I. and EUNICE W. SMITH. "Chicago Housing Conditions Among the Slovaks in the Twentieth Ward." *American Journal of Sociology* 20 (September, 1914).

WOLFSON, THERESA. *The Woman Worker and the Trade Unions.* New York: International Publishers, 1926.

Women's Educational and Industrial Union. *Report of an Investigation of 500 Immigrant Women in Boston.* Cambridge, Mass.: Schlesinger Library, Radcliffe College, June, 1907.

————. *Immigration as a Source of Supply for Domestic Workers, 1905.*

————. *Immigrant Women and Girls in Boston, 1905–06.*

YEZIERSKA, ANZIA. *Children of Loneliness: Stories of Immigrant Life in America.* New York & London: Funk & Wagnalls, 1923.

INDEX

Abbott, Edith, 89
abortion, 2, 3, 4–6, 55
Adamski, Mary, 195–196
advertisements, 4, 16, 47, 132
Allegheny, Pennsylvania, 9
ambivalence, 2, 42, 47, 56, 65, 68,
   101, 138, 142, 190, 234, 237, 238,
   240, 246, 249
American Medical Association, 14
amulets, 47
Anguini, Lola, 4
animals, 159–160, 163–165
Arkansas, 10
Armenians (Armenia), 116, 204, 227
Arnegaard, Margit, 59
artificial flowermakers, 105, 113–114,
   124, 129, 144
assimilation, 234–238
Austrian (Austria), 111, 184, 209, 242
Austro-Hungarian Empire, 172

Badad, Rachel, 178
Banir, Mrs., 178
Baptist, 28
baths, 17
Bauer, Lotte, 219
Bazanoff, Anastasia, 56
Belgium, 204
Belmont, Mrs. O. H. P., 142
Bergen, 68
Berlin, 6, 150
Bernstein, Sylvia, 184
bigamy, 194–196, 199
birth control, 3–5
blizzards, 83, 158, 163
boarders, 59, 105, 107, 112, 119–121
Bohemian (Bohemia), 21, 32, 34, 89,
   91, 108, 115, 123, 131, 138, 166,
   195, 205, 208, 213
Bond, Katherine, 23, 156, 163, 240
Borkowska, Teofila, 197–198
Boston, 94, 132, 143, 144, 146, 192,
   248
box factories, 124
boycott, 143
Brady, Mrs., 55
Brandt, Mrs. R. O., 83, 88, 157, 158
bread-baking, 70–71
Bremer, Fredericka, 163
bribery, 192

British (Britain), 116, 124, 137, 172,
   173
Brooklyn, 45
brothers, 110, 215, 224, 227
Brunig, Mrs., 45
Budapest, 173
budgets, 74–75, 98, 102, 104, 106,
   107
Buffalo, 187
Bursova, Getta, 111
Butterworth, Rebecca, 10

California, 11
Canadian (Canada), 52, 58, 193, 208
candy makers, 114–115, 241
Capek, Thomas, 32
Castle Garden, 178
Catholic, 31, 33, 36, 50, 93, 94, 147
Cavalleri, Rosa, 11, 12, 13, 38, 39, 49,
   50, 68, 72, 80, 92, 99, 113, 133,
   149, 185, 198, 219, 226, 238, 241
celibacy, 3–5
charity, 54, 72, 185, 195, 228
Chicago, 13, 41, 49, 54, 59, 62, 74,
   79, 113, 118, 120, 123, 131, 133,
   139, 146, 174, 176, 187, 192, 194,
   213, 218, 243
Chicago Commons, 80
Chicago Domestic Relations Court, 53,
   211
Chicago Vice Commission, 4, 6, 61
child care, 92–96
childbirth, 2, 7–15, 87, 224
Chinese, 247
Chotzinoff, Samuel, 88, 186
Christmas, 31, 72, 201, 221
church attendance, 27–30, 32, 34
cigar makers, 115–116, 122, 205
Cincinnati, 64
Civil War, 147, 160, 163, 164, 221,
   231
clothing expenditures, 96–99
Cohen, Rose, 15, 27, 30, 33, 37, 42,
   72, 77, 84, 98, 112, 126, 128, 132,
   140, 154, 156, 181, 183, 184, 185,
   190, 191, 204, 205, 214, 217, 219,
   234–236, 245
collar starchers, 118–119
Colorado, 10, 11, 143, 226, 227
Coney Island, 98, 248

Congress, 173, 174, 196, 229
Connecticut, 123, 156, 174, 240
contentment, 247–249
Contract Labor Law, 173, 174
cooks, 148, 154
courtship, 36–43
Croatian (Croatia) 41, 74, 122, 199, 201, 211, 243
Cubans, 115
czar, 172, 194, 245
Czech, 32, 166, 211, 229

Danish (Denmark), 126, 230, 242
daughters of immigrants, 4, 37, 109, 110, 111, 214–215, 217, 223, 224, 227, 234
Davousta, Molly, 111
Demirjian family, 204
Denver, 11, 226
deportation, 178–180
Depression of 1893, 33, 72, 133
desertion, 6, 47, 51–56, 193–199
Detroit, 13
diet, 68–77
discontent, 243–245
divorce, 48–50
domestic workers, 57, 63, 100, 146–156
dowries, 36, 42, 217, 237, 242, 243
dress, 96–101
Drier, Mary, 141
dugouts, 83
Dutch, 162, 236

elderly, 217–218, 244
Ellis Island, 56, 96, 173, 174, 177
employment agencies, 132, 146
Endresen, Guri, 161
English (England), 8, 10, 23, 24, 28, 31, 45, 59, 75, 86, 114, 116, 147, 156, 163, 187, 198, 209, 228, 240, 242, 247
Evil Eye, 7, 8, 15
extramarital relations, 58–60

Fall River, Massachusetts, 75, 116, 140, 222
family structure, 210–223
farming women, 166–172, 200, 211, 229
fatalism, 2, 6, 11, 23, 33, 47, 133, 145, 156, 193, 234
feeble-mindedness, 173
Finnish, 81
fires, 79, 135–137, 157, 160

Fitzgerald, Bridget, 151
Florida, 115
Foundling Asylum of the Sisters of Charity, 58, 122
fraud, 126, 153, 186
French (France), 36, 61, 62, 204, 228, 241, 242
French Canadian, 18, 20, 116
frontier, 23, 26, 28, 157–166, 209
Frowne, Sadie, 97, 106, 231
funerals, 25–26, 188

Galicia, 218
gardening, 75, 77, 84, 121, 167
garment manufacturing, 113, 117, 120, 127, 131, 139–42
Gaszynski, Mrs., 47
German (Germany), 2, 3, 5, 6, 8, 12, 23, 26, 29, 31, 34, 40, 41, 45, 51, 63, 86, 87, 108, 114, 116, 117, 122, 130, 131, 138, 147, 148, 150, 151, 160, 172, 176, 203, 210, 213, 218, 219, 237, 241, 242, 244, 248
Gorgini, Rose, 132
Goritzina, Kyra, 148, 154, 204, 230, 236
Great Depression, 32, 73
Great Lakes, 189
Greek (Greece), 116, 187
Greenwich Village, 105
grocery budgets, 74–75
Grossinger, Jennie, 121
Groth, Mrs. Assur, 162
Grubinsky, Mary, 212–213
Gutowski, Martha, 48

Halperin, Katia, 107
Hamburg, 184
Hasanovitz, Elizabeth, 124, 129, 138, 184, 193, 222, 244, 245
hats, 97, 101, 113, 114, 126, 245
Hebrew Sheltering Guardian Society, 95
Heckert, Margaret, 56
Hertman, Lisa Jonsdotter, 247
Hjort, Caroline, 190
Holyoke, Massachusetts, 18, 73, 93, 116, 138, 139
home contract work, 105, 119
home ownership, 85–86
homesickness, 10, 237, 239, 241, 249
Homestead, Pennsylvania, 90, 143, 205
Homestead Act, 165
hospitals, 15

housework, 87–92, 144, 146
housing, 77–86
Hughes, Mary Paul, 221
Huhtasaari, Emma, 81
Hungarian (Hungary), 114, 118, 122, 173, 205, 209, 212, 243, 248
hunger, 33, 72–73, 154, 243
Hvistendahl, Rev. Mr., 29

illegitimacy, 57–60
Illinois, 28, 163
illiteracy, 172, 191, 199, 213, 220, 235
Immigrants' Protective League, 40, 57, 192
Indiana, 87, 126
Indians, 7, 126, 160–162
industrial health and safety, 134–137
infant mortality, 14, 20–23, 188–89
infanticide, 2
inland journey, 185, 187, 189–190
insurance, 26, 107, 127
International Silver Company, 124
Iowa, 22, 24, 82, 160, 162, 187
Irish, 8, 18, 20, 23, 31, 34, 36, 41, 45, 46, 60, 64, 73, 75, 86, 97, 99, 100, 106, 108, 116, 117, 118, 130, 139, 145, 147, 148, 151, 187, 208, 209, 214, 220, 221, 236, 239, 242
Irish-American, 100
Isely, Elise, 28, 121, 158, 162, 166, 180, 182, 184, 209, 236
Italian, 2, 4, 5, 8, 11, 14, 15, 17, 20, 31, 32, 34, 36, 37, 43, 46, 58, 59, 64, 70, 72, 73, 74, 90, 91, 97, 98, 107, 108, 111, 113, 114, 115, 116, 123, 125, 127, 129, 130, 136, 139, 142, 144, 148, 167, 175, 185, 193, 205, 209, 210, 211, 214, 215, 217, 218, 221, 226, 227, 228, 238, 239, 240, 241, 242

Jacobsen, Mrs. Ole, 158
Japan, 203
Jewish (Jews), 3, 14, 15, 18, 19, 20, 30, 31, 32, 33, 37, 48, 52, 53, 56, 59, 61, 63, 72, 91, 97, 106, 107, 111, 112, 113, 117, 121, 128, 136, 138, 141, 143, 144, 148, 153, 175, 185, 186, 191, 194, 202, 203, 218, 220, 225, 228, 238, 239, 243, 245
Jewish Daily Forward, 49, 175, 177
Jons Dotter, Kare, 202
Johnsson, Maja, 244

Kansas, 23, 28, 156, 158, 163, 240

Kapolo, Mrs., 174
Kellor, Frances, 132
kitchens, 77, 78, 82, 83
Klotin, Anna, 139
Know-Nothings, 236
Koenig, Emilie, 87, 150
Koenig, Leopold, 56
Kohut, Rebekah, 219
Koren, Elisabeth, 22, 27, 71, 76, 81, 82, 83, 84, 159, 164, 240
Kosice, Katerina, 174
Kulas, Mrs., 54

language, 13, 50, 87, 119, 131, 148, 173, 239, 241
laundries, 88, 91, 118–119, 130
Lawrence, Massachusetts, 2, 20, 73, 117, 135, 142, 210
Lazowska, Maryanna, 200
LeHavre, 185
life expectancy, 20
Lindgren, Ida, 243
Lithuanians (Lithuania), 18, 42, 59, 63, 74, 78, 85, 126
locusts, 158
London, 111, 185, 186
LoPezzi, Annie, 142
Los Angeles, 226
Ludlow, Colorado, 143
Lutheran, 6, 22, 27, 29, 31, 225

Magyars, 239
Malkiel, Theresa, 219
marriage, 36, 42, 43–48, 56, 60, 110, 152, 193–206, 209, 210, 222, 223, 224, 227–228, 229
Marseilles, 204
Massachusetts, 2, 14, 18, 20, 73, 93, 107, 117, 139, 142, 167, 210
matchmaker, 42, 63
maternal death, 9, 14
medical expenditures, 17
medical profession, 4, 13, 14, 16, 17, 19, 123
metal industries, 122–123
Michigan, 74, 81, 143, 162
Midwest, 18, 26, 34, 71, 123, 157
midwives, 13–14, 19
milk, 70
mill towns, 78, 80–81, 85, 104
milliners, 112, 126, 151, 242
ministers, 6, 22, 28, 30, 120
Minnesota, 87, 160, 189
Missouri, 50, 121, 185, 209
Montreal, 189

Morgan, J. P., 142
Mormons, 228–229
Morris, Jane, 247

Nakov, Elena and Gerda, 134
Naples, 175
National Desertion Bureau, 49, 53
Nebraska, 40, 157
Newark, 14, 180
New England, 7, 90, 113, 116, 117
New Jersey, 85, 113, 167, 213
New York, 129, 247
New York City, 4, 20, 31, 58, 61, 78,
    79, 86, 100, 111, 112, 113, 114,
    115, 117, 121, 122, 126, 127, 129,
    130, 141, 142, 146, 147, 148, 150,
    177, 178, 185, 187, 191, 192, 193,
    205
New York City General Labor Union,
    138
New York Times, 137, 141
North Dakota, 83, 109, 157, 247
Norwegian (Norway), 2, 6, 18, 20, 22,
    29, 59, 68, 69, 71, 72, 76, 81, 82,
    83, 84, 87, 88, 100, 109, 146, 157,
    158, 159, 161, 162, 165, 166, 189,
    191, 210, 220, 236, 240, 246, 247,
    249
Nova Scotia, 173
nuns, 64, 93, 222, 226, 227
nursemaids, 147, 151, 242
nutrition, 69–76

Oleson, Anna, 187
Omaha, 62
orphanages, 93–95, 122, 220
overcrowding, 78–79, 81, 119

Pagano family, 10, 11, 77, 144, 215–
    217, 226
Paris, 242
Parker, Cornelia, 97, 114, 129, 130,
    134, 138, 144
Paterson, New Jersey, 85, 113
Pearson, Mrs. George, 173
Pehotsky, Bessie, 33
Pennsylvania, 9, 97, 113, 119, 201,
    205
Peppo, Rafella, 193
Philadelphia, 78, 104, 123, 203
Pittsburgh, 113, 114, 122, 130
pogroms, 175, 202, 238
Polish (Poland), 4, 13, 17, 20, 32, 36,
    40, 43, 47, 54, 59, 60, 74, 75, 79,
    86, 89, 112, 116, 120, 122, 130,

131, 135, 174, 195, 199, 200, 203,
    205, 209, 227, 229, 231
polygamy, 228–29
Portuguese (Portugal), 20, 75, 241
Prague, 174
prairie fire, 157
pregnancy, 2–15, 56, 88, 195
pregnancy desertion, 55
pre-marital relations, 56–58
Preus, Linka, 6, 22, 46, 82, 84, 100,
    166, 189, 225, 228, 231, 236
priests, 32, 50, 60, 94, 120, 172, 195,
    222
prostitution, 60–65, 141
Protestantism, 28–33, 93, 94
Providence, Rhode Island, 36, 123,
    135
Pure Food & Drug Act, 21
Puritans, 145

Quaker, 76
quarantine, 16, 18, 192
Quebec, 189, 191
quota system, 175–176, 204

Raaen, Aagot, 109, 149
Raaen, Kjersti, 149
rabbis, 32, 48, 195, 202, 212
railroads, 117, 163, 187, 189–190
rats, 80
Reid, Hattie, 45
Reilly, Mrs., 99
religion, 27–35, 36, 228–229
rent, 30, 42, 84–86, 104, 243
returning, 239–245
Reverez, Mrs. Joseph, 176
Richardson, Dorothy, 129
Riis, Jacob, 58, 129
Ronaldson, John, 199
Roos, Rosalie, 246
Rosenbaum, Rachel, 173
Rosorzki, Maryanna, 176
Russian (Russia), 30, 54, 56, 72, 89,
    111, 125, 130, 134, 141, 148, 153,
    172, 175, 176, 186, 191, 192, 193,
    194, 197, 202, 203, 204, 209, 217,
    222, 230, 235, 236, 245
Russian Revolution, 175, 179, 236
Ruthenian, 89

Sabbath, 27, 28, 32
Saehle, Jannicke, 68, 187
Salt Lake City, 226, 229
Sandoz, Jules, 40
Sandoz, Mary, 157

San Francisco, 29
sanitation, 80–81
savings, 98, 107, 111, 151, 152, 221, 242
Scandinavian (Scandinavia), 19, 26, 27, 29, 34, 117, 139, 148, 158, 160, 210, 230, 234, 242
scarcity of women, 119, 208–209
Schaddelee, Cornelia Slag, 162
Schneiderman, Rose, 95, 127, 137, 192, 197, 236
Schultz, Katie, 173
Schwandt, Mary, 161
Scotch (Scotland), 32, 138, 147, 192, 196, 199, 209, 239
seamstresses, 112, 117, 242, 244
Segale, Sister Blandina, 64, 227
Senate, 114, 116, 122
servants, 21, 146–156
sexual harrassment, 128–129, 184, 187, 189
siblings, 109, 111, 219–222, 227
Sicilian (Sicily), 7, 8, 88, 100, 133
Silberman, Sarah, 111
silk makers, 85, 113
Sinclair, Upton, 13, 14
Sioux, 160–161
Slavic (Slavs), 16, 34, 59, 61, 86, 89, 100, 104, 119, 120, 122, 130, 167, 205, 230, 237
Slokowski, Henry, 54
Slovak, 97, 174, 195
smallpox, 16, 18
snakes, 83, 159–160
social work/sociology (social workers/sociologists), 4, 6, 15, 21, 22, 25, 31, 41, 44, 45, 46, 48, 51, 52, 53, 55, 59, 60, 69, 72, 78, 80, 89, 91, 93, 94, 105, 110, 121, 125, 129, 134, 144, 152, 155, 173, 194, 196, 208, 214, 228, 240
Socialists, 142
Society for the Prevention of Pauperism, 132
sod houses, 83–84
Solomon family, 178, 223
South, 115, 246
Spanish, 114, 115, 209
Starkiewicz, Zofia, 203
steerage, 62, 181–185
Steffansson, Maria, 247
Stenhouse, Fanny, 228
stepmothers, 218–219
Stern, Elizabeth, 3, 18, 21, 214
St. Joseph, Missouri, 121, 209

stores, 57, 127–128
strikes, 137, 138, 139, 141–144
Strucinski, Adam, 197
suffrage, 142, 213
surgery, 16
Svendsen, Gro, 2, 19, 24, 28, 59, 70, 76, 87, 100, 157, 160, 162, 165, 167, 188, 220, 230, 236, 237
sweatshops, 16, 117, 128, 131
Swedish (Sweden), 39, 81, 112, 114, 130, 139, 163, 182, 202, 243, 244, 246, 247
Swiss (Switzerland), 28, 40, 121, 157, 166, 180, 209, 228, 236
Syrian (Syria), 5, 116, 204, 223

taboos, 7–8
tailors, 108, 113, 117, 121, 128
Tampa, Florida, 115
Texas, 22, 29, 71, 84, 159, 164, 246
textile workers, 90, 113, 116–117, 124, 135, 139, 140, 142, 247
ticket problems, 185–186
toilets, 80
Tongate, Emily, 247
Trentino, Louise, 107
Triangle Fire, 136–137
tuberculosis, 17, 19, 70, 79, 117, 242
Turks, 204, 239

Ukrainian People's Home, 180
unemployment, 108–109, 131–134
unions, 137–144, 173
United Garment Workers, 139
United States Department of Labor, 116
United States Immigration Commission, 62, 172, 239
unwed mothers, 56–58
Urosova, Natalya, 127, 141, 144
Utah, 10, 11, 229

vaccination, 18–19
ventilation, 17, 117
Vice Commission of Chicago, 4, 6, 61
Vienna, 111, 212, 240
Virginia, 166

Waerenskjold, Elise, 22, 25, 29, 71, 75, 81, 84, 158, 159, 162, 164, 165, 240, 246
wages, 26, 60, 105–111, 113–126, 129, 133, 139, 140, 152, 153, 242
Wallas, Graham, 144–145
Walther, Anna, 126, 242

Warsaw, 198
Welsh, 147, 209
West, 29, 94, 120, 126, 146, 163, 190, 208, 209
West Virginia, 40
wet-nurses, 121
"white slavery," 62, 64, 177
Whittaker, Ann, 28, 163
widows, 19, 26, 95, 108, 144, 165, 221
Wilson, Aaste, 26
Wisconsin, 6, 20, 68, 69, 82, 133, 146, 163, 189
witching women, 16, 19
Women's Trade Union League, 141, 142
Working Women's Society, 129

World War I, 147, 175, 178, 179, 200, 203, 204, 216, 222, 231, 240

xenophobia, 175, 179

Yankees, 29, 83, 100, 116, 146, 209, 234
Yezierska, Anzia, 153, 212
YMCA, 17
Yonkers, 123
Yugoslavia, 176
YWCA, 111, 125, 132, 155, 205

Ziejewski, Lena, 47
Zielinski, Charles, 58